CONTENTS

1/Early Days

History of Badminton 7
The Badminton Association of England 12
The International Badminton Federation 14
War Years 17
Famous Clubs 18
Halls—Ancient and Modern 22

2/Equipment

Rackets 27
Shuttles 32
Clothing 37
Shoes 40

3/Badminton and the Media

Press and Television 41
The Badminton Gazette 43
Letters to the Editor 47
Laughter in Court 51
Verse—or Worse 57
Action Snaps 60

4/Coaching and Training

The Development of Coaching 63
Books 66
Tips from the Top 68

5/Junior Badminton

With the Juniors 73
English Schools' Badminton Association 79

6/England's Major Events

Inter-County Championship 81
English National Championships 86
The All-England Championships 87
Twenty Years of All-England Highlights 90
All-England Winners 106

7/International Events

World Championships 109
World Games 1981 111
Friends' Provident Masters Open
    Championship 111
Commonwealth Games 113
European Championships 114
Olympic Games 116
Nordic Games 117

8/The Team Events

Thomas Cup 119
Badminton's Day of Shame 129
Uber Cup 130

9/Famous Names and Games

Memorable Matches 137
Famous Officials 142
Great Players 148
Stars to Be? 163

Index 164

ACKNOWLEDGEMENTS

Grateful acknowledgement is made to:
Mervyn Rees and Louis Ross, cameramen
extraordinary: for providing superb photos.
The Badminton Association of England and
The International Badminton Federation: for
their generous permission to use extracts and
photos from the *Badminton Gazette* and
World Badminton respectively. Ian Maconachie
and Peter and Ken Milroy of Reinforced
Shuttlecocks Ltd: for allowing me to obtain
photographs of the manufacture of the world's
finest shuttles, the RSL No. 1.
Pip Pearson and Carlton Sports: for allowing
me to obtain photographs of the manufacture
of their fine range of rackets.
Mike Griggs of Dover and Gordon Ridgewell
of Saffron Walden: for their expert photo-
graphy of the above processes.
Humphrey Chilton (Vice-President of the
BA of E), Craig Reedie (President of the
IBF), Ian Maconachie (RSL), Nev
Macfarlane (Chairman, English Schools'
Badminton Association), Larry Landrey
(BA of E Administrative Secretary) and
Betty Scheele: for vetting relevant chapters.
Ronnie Rowan (IBF General Secretary): for
supplying much useful information.
Untold thousands of friends and players I
have met on court and off: for helping to keep
alight my enthusiasm and delight in all facets
of a marvellous game for more years than I
care to remember.

Acknowledgement is made to the following
for the reproduction of illustrations on the
pages indicated:
Badminton Gazette: 13, 19 (both), 20 (both),
23, 26, 29, 38, 43 (lower), 44, 45, 47, 51, 65,
71 (lower), 82, 88, 112, 131.
Basle Sports Museum: 8. BBC: 10. BBC
Hulton Picture Library: 11. Carlton Sports
Ltd: 30–31. Hugh Forgie: 54. Mike Grigg:
28, 33, 34–35. International Badminton
Federation: 15 (right). Litesome: 39 (right),
40. Preben Seborg: 16, 24. Mervyn Rees: 98
(lower), 99, 100, 101, 104. P. Richardson: 43
(upper). Robinson's Barley Water: 64. Louis
Ross: 43, 65, 71, 98 (upper), 102 (upper right
and lower), 103 (upper), 129, 147. RSL: 34–
35. *World Badminton*: 9, 12, 16, 24, 147.
Every endeavour has been made to
acknowledge illustrations where possible.
Quotations in the text, unless otherwise
specified are from the *Badminton Gazette*,
Badminton or *World Badminton*.

Abbreviations, except for England (not
indicated), are as follows:

C	=	Canada
Ch	=	People's Republic of China
D	=	Denmark
GFR	=	German Federal Republic
I	=	Indonesia
Ind	=	India
Ire	=	Ireland
J	=	Japan
K	=	S. Korea
M	=	Malaya/Malaysia
N	=	Netherlands
Nor	=	Norway
NZ	=	New Zealand
S	=	Sweden
Sco	=	Scotland
Swi	=	Switzerland
T	=	Thailand
USA	=	United States of America
W	=	Wales

The Guinness Book of
Badminton

Pat Davis

Guinness Superlatives Limited
2 Cecil Court, London Road, Enfield, Middlesex

Dedication
This book is dedicated to another Pat Davis, my wife and P.A.
Without her help and inspiration this book would have been
a pale shadow of its present bonny self

Editor: Alex E Reid
Design and layout: Michael Morey

Copyright: © Pat Davis and Guinness Superlatives Limited 1983

Published in Great Britain by Guinness Superlatives Limited
2 Cecil Court, Enfield, Middx

British Library Cataloguing in Publication Data
Davis, Patrick
The Guinness book of badminton.
1. Badminton
I. Title
796.34'5   GV1007
ISBN 0-85112-271-X

Printed and bound in Spain by TONSA, San Sebastian

One/**Early Days**

History of Badminton

There seems to be little doubt that badminton's lineage is aristocratic. But the facts as to precisely who invented the game, where and when, are still veiled in some doubt. They seem likely to remain so though badminton certainly made its bow less than 150 years ago

The origin and development of badminton's sister game is much more clear cut. Real (or royal) tennis originated first in monastic cloister, then in aristocratic castle before being played in the palaces of French kings—and forbidden by law to the *hoi polloi*. Shakespeare recorded the Dauphin's gift of tennis balls in 1414 to Henry V:

> When we have match't our rackets to these balls
> We will, in France, by God's grace, play a set
> Shall strike his father's crown into the hazard.

But *lawn* tennis was a Victorian middle-class adaptation. Although Major Gem, Clerk to the Birmingham magistrates, pioneered the outdoor game in the 1860s, the accolade has been given to a Major Walton Clopton Wingfield. By strange coincidence he was a distant descendant of John Wingfield who was gaoler of Charles D'Orleans, an enthusiastic tennis player—who had been taken prisoner at Agincourt. It was the Major who produced his invention 'Sphairistiké' (on an hour-glass shaped court!) at a Christmas party at Nantclwyd in 1873. It is the bust of the Major, inscribed 'Inventor of Lawn Tennis', which stands in pride of place in the Lawn Tennis Association's offices.

Milton Keynes, the Badminton Association of England's headquarters, can boast no such bust or clear-cut pedigree. Badminton's inventors could be as diverse as the seventh Duke of Beaufort's numerous children, Indian Army Officers, or a London club-man, John Loraine Baldwin. The only certainty is that, as lawn tennis sprang from real tennis, so badminton originated from battledore and shuttlecock.

The latter's history dates back to Ancient Greece, Sumeria and the early Far Eastern civilisations including Japan, India and China (where Oriental dexterity often used feet rather than hands or rackets). That it was equally popular in Europe is proved by medieval woodcuts which show peasants at play. With home-made, all-wood bats and crude shuttles it became a popular children's game as it could be played on any small patch of open ground.

Strutt's *Sports and Pastimes* went further. Badminton (*sic*) was popular among grown persons in the reign of James I. Indeed, the latter's son, Prince Henry, is recorded as 'playing at shuttlecock with one far taller than himself and hitting him by chance with the shuttlecock upon his forehead'. And the comedy of *Two Maides of Moreclacke* (1609) declared 'to play shuttlecock methinks is the game now'. Pepys too found time, doubtless from other more amorous pastimes, to mention 'shittlecock'.

By the 17th century, *le jeu de volant* had become an aristocratic pastime. It has been recorded that Catherine the Great enjoyed it. In neighbouring Sweden, Queen Christina played *featherball*, in which a soft ball of chicken feathers replaced a shuttlecock, on a court (now a church) near her Stockholm palace. Charming illustrations from the Basle Sportsmuseum show that it was played with a maximum of elegance but a minimum of activity by ladies and gentlemen of rank and of such rich apparel that swift or energetic movement must surely have been impossible. Watteau depicted it with his delicate, silken touch.

No activity was needed because the aim was to hit the shuttle *to* one's partner (he can hardly be called an opponent) not to beat him. Or one could play oneself—a racket in each hand!

In 1767 M de Garsault in the *Art of the Tennis Racket Maker* devoted 147 paragraphs to 'Royal Tennis' and but six to 'Concerning the Shuttlecock'. Used instead of a ball, they were, he bemoaned, extremely tiring to hit and, at 20 sous each, extremely expensive as three dozen could be

Strung rackets flank older vellum-covered battledore in RSL museum.

'quickly spoiled'. (How little times change!) As in tennis, the opening stroke of the game was made by a servant (hence, 'to serve'). The latter *threw* the shuttle into play reverting to the crank or catapult when he tired! Six or eight players were customary: shuttle-bases were 2 in *25 mm* in diameter, shades to come of the 'Cauliflowers' used in India a century later.

American Uber Cup player Diana Hales records that in 1864 in America it was played by teams of three or four who struck the shuttle in turn. And that—rather as William Webb Ellis, who with a fine disregard for the rules made handling-runs in football at Rugby in 1823, was frowned upon as 'taking unfair advantage'—so too were the growing number of players who actually tried to make their opponents *miss* the shuttle.

Conjecture gives way to incontrovertible fact. And the shape of things to come slowly emerges. At Badminton House, no less, on the vellum of an old-fashioned battledore is inscribed 'Kept up with Geraldine Somerset on Saturday, 12th January, 1850, to 2117. Henrietta Somerset.' And 'The Lady Henrietta Somerset in February 1845 kept up with Miss Sybil Mitchell 2018'. Listen—and you can still hear echo in the spacious front hall of Badminton House the boom of clumsy shuttle on tight stretched vellum, the chanted tally, and perhaps the childish woe when the so-near record, laboriously and carefully striven for, was not achieved.

Amazing that children could play with such disciplined care. Still more amazing that as yet no high-spirited youngsters had hit the shuttle *away* from, even at, their playmates; had never felt the urge to send them careering desperately, foolishly, hilariously, after an elusively placed shuttle.

Yet, surely now, badminton cannot be far away?

The Duke of Beaufort, Master of the Queen's Horse and a man who has hunted almost daily (as did his father before him) throughout 47 seasons—give or take a couple of wars in which he was actively engaged—will tell you positively that it was Lady Henrietta Somerset and the other seven daughters of the seventh Duke who invented the game in the 1840s or 1850s at Badminton House.

In his recent autobiography he writes:

'My parents habitually used the Front Hall as a sitting-room and it was also put to another good use by a previous generation. One rainy day in the middle of the last century, my great-aunts were feeling rather bored, so they rigged up a string from the front door handle to the fireplace to try out the battledores and shuttlecocks that they had devised for themselves with both ingenuity and patience. They then proceeded to play a new game, making up the rules as they went along. At first, their aim was to keep the shuttlecock in the air for as long as possible, but the rules became more and more sophisticated as their skill grew, and eventually between them they had invented the game of badminton.'

And at a dinner at the Mansion House in 1980 when he resigned as President of the British Field Sports Society he refers to the guests at a similar dinner in 1884 held to honour his grandfather:

'I see the names of many of my own family, including that of my great-aunt *who was responsible for inventing the game of badminton* in our front hall when she was a child. We still have her battledore—home-made with great ingenuity...'

There appears to be no doubt there. So, do we owe badminton to a woman?

Nevertheless, backed by no less an authority than badminton's first and greatest player and administrator, Sir George Thomas, (who himself played in his parents' home in Constantinople with tennis rackets and huge shuttles) there is another story. That of a day too wet for croquet when bored house-guests picked up the children's discarded battledores and shuttlecocks and played a form of badminton in that same front hall (1863–8). Its measurements would certainly allow for a court.

But two other claims, apocryphal perhaps, seem worthy of dismissal. With the children's well-made shuttles to hand it would surely have been unnecessary to make others out of champagne corks and chicken feathers. Nor would the hour-glass shaped court have been a necessity for only on one side-line do doors open inwards, on the other stands a very solid marble fireplace.

In this connection there arises the chicken and

J L Baldwin, founder of I Zingari and the 'Old Stagers', who may have drafted the game's first laws.

egg conundrum. Army officers, Indian army officers at that, might well have been among the guests. Had they, as some suggest, having learned the game in India brought it to Badminton House for its christening? Or, having played it first at Badminton, did they take it back to India as a social game to break the tedium of exile?

There is yet another alternative. It detracts none of the glory from Badminton House but focuses the spotlight more sharply on a middle-aged man, John Loraine Baldwin, rather than on a young girl.

S M Massey, one of the first All-England champions, unequivocally states 'badminton's origin was due to the late Mr J L Baldwin who first played it at Badminton House'. Born in 1809, a member of the gentry and later a friend of the Prince of Wales, 'kindly, handsome and dignified', he was undoubtedly a welcome guest at Badminton House. Indeed, he lived only 20 miles *32 km* away at Tintern Abbey and even became affectionately known as the 'Bishop of Tintern'! As further proof a photo shows him in stately recumbence, in front of a cricket group taken outside the House itself.

Indeed, cricket, and acting, were his great loves. He was one of the four founders of the socially exclusive I Zingari (Egyptian: Wanderers). And, after stage experience at Oxford, he helped to found the 'Old Stagers' who for more than a century have produced plays (to say nothing of a witty and topical Epilogue) during Canterbury Cricket Week.

More pertinent, he was a confirmed club-man, hailed indeed as the 'King of Clubs'. It was he who wrote the *Revised Rules of Short Whist* as well as some rules for the 'Four in Hand Club'. What more natural than that it was his fertile and meticulous mind that devised badminton and its first laws when he saw a haphazard game during one of his visits to Badminton House?

Ken Davidson in *Winning Badminton*, written with Lealand Gustavson, states that 'badminton as we now know it was played in England in the 17th century. It must have been played in other parts of Europe since a portrait by Adam Manyoki of 'Young Prince Sulkowski' who lived in the late 17th and early 18th century, shows that young scion of the Polish Royal Family holding a shuttle-cock and racket'. About 1740, the youthful Earl of

Judy Hashman and Kathy Tredgett, in period costume and with long-handled battledores, re-enact Badminton's infancy in the hall of Badminton House.

'The New Game of Badminton in India' : *clothing seems as unsuitable for India as for sport.*

Dysart was similarly depicted—together with a frisky dog wanting to be in the act also! Battledore and shuttlecock 'yes'; but badminton, surely 'no'.

England's greatest pre-Second World War player, Betty Uber, in *That Badminton Racket* states 'Badminton was introduced about 1870 by the Duke to his guests—Army officers on leave from India'. It might well be that the fond father watching his children at play had seen the game's possibilities—and offered them as an acceptable means of alleviating his rain-bound guests' boredom. Margaret Tragett, Betty Uber's great forerunner, suggested India as 'the country in which the game originated'.

Perhaps Massey neatly encapsulated the dilemma when he wrote 'The germ of the game and the name are due to England; its rapid evolution to India'.

Lawn Tennis, Croquet and Racquets, etc. published in 1883 called badminton 'lawn tennis played with shuttlecocks' and ranked it amongst the 'etceteras'. It put the cat among the pigeons too (or should it be 'the cart before the horse') by stating 'badminton, lawn tennis with shuttlecocks, was first played, I believe, in India, and introduced into England by the Duke of Beaufort'.

Its existence in India is well documented by *Badminton Gazette* correspondents. Captain Coupar played in Lahore in 1868; Colonel Arthur Hill at his Calcutta home, Colonel Deane in Simla and R H Abbatt in Allahabad in 1872; Sattara in W. India in 1873, and Karachi in 1874 are also mentioned. And it was of course in Poona (now Pune) that not only did Sir Edward Henry revolutionise the game with the first drop-shot, but the first laws were drawn up in 1873 by Colonel S S C Selby, RE. (Was his fly-leaf inscription 'Here's law and warrant, lady' a generalisation or a barbed arrow flighted at ladies who violated them'?) And 4 years later the *Times of India* reported that the Bishop of Madras had made a vehement attack from his pulpit on badminton played on Sunday mornings.

One wall of King's School's court is part of the ancient City wall of Canterbury, dating back to the Middle Ages.

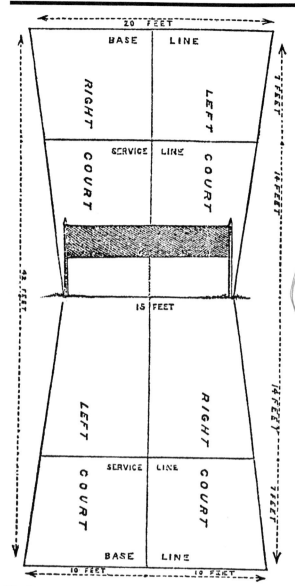

The hour-glass shaped court shown in 1876 in a booklet entitled Rules for the New Games of Tennis and Badminton.

A photo in Bernard Adams' excellent *Badminton Story* shows six bowler-hatted gentlemen playing outdoors over a net strung across the middle of 11 ft *3.4 m* high posts—to the strains of a band. Other intriguing photos show several well-worn courts at Peshawar; strategically placed, tiny, turbaned 'shuttle-boys'; and a game played over a volleyball-height net amid exotic palms, whilst servants waited court-side with fresh supplies of rackets and shuttles.

It was in Poona that a tennis court was set aside for badminton 'duffers' who got their own back by referring to badminton as 'push-feather'. Even less happy were the natives' unwitting name 'Tomfool' (derived from 'tam-tam', the bat of a native game, and 'Phul', a flower: tamphul);

'bumble-puppy'; and 'hit and scream'. The latter because of the histrionics of long-skirted ladies when the shuttle was homing in on face or hat high piled with artificial fruit or flowers. It was this perhaps that put tennis again in the ascendant just as badminton had supplanted croquet.

Not surprisingly, most of such courts were out of doors. But the hour-glass shape court may well be attributed to the game being played in Karachi in an old barracks only slightly wider than a court. In it there were swing doors opening onto the side-lines. To avoid danger or interruption of play, the side-line was angled in to join a short service line 4 ft *1.2 m* shorter than the base-line. 'In India', it was said 'the court, like ladies, had a waist'.

To which person or country goes the credit for inventing badminton is conjectural. But that it has given pleasure to millions and is today played in over 60 countries is incontrovertible fact.

The Badminton Association of England

To many players the BA of E is a remote body, far removed from the problems of everyday club play, that rapaciously demands ever higher affiliation fees yet gives little if anything in return. Nothing could be further from the truth!

Had it not been for the vision of stocky, walrus-moustached, balding enthusiast Colonel S S C Dolby who first banded fourteen clubs together at Southsea on 12 September 1893 to form the Badminton Association we might still be horrified to find league opponents playing on a court twice the size of ours, shuttles twice or half the speed we are accustomed to, and short service lines at varying distances from the net.

Nor should we have the modern wealth of badminton amenities: leagues and tournaments, international and exhibition matches; Badminton magazine and TV coverage; coaching and schools' play; insurance policies and cheap clothing . . . The benefits are many. Though affiliation should surely be *giving* to the game (as three generations of honorary officials, from the humblest club secretary to the BA of E President himself, have so generously done) rather than merely receiving from it.

Colonel Dolby was just such an enthusiast. Not merely did he accept the Presidency but he also undertook the duties of Honorary Secretary and Honorary Treasurer. The latter positions he held until the call of duty swept him off to the Boer War.

Colonel S S C Dolby : Founder of the Badminton Association of England. (President 1893–8; Hon Secretary and Treasurer 1893–9)

Maybe it was a matter of rank for the Committee elected included three Lieutenant Colonels, two Majors and only two 'Misters', mainly from clubs in Hampshire and Devon. Ireland, 1899, and then Scotland, 1911, formed their own unions. But they, like clubs world-wide, affiliated to the Badminton Association. The first foreign club to do so was that run by Baron von Maltzhan at Homburg Spa.

At first, few clubs either cared or were even aware of the Association's existence. The 1903–4 BA Handbook showed, amongst others, 13 affiliated clubs in Devon, 21 in Middlesex, 19 in Surrey—and 13 in Dublin, where badminton was thriving. By 1914, the number had grown to 467, and in 1923, to 550. By 1938, it had risen sharply to 1296 clubs with an estimated 42 000 players. Now in 1982, there are well over 5000 clubs and some 125 000 affiliated players.

Such, sadly, are merely the tip of the iceberg. Below is a great number of clubs and an estimated 1 500 000 players who feel little or no responsibility for the game as a whole—or are horrified by a modest affiliation fee of a pound or so. Less than the cost of a lipstick or a packet of cigarettes. Far, far less than the £5–£6 that European players pay without demur.

'Affiliation fee' has long been a dirty word. Parochially-minded clubs saw no benefit to themselves in the *Gazette*, or in the Inter-County Championship and international matches that it reported. Annual general meetings became a battleground where county secretaries sprang desperately to the defence of their invariably 'poverty-stricken' clubs against that marauding monster—the harassed Honorary Treasurer of

the BA of E. In 1962, they turned down a 3d *1½p* increase per head 'thereby denying future generations a chance of new halls'. In 1967, the fee was upped to 2/6d *12½p* per head from 17/6d *87½p* for one court or 1/- *5p* per head (18/- *90p* min). The first increase for 10 years during which costs had risen 75 per cent! The skirmishing continues today.

Not long after his appointment in 1978, Chief Executive Air Vice-Marshal Larry Lamb, doubtless used to dealing in millions, saw his urgent plea for an increase grudgingly accepted—but only at the cost of axing the free issue of the *Gazette* to affiliated clubs after a run of 60 years. Today, as then, the BA of E is living far beyond its own means. It relies heavily on the suddenly terminable support of the Sports Council, on equipment manufacturers, TV fees and commercial sponsorship.

The formation of County Associations in the '20s was a great filip to the game in general as well as the springboard for the promotion of the Inter-County Championship (1928) which did much to raise both standards and interest. They looked after club interest, ran open and restricted tournaments as well as leagues, produced their own handbooks—and later, newsletters.

Progress on a wider front was steady if unspectacular until the '70s. Tournament players were co-opted onto a committee of enthusiastic 'veterans' (1939); the BA of E, nominated All-England pairs to ensure the strongest possible partnerships (1948); a tournament levy was introduced (1948); a Publicity Officer, S Lyle Smythe was appointed—at a fee of £30 (1952); the English Invitation Tournament was instituted as a means of ranking and selecting (1953).

Less important but perhaps the end of an era was the disappearance of the blazer. The ubiquitous tracksuit, attractive and utilitarian in itself, usurped its place. The two BA of E blazers had long been a mark of honour and of distinction. That awarded to players chosen for England had narrow green, white and blue stripes on a dark red ground; with a red rose and BA of E in words on the pocket. That most coveted of all, to be worn only by All-England champions, had red, white and blue stripes on a green background with a white rose and AEBC on the pocket. These remnants of Edwardian and pre-War glory, once so proudly worn, are now seen only on ceremonial, pre-match line-ups.

In 1967, larger premises were rented in Bromley, Kent, as HQ offices. Prior to that, Herbert Scheele had worked from his own home (with only the

From a derelict farm at Milton Keynes has arisen the BA of E headquarters and the National Badminton Centre.

help of his wife, Betty). So too had Coaching Secretary Nancy Horner; the Honorary Treasurer from his own office; the business side of the *Gazette* was run from RSL premises. The BA of E was still very much an *amateur* organisation—in the best sense of that word.

But with the '70s and under the shadow of Open Sport, the organisation became much more professional. A Coaching Secretary, another ex-RAF man, jovial Flight-Lieutenant Ollie Cussen joined Squadron-Leader Larry Landrey, Administrative Secretary. A full-time Chief Coach too, Ken Crossley, to be followed by Roger Mills, was appointed. In 1977 came Nick Budibent, Development and Publicity, who was responsible for an increase in sponsorship. But it was nothing like the kings' ransoms flooding into much televised Lawn Tennis and Golf, nor sufficient to send top players racing to the flesh-pots. In 1978, to do justice to the increasing number of sponsored events, a Cumbrian with a distinct sense of humour and a flair for organisation was appointed Promotions Manager —Tommy Marrs.

In the same year, PA Management Consultants and a BA of E Committee sifted through over 400 applicants to get just the right man to see them through the 'Open' traumas that had afflicted Lawn Tennis. Air Vice-Marshal Larry Lamb, CB, CBE, AFC, FBIM was the man chosen. And things began to hum!

Bigger, more central offices were constructed from a derelict farm just outside new town Milton Keynes. And within 18 months a three-court hall was ready for play. Still to come to complete the National Badminton Centre are a hostel and bar, a library-cum-museum and a lecture theatre.

More staff were added; Derek Betley, an accountant, to keep a finger on the financial pulse; on Cussen's retirement, Barbara Wadsworth, ex of the BBC and a Cheshire county player, became Coaching Administrator, and Ciro Ciniglio, who had played top badminton for no fewer than five counties, took on the vital role of Coaching and Team Manager. Paul Whetnall did much coaching but no new Chief Coach was appointed after Roger Mills' departure.

Training support grants were given to top and promising players; closer liaison made with the English Schools BA; an under-23 B Squad formed; more and more tours arranged both in England and abroad; Committees streamlined; a glossy new look *Badminton* magazine published; more benefits thought up for grass-roots players. Things were on the move. And yet—All-England's men's titles, and Thomas Cup and Uber Cup triumphs were still beyond our grasp.

Early days perhaps but surely the day will soon come when the Association that nurtured the game, then gave it freedom, will reap its reward in terms of on-court success. Against nations such as Indonesia and China, where government support is high for sports which bring national prestige, the task is immense. The struggle will be hard!, And will need the backing of every badminton enthusiast.

The International Badminton Federation

With badminton most certainly christened, if not born, deep in the heart of the English countryside, it is not surprising that English officials held badminton's leading-reins for many years.

First Ireland and Scotland affiliated to the generally titled Badminton Association. Then, as the game spread, followed individual clubs in Canada and Australia, New Zealand and USA, and later still overseas nations: France, New Zealand and Denmark.

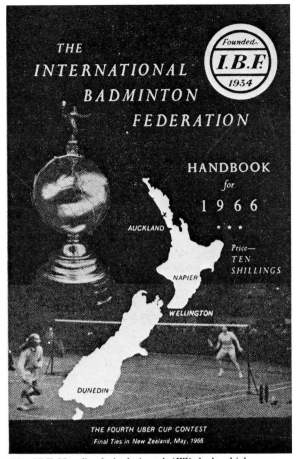

It was not until 1932 that there was the first hint of rebellion against virtual English dictatorship. And that was not unwarranted because on the 22-man Committee, Ireland, Scotland and Wales could hope for no more than one representative each. So, completely outnumbered, they eventually got together (during the Welsh Championships at Llandudno's Craigside Hydro) under the chairmanship of Ireland's team manager John Plunkett-Dillon to formulate a demand to be 'given the key'.

Duly briefed, Plunkett-Dillon, a solicitor, approached the BA of E's most influential figure, Vice-President Sir George Thomas. The latter courteously listened to their proposals, laid them before his own committee and, with Plunkett-Dillon and A D Prebble, worked zealously to reverse the initial horrified BA 'thumbs down'. Prebble was a leading international and administrator at both tennis and badminton. Having seen the wrangling when the International Lawn Tennis Federation was formed, he worked enthusiastically for better things for badminton.

Fierce debate raged but in March 1934, despite a vehement last-ditch stand by the die-hards, it was resolved to call a meeting of the four Home Countries, with Denmark, Canada, Netherlands, New Zealand and France. So it came about, in July, that after 41 years of uninterrupted rule, England handed over control of the laws and the international game. The latter's proposed rules were adopted and its 'christening spoon', a generous donation of £200, gratefully accepted. The International Badminton Federation was in being. Seven out of the thirteen strong Executive Committee, however, were English and only two came from outside the UK. And any other President than Sir George Thomas would have been unthinkable.

The first of so many new member nations, India, was elected in 1935; fitting indeed since in that country the game certainly flourished and may well have been born. The following season, the first slim Handbook of 63 pages was compiled by the BA of E's (and now IBF's) Secretary, F W Hickson.

The IBF Handbook, badminton's 'Wisden', which grew from a slender 63 pages to a rotund 400 under Herbert Scheele's editorship.

Sadly, Hickson died before he could make his mark on the new Federation. And so, in 1938, from a two-man field, the IBF appointed Herbert Scheele as its Honorary Secretary, a choice they surely can never have regretted for in that position he gave them 38 years of loyal and distinguished service.

Much of the Federation's initial work was to be in connection with the Laws and the Thomas and Uber Cup Championships. (Full details of these are dealt with under those headings). An AGM was held in 1940 but it was to be the last until 1946 when seven of the fifteen member nations agreed that subscriptions for 1942–5 should be waived. A year later came the first handbook for 7 years.

Verna Keddie of Bunbury, West Australia, travelled to and from Ballarat to play for her country; the match and overall journey of 4780 miles 7690 km took 19 days. Not bad for a home fixture?

IBF Council at work. Indonesia's Dr Sudirman, Denmark's Poul-Erik Nielsen, President Stellan Mohlin, his successor Scotland's Craig Reedie, efficient Secretary Ronnie Rowan.

Edited by Herbert Scheele, it had grown lustily to 117 pages, filled with the first of the detailed national and international records and the editorial notes which became such invaluable features.

In 1955, Sir George felt that 21 years in office was enough both for his good and that of the Federation. That he was no titled figurehead is boldly underlined by the fact that in that time he had missed but one meeting of the various committees, and even sub-committees, which he chaired with both charm and efficiency. And *that* one meeting had been held while he was on the high seas returning from Singapore, where he had watched all the Thomas Cup inter-zone ties, presented his trophy, and been accorded a rapturous reception. That he still had much to give the game at the age of 74 is evidenced by his being given the right (as Founder President) to attend the AGM and Council Meetings.

Honorary Treasurer D L H Mercer also retired after 21 years of increasingly onerous service. An indefatigable sportsman and spare time worker but no accountant, the actual book-keeping was left largely to former international A W Goodfellow whose firm generously audited the books for 28 years—for a guinea a year in the early days! He was made an Honorary Life Vice-President and was succeeded by Lancashire's former international Harold Morland, a practising accountant.

By 1954 membership had again doubled to 31 which included 11 Eastern countries. And by 1958, the game had grown so much that to prevent a log-jam of fixtures, permanent dates were allotted to the major European Championships and a specific date for National and Restricted Championships.

A year later on 1 July, the Federation celebrated its Silver Jubilee at the Hyde Park Hotel with Sir George as the Guest of Honour of the 20 national organisations represented. A few months later still, a Council meeting was held for the first time ever outside London, in Amsterdam. But it was not until 1976, 42 years after the foundation of the IBF, that an AGM was held abroad, in Bangkok. Thereafter, it was held in conjunction with a major event.

1963 signalled another important jubilee, that of Herbert Scheele's appointment, marked by the presentation of a silver salver and cheque.

Minor as well as major matters had to be dealt with. 500 was decided on as the minimum number of affiliated players acceptable for a nation to be entitled to full membership. Lesser numbers warranted only Associate Membership. A glance at the names of some such members gives a striking idea of badminton's expansion to some of the remotest corners of the earth: Kuwait and Tobago; Bahrain and Sarawak; Seychelles and Vietnam; Falkland Islands and Iceland; Sabah and Peru.

Other minor yet necessary legislation involved a switch to metric weights and distances; stipulation of a minimum height of hall for international play—26 ft 8 m; Bisgood's proposal to restrict the height of all badminton halls to a common one had been rejected as impracticable.

With the shadow of Open badminton and its attendant pitfalls about them, legislation was enacted on amateur and international qualifications which had to be such as to allow for badminton's possible grasping of its long-wished-for holy grail, inclusion in the Olympic Games. Players were divided into two categories: amateur and licensed. The former were granted increased prize money up to £100 and with it Olympic eligibility; the latter, eyes hopefully on the golf and tennis millionaires, could win whatever prize money was going but became Olympic outlaws.

Today top prize money for one event is the £3000 offered at the London Friends' Provident Masters, a welcome but almost derisory amount compared with that pocketed by Wimbledon winners. In December 1983, Pro-Kennex Grand Prix prizes will be $10 000 and $6000 for the singles winners.

Sponsorship brought in its train greater efforts to catch the TV eye: advertising on tracksuits was, subject to official approval, permitted; but limited on whites to 2 emblems neither exceeding 20 cm²; the former of course had to be discarded once play began and 'predominantly white' was still the order of the day unless international team colours had been approved.

The prohibitive cost of production of a 400 + page handbook sadly left the game without its 'Wisden'. As some small recompense an annual Statute Book is published. And the quarterly *World Badminton* launched and edited by Herbert Scheele in 1972, gave the ever-growing list of international events and news greater scope than could England's *Badminton Gazette* which had hosted it for many years.

After nearly 7 years, during which *WB* grew from twelve to twenty pages, Mr Scheele handed over the reins to Lorne Wortman of Canada. All member nations now had to buy a proportionate quota of copies, and editorials were to voice Council's opinions, not the editor's. (Herbert Scheele had occasionally fallen foul of his 'masters' by his outspokenness). Assistant editor Rupert Mee was tragically killed in a car crash, and in March 1980 control passed to the Scottish Badminton Union who appointed Craig Reedie, Judy Budge and Willie Kemp as the Editorial Committee who have produced a lively, well illustrated magazine.

One of the joys of badminton has been its tradition of keen but friendly international rivalry. But with the advent of the '70s the snake glided into badminton's Eden. The 'Apartheid' question gave rise to sporadic demonstrations, player walkouts, and national outcries for South Africa's expulsion. Today, an uneasy truce exists: the South African Badminton Union, SABU, has given an undertaking not to enter for Thomas or Uber Cups.

The major conflict, as in other sports, has been the acceptance of China as a member. The IBF

King Gustav of Sweden, a first-class tennis player, took up badminton on his 75th birthday.

rightly and resolutely refused her conditional demand for the expulsion of unoffending Taiwan, a member since 1957. A secondary bone of contention that arose was the voting scale: one vote on affiliation for all; an extra vote for larger badminton nations with more than 10 000 active, affiliated players; and a third vote if a country had participated in two of the three most recent Thomas or Uber Cup competitions. Recently elected smaller nations, mainly African and Asiatic, demanded equality with their bigger and more knowledgeable confrères. 'One nation, one vote' was the cry.

Impasse arose. Relations worsened. The Asian Badminton Confederation attempted a partially successful boycott of the All-England Championship. (The Home Countries each with three votes were held to be a mischievous cabal who had united to thwart these two moves). It was also unsuccessfully proposed that only countries with individual political status be members. In 1977, Taiwan was expelled but an appeal to the English courts backed her stand that such an act was unconstitutional. In 1978, a breakaway World Badminton Federation was formed, and it took some 3 years of patient negotiation before the Chinese dragon and the Taiwan lamb lay happily together in the IBF fold, and with WBF and IBF unified.

With Open badminton accepted in 1979 surprisingly meekly by 54 votes to 0 and in just 25 minutes, world badminton looks set for another concerted advance. World rankings have been computed; a world schedule of major tournaments agreed; three successful World Championships held; a World Team Championship mooted as are revamped Thomas and Uber Cup Championships to encourage entry by smaller nations.

The IBF has constantly urged the claims of badminton for inclusion in the Olympic Games. But, although it was chosen as a demonstration game in 1972, these pleas have fallen on deaf ears. And with the astronomically escalating size and cost of the Games, probably will continue to do so. Despite that, thanks to the IBF, badminton is a truly international game.

War Years

Naturally, the two World Wars brought badminton virtually to a standstill. But even amid its horrors and tragedies, relaxation had to be sought. Badminton played its part.

The *Gazette*, the BA of E's official publication, soldiered on until April 1915. Its editor appealed for news of players who had joined up. A Gazette War Fund was started: Bolton BC raised 16/- *80p* by entrance fees from an American tournament; leading players took part in an exhibition for War Refugees at Richmond Baths (Admittance 1/- *5p*) but 'were sadly out of condition'.

Appeals were made for rackets for the 12 000 soldiers in training at the White City. There the game reverted to its infancy with three, four or even more players a side; in odd corners 'singles without a net found favour'. Major McCallum, later of Strollers (the Irish touring team) fame, unperturbed by a few snags, kept the game going at Ballykinlar Camp in Ireland: 'The huts are 20 ft *6.1 m* wide and 60 ft *18.3 m* long—but only 10 ft *3.0 m* high! The light is from a few oil lamps— and a stove rather gets in the way'. But they pressed on!

It was even chauvinistically suggested that the French C. in C. Marshal Joffre's 1914 stonewall tactics were based on those of ladies' doubles!

The Second World War brought ever greater dislocation. The blackout caused both lighting and heating difficulties. Local travel was by bicycle. Betty Uber recalls an unhappy 1940 visit to front-line Herne Bay: frozen pipes festooned with icicles in a deserted hotel; anxious play on a mile-long pier liable to instant demolition if invasion threatened!

The best of such shuttles as were made went to the Forces; civilians played with brown or black feathered shuttles of disconcertingly variable speed. In the 'phoney war' days, Reinforced Shuttlecocks Limited, (hereinafter abbreviated to RSL), later to suffer air-raid damage during the London blitz, advertised: 'Badminton players will be as relieved as RSL to think that the only gun in action is their shuttle-gun'. That was too good to last: after an air-raid a Leicester Club had its courts commandeered as a mortuary; Alexandra Palace's courts disappeared beneath mountains of bombed out furniture.

But even in prisoner-of-war camps badminton could flourish if there was an enthusiast such as Peter Birtwistle, now a BA of E Vice-President, in

During the Second World War, at King George VI's command, courts were marked out in Windsor Castle State Apartments so that the present Queen and Princess Margaret could play.

charge. At Oflag VIIC, Laufen, the Bishop of Salzburg's Palace, three courts were marked out in the old coach-house. Rackets, gut and shuttles were sent by RSL's Frank Henley and Denmark's A C J van Vossen; the latter also sent food parcels when he could. At Biberach, 60 miles *97 km* North of Lake Constance, play was outdoor but forbidden if it was windy for fear of mishits damaging irreplaceable shuttles. At Eichstatt, 2 ft *0.6 m* extra width attempted to compensate for a 12 ft *3.7 m* lack in length. Despite that, a pillar in the middle of the base-line, a low ceiling and still lower beams, 400 members played under a comprehensive booking system that ensured fair shares for all from 7 am to 8 pm in league matches and tournaments. The courts were put out of bounds after discovery of an escape tunnel leading from an adjoining room. (And the supreme accolade for Sheffield rackets: after 5 years they were all still in use!)

In 1946, the slow derequisitioning of halls brought a vitriolic outburst from an incensed Herbert Scheele: 'It is deplorable in the extreme that the use of halls is being governed by the despicable desire of their owners, often official bodies, to increase their bank balances. Drill Halls are being used for bazaars and whist drives, not for military purposes'.

Shuttles were virtually 'export only'; petrol unobtainable. (In the Philippines original corks were constantly refeathered).

Happily there was a lighter side. It was recorded that English players frequently mis-sighted shuttles when playing in Denmark. Was this due to the unaccustomed richness of the enormous Danish meals? Would it be advisable for the Danes' return visit to start earlier—so that they could acclimatise to *our* rations?

And the last word (no unusual occurrence) with England's Warwick Shute: 'My cabin-mate returned from Jutland with an eight-year supply of eggs'!

Famous Clubs

Although, as in India, badminton was initially a garden game (weather permitting), the club system became the foundation of British badminton proper. And it was of prime importance in the game's early days when county matches were unthought of and tournaments were few. Then, and later in the heyday of the London League, club teams were star-studded with internationals and near internationals.

Today, club badminton is more run of the mill stuff ranging widely and wildly from virtual beginners to county players. Not surprisingly modern clubs do not feature as prominently in the news as the old timers did. Perhaps the quest for the Europe Cup may lead to greater club consciousness as the search becomes more intense to find Britain's top club team.

The two Palace clubs, Crystal and Alexandra, loomed large in the early years of the century. The latter club's seven courts were marked out as early as 1902. In the First World War they were occupied by Belgian refugees; in the Second, in 1941, by furniture from bombed houses. On the advent of peace, the Trustees stonewalled all Alexandra Palace's efforts to return to the building despite a 1947 agreement to restore the courts to the Club. Eventually, bureaucracy won. The BBC was granted the lease, a rent of £15 000 for the two rooms *below* the courts and £1000 for the playing hall itself wanted only as a means of ensuring absolute quiet. Alexandra Palace BC received a beggarly £200 compensation and had to settle for Finchley Drill Hall.

All this was a sad waste of many improvements which the Club had made. Unhealthy gas had been replaced by daylight electric lighting, disliked by visiting teams and soon altered. Walls had been painted brown; ceiling, biscuit. And a Columbian pine floor had been laid on a cork underlay. A worthy setting for players of the calibre of Hume and Nichols, Jean Stewart and Nancy Horner, and for the North London Championships.

One badly lit court in a Baptist Chapel schoolroom: such was the birthplace of Upper Norwood BC in 1897. When it moved soon after to a swimming bath and then to the nearby Crystal Palace it was to become the most influential club in England: to rank among its members such pioneers as J H E Hart and G W Vidal, a young enthusiast Margaret Larminie, the non-pareil Sir George Thomas, and the all-conquering Irishman, Frank Devlin.

Its first three courts were in the South Gallery (next to the stuffed wild animals) where an over-enthusiastic smash might well float down to the Main Hall. Tea was served at the end of the gloomy Jungle Gallery! After several moves, five courts were laid in the old skating rink. In 1922, a further and final move was made to the separate Canada Building where eleven (later thirteen) fine courts,

The oldest club in Ireland is the Dublin Ailesbury BC founded in 1903.

G W Vidal, BA of E Hon Secretary 1899–1906.

J H E Hart: another of the pioneers of the game 'whose names will always be honoured'.

partitioned by green curtains, were available every weekday from 2–10 pm. Here, on the half-hidden 'Shy Ladies' court, Betty Uber tirelessly perfected her serving. And here the South of England Championships were held for many years.

Fortunately the holocaust of 1936 destroyed only the Crystal Palace itself. And the Club quickly denied rumours that the building's escaping rats had swept into new quarters with them. After the War, Crystal Palace Badminton Club, with the neglected Canada Building crumbling round their ears, had hoped to use Dulwich Indoor Tennis Courts but despite verbal agreement nothing came of the proposal.

Almost equally famous was the Logan Club, the third of the élitist clubs. It was founded by the Baddeley twins, Wilfred and Herbert, of Wimbledon tennis fame (Wilfred, at 19, was the youngest

Four-a-side was the order of the day on the huge 60 ft × 30 ft 18.3 m × 9.1 m court at Ealing BC.

Southsea BC 1st Team. Leg of mutton sleeves, black ties and oddly-shaped racket-heads are much in evidence. Colonel Dolby is third from the left.

ever singles winner) not merely for badminton—but also for bridge and billiards. It moved to Earls Court where an extra court and bridge-room were added in 1912.

During the First World War the courts were often taken over by Hazel Hogarth, originator of the backhand serve, to make sun-flaps for the troops. 1931 saw the first Logan Invitation (Doubles) Tournament. To be one of the 16 men or women invitees with a chance of winning the coveted silver shuttle was the badminton player's cachet. The London Championships were held here between the Wars; it was apocryphally rumoured that, because of restricted space, they were run by Colonel R Bruce Hay from a telephone booth in the lounge. The club which had boasted such great names as Sir George Thomas and Margaret Tragett was wound up in 1947.

If the recurrence of these names at different clubs sounds odd to modern ears it should be remembered that at that time players often belonged to two or three clubs. And, until checked by London League rules, played matches for all of them!

Cazenove, despite its name, was East End born, in 1909, in the Orion Gym, Hackney. W H Clarke probably set up a record for long-time serving Secretaries—over 40 years, during which he twice resuscitated an almost moribund club.

Ealing BC's boast was that it was one of the oldest clubs in the country. It was founded early in the 1890's by R F St Andrew St John, a retired professor of Hindustani in the Indian Civil Service. As in India the court was hour-glass shaped and Sirdar rackets—2/6d *12½p*—and fluffy shuttles from the Army and Navy Stores were used. After a spell in Ealing Baths playing on a 30 ft by 60 ft *9.1 m × 18.3 m* court (twice today's area) they built, in 1903, for £450, their own courts. These, although they paid a steady 5 per cent dividend, were condemned for lack of run-back and changing accommodation.

S M Massey was Secretary when they won the London League Shield in 1909 and 1910; Colonel S S C Dolby, one of the founders of the game, kept it open throughout the First World War. It was Ealing who pioneered tournaments 'restricted' to non-open event winners.

Richmond BC in 1900 planned to use the Star and Garter Hotel ballroom but had to content themselves with Townsend Terrace Drill Hall until 1911. The sub for the whole family was set at 7/6d *37½p*. In 1901 they had been challenged by Ealing but the match was postponed for a month 'to get more practice in'. In 1912–13 they beat

the powerful Logan side to win the Championship of London. Richmond was undoubtedly a name to conjure with!

Claim and counter-claim have been made as to which were the first clubs in this country. An article based on the memories of Major C H Hannington and Sir George Thomas gives the accolade to Southsea where the game was played in 1888 on South Parade Pier (burned down in 1904). Bath had a club in 1890 and the two played matches in that year though a month or two earlier Southsea had beaten Caledonians in what was claimed to be the first ever Club match. Clubs quickly followed we are told in Southampton, Romsey, Bognor and Guildford.

This is supported by the fact that badminton undoubtedly was first played largely by retired Indian Army Officers and Indian Civil Servants who tended to settle along England's sunnier South Coast. Massey in his book *Badminton* (1911) however claims that in 1875 'Tea and Badminton' was the order of the day in the ball-room of the West Cliff Hotel, Folkestone, where a Services Club played.

This was countered by Miss D Baker, Honorary Secretary of Teignmouth BC, who claimed the honour for her club 'in the early '70s (when shuttles were £1.50 a gross and tea 11d *5p* a pound)'. It had been founded by the Lucas family, of whom Meriel Lucas won six singles and ten ladies' doubles All-England titles between 1899 and 1910.

Back came the *Gazette* with still other claims. St Andrews BC alone had *documentary* proof—in its Club Rules dated 1884–5 when badminton ousted tennis from a specially built hall. Guildford started in 1891 or 1892 and a minute records '1/- *5p* for four shuttles'. Tavistock BC (1901) spent nearly as much on marking chalk as on shuttles.

No matter which club can claim the title these were the pioneers. They fought it out, three or four a side on hour-glass courts of varying dimensions with shuttles of varying sizes and speeds. Play can never have been dull. Especially when ladies' pairs played men—and beat them!

But even older than these is the New York BC. Founded in 1878, membership carried great social distinction. With a waiting list of 300, many of

Lensbury & Britannic House BC played 1131 matches between 1950–8 (170 in one season); Occasionals BC played 2000 matches in 18 seasons.

Canada's oldest club, 'Montreal Ladies' Tennis and Badminton Club', was founded in 1908. Regulations then stipulated that 'skirts must be full and not more than 8 in above the floor'.

them débutantes, the committee could afford to elect 'only the good-looking ones'. (Of applicant J Smith it was tersely and unflatteringly recorded: 'Not much'). There was a profusion of tea, flowers, whist and gossip—but little badminton. At least until 1904 when Ted Van Winkle decided they were playing incorrectly—and provided a set of rules!

The ladies wore trains and picture hats; the men top hats, chokers, and Prince Albert coats. Not surprisingly 'no one ran'—though one male was expelled for the heinous impropriety of removing his coat. 'Badminton' it was opined, 'is an easy game not demanding the same exertion as bowling'. With four-a-side that was a distinct possibility.

When a bell rang, activity reigned for the first to finish had choice of lavish prizes: often silverware; once, even, US Steel Corporation Stock. If a girl was distressed that she had not won a prize she was paired with the best player so that the situation could be tactfully remedied.

Shuttles were so slow it was impossible to kill them 10 ft *3 m* from the net. So when the sisters of the founders saw that the cup they had presented was likely to be won outright they imported a 6 ft 7 in *2.0 m* tennis giant, Mahan. Driving his opponent to the base-line by sheer brute strength, he pinned him there and waited at the net to make the inevitable kill. He certainly saved the cup that day—but won it outright himself with two more victories!

Amongst other clubs in USA are recorded the Bird 'N Bat Club and, worse still, the Gut 'N Feathers Club! In the 1930s, nearly every new house in California was designed with an outdoor court. In Canada, the game was played in its major cities in huge clubs with superb facilities, and with coaches such as J Frank Devlin and G S B 'Curly' Mack. Denmark had not been slow to build fine halls used seven days a week, morning, noon and night. Hvidovre BK, Kobenhavns BK and Gentofte BK are famous names who have long fought for Danish supremacy. In the Far East, still evenings precluded the need for halls; any bit of level ground became a court.

England's biggest and most powerful club to which top players inevitably gravitate is Wimble-don boasting a membership of 870. Other Surrey clubs follow: Coulsdon and Purley (330) and Ebbisham (258). Littlehampton has 200 then the North takes over with Bolton's Markland Hill (174). Even little Spalding has 116 enthusiasts.

Other club names to conjure with are the famous Irish and Scottish touring teams, the Strollers and the Wayfarers respectively. The Occasionals (Middlesex) played matches only: 2000 plus in their first 25 years, all organised by disabled Percy Emms. The Wizards and the Witches are the Elysian Fields where top players past their best (Gerald Tautz was playing when he was over 70) still browse happily. The Challengers, a team of the best Glasgow men, played in a police station. Gnomes and Jovials speak for themselves.

And it is in clubs such as these—over 5300 are affiliated to the BA of E—that badminton is enjoyed in almost every village and town of any size throughout the country.

Halls – Ancient and Modern

Few sports can have flourished so richly in so barren a desert of facilities as has badminton. Few have been played in so divergent a range of unsuitable halls that have included prisons and work-houses.

Before the First World War only a handful of clubs could boast a hall built specially for the game. Ealing Badminton Club, in 1903 was the first to build its own hall (£450) but it was subsequently villified as 'with little run back; it could have been much better'. St Marks, Kensington was built by B Narischkine, whose father had owned large Russian estates and been connected with the Imperial Court. Later, it fell on hard times and became a billiard hall.

The famous Logan BC added an extra court whilst Cazenove, ejected from the Orion Gym, Hackney, joined forces with the homeless gymnasts to build Orion Hall, at Stamford Hill, only just before the War put an end to badminton.

The period between the Wars showed only a little improvement. Fine halls were built by Ebbisham (Epsom), Littlehampton and Hull. So too at Wimbledon where Noel Goddard master-minded the now famous Squash and Badminton Club. Lytham St Anne's, ousted by a bakery from

England boasted courts in disused 'tunnels' at both Waterloo and Liverpool Street Stations.

its eleven courts in a disused air-shed, built its own five-court hall, opened by Mrs Tragett and venue of the first Uber Cup final. Slough's excellent courts were part of a Community Centre—and there the Queen was much captivated by Humphrey Chilton's (now a BA of E Vice-President) nimble footwork!

A few more halls were built after the Second World War. But it wasn't until the '70s that there was a major change. Then every town and most schools decided that Sports Halls were essential not only to physical fitness but also to local prestige. But multi-sport halls with their generalised lighting, bewildering maze of lines, light coloured backgrounds, and bedlam of karate grunts, five-a-side football imprecations, and thunder of bouncing basketballs were not ideal.

By not building halls designed solely for badminton in an era of comparatively low building costs England lost its chance. The Danes, more far-sighted, seized theirs. For example Hvidovre with a nightly and week-end rota of 22 players, helped by two skilled men, built their own three-court hall—in 6 months. Such purpose-built halls

As an economy measure the ballroom of the British Embassy in Paris was turned into a badminton court (1953). So too was the old ballroom at London's Mansion House by the Lady Mayoress.

did much to give them a generation's dominance. The Netherlands too were to the fore with prefabricated 'Pelikan' halls which could be erected for £30 000 in 3 months. Over 100 had been built by 1969.

In this country it was too often a case of 'make do and mend', of living on the bounty of other sports. Roller-skating rinks were gratefully taken over when that boom ended (1911); though it is recorded that at Surbiton BC a megaphone had to be used to announce 'the next game' so far distant were the players.

Later, swimming baths, boarded over during the winter close season, were a godsend. But for the most part badminton relied upon a range of church halls (not churches themselves as a stunned Austrian was led to believe), village halls and

The Horticultural Hall, London (1913). 'Some of the best of English badminton' was played here.

23

The Great Dane, Svend Pri, played a farewell game near his own store in Copenhagen's Amagercentret.

school gyms. Each had its own personal hazards from a cat's cradle of beams, fluorescent lights and gas heaters in dim and dusty territory overhead to a skating-rink of a floor underfoot.

Many clubs sought sanctuary in drill halls. Often they provided reasonable height and space but they were grey, bleak and unfriendly places. Betty Uber herself started at Sutton in such a hall, typical of many, before she moved on to the luxury of the Crystal Palace which, like the Alexandra Palace, was one of the few to provide first class facilities in London.

For those who know only modern sports centre comfort and amenities, her description shows the spartan spirit of their forebears. Without heating, it was cold and dreary (though Mrs Uber's own enthusiasm burned too bright for her to notice it). The courts perilously shared a common side-line; whilst the outer lines were strategically infiltrated by disused radiators. Two doors opened off from

At the inauguration of the Brussels Metro, badminton was played in the booking hall of Delta station. And in a Paris Metro station during a National Week of Sport.

these so play was interrupted every time men sought the sanctuary of their changing rooms, an ice-cold shooting range, or, sheepishly, the lavatory. The ladies fared even worse: a half-curtained off sergeants' mess. Lukewarm tea and biscuits were provided by the caretaker's wife at 8.30 pm in a spartan 8 ft × 6 ft *2.4 m × 1.8 m* room. And yet play flourished!

Floors ranged from dropped-arch-inducing concrete to highly polished timber with ballroom aspirations. Lethal ones in the latter category were a constant source of correspondence in the *Gazette* columns. For years, Club Secretaries eagerly sang the praises of their pet panaceas which ran the gamut from branded remedies such as Vim and Soako, Glitto and Stearine, Boval and Marspan to the down-to-earth, old-fashioned remedies of soda, powdered pumice stone, brick dust or resin. The latter, used even at the All-England on a parquet floor, resulted either in glare, suffocating dust-clouds, fly-paper tackiness, or even all three.

Nor was the alternative, a drugget or stretched canvas, more successful:

> Little Miss Muggett
> Slipped on the druggett
> Playing in Handicap 'B'.
> Her racket hit space
> Which lost her the ace
> And the floor was much harder than she!

It is recorded of fast-moving English international Donald Hume: 'It took four rushes, five smashes and half a game to tear apart every seam on his side of the net. And that was that!'

Today, Hova courts are much less wayward. Brain child of T R Humble, Borough Surveyor of Hove, they were conceived after drugget had again taken a hammering on the highly polished floors of King Alfred Baths, a wartime Naval OCTU. A trial strip, 6 ft × 3 ft *1.8 m × 0.9 m*, made from an old indoor tennis court surface, was tested by Sussex international F C Sharp, returning shuttles thrown to him by Mrs Thornhill, the President's wife. And it was not found wanting!

Lighting too had its foibles. An international match in Sweden was played by the light of a chandelier above the court; a village match by oil-pressure lamps on a mantelpiece. Ian Maconachie playing in the wilds of Ireland heard a crash as the village hall was plunged into darkness; a car jacked up outside with engine running to drive a dynamo had collapsed!

In its infancy, badminton was played by gaslight—but the new-fangled incandescent mantles in the early 1900s were horribly vulnerable to the wilder sling or mishit, or the drive played with less than Thomasian accuracy. Even mighty Alexandra Palace BC piped its gas cross-court through rubber tubing; over enthusiastic lunges by an energetic player could plunge the court into temporary darkness!

That 'exception was the rule rather than the rarity' was proved by the author's own experience even in the comparative civilisation of the Lancaster League. His own club, Kendal Zion, had a 15 ft *4.6 m* high ceiling and a radiator across one backhand corner (he has the scars to this day to prove it!); Wesleyan, a gallery, with two supporting pillars on the base-line, that overhung the back 'tramlines'; Centenary, base-lines marked 18 in *45.6 cm* up the back walls; Red Rose played in a boarded over swimming bath with changing cubicles so near the side-line that males who favoured the half-court game were frequently accused of being 'dirty old men'.

Mary McCallum's Glasgow Churches League experiences were even more hair-raising. A slow-combustion stove under the net did at least make the concession of allowing the removal of the centre section of its tri-partite 18 ft *5.5 m* stove pipe. A massive pulpit just 6 in *15.2 cm* behind the base-line led to the coaching dictum: 'When in

Amager BC (Holland) courts were built in the courtyard of a block of flats.

trouble, clear to the centre'. Horror, as well as defeat, doubtless stared players in the face at a club that had a mirror across the width of the back wall. A sense of balance was needed where one side-line was a foot higher than the other. Shades of the panto Demon King prevailed at yet another where a railed off circular staircase emerged in one corner 4 ft *1.2 m* from the base-line and 2 ft *0.6 m* from the side-line. Considerable care or circulatory nimbleness was needed to avoid cracked ribs in returning the home players' thoughtfully placed clears and lobs.

Other Chambers of Horrors were courts that had: a coal fire (mercifully unlit) and fender 6 in *15.2 cm* over the base-line; a shared 6 in *15.2 cm* communal strip down one side-line; a forecourt so shortened to squeeze it in the room's confines that the receiver's racket practically touched the net; and a mantelpiece on which the umpire crouched whilst the remaining players sat in another room altogether.

But on the brighter side there were halls of generous girth. Albert Park in Melbourne had 15 courts, to say nothing of 44 table tennis tables

A scene of magic : all seven courts at Wembley Arena in full swing during the All-England Championships.

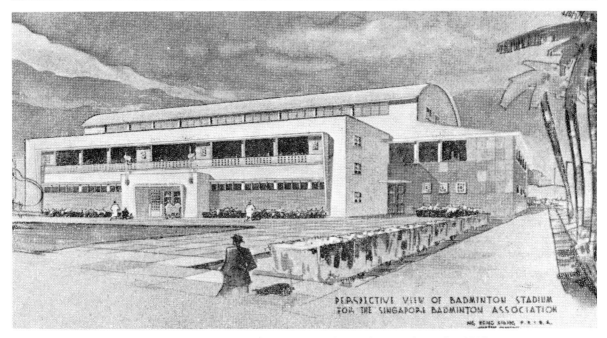

PERSPECTIVE VIEW OF BADMINTON STADIUM
FOR THE SINGAPORE BADMINTON ASSOCIATION

Singapore's fine Happy World Stadium. Housing 9000 spectators, it cost, in 1952, just—£60 000!

and 7 basket-ball pitches. Vast American armouries invariably housed over 20 courts. So did RAF St Athan (Wales) and the Worms Club in West Germany.

Portugal boasts a club, Futebal Clube de Porto, where, despite its title, badminton is played; it has a trophy room containing 2500 items, including a monster cup to record their defeat of Arsenal, 3-2. University of Mexico courts are in a pyramidal building; Puebla's look out on a snow-capped volcano, and Racing Club de Paris had a panorama of Paris from seven floors up in a garage.

Halls of international fame are numerous. Singapore's 'Happy World Stadium' speaks for itself. Negara Stadium in Kuala Lumpur is the heart of Malaysian badminton. Senayan Stadium in Jakarta fulfils the same function for Indonesian badminton; a training camp and hall in which 14 000 avid enthusiasts will happily sweat, cheer and barrack in an auditorium planned for 10 000. Peking's Capital Stadium and Tokyo's Municipal Gym have vast floor areas in which a single badminton court seems no bigger than a postage stamp.

Nearer home, Belfast has long enjoyed its McCallum Hall, and Dublin its Terrenure Hall. They commemorate respectively the magnificent

Members of Abingdon BC played in the Old Gaol—and changed in the fuselage of an ex-RAF glider.

financial exertions of those great players Tommy Boyle (the only man ever said to have wrong-footed Wong Peng Soon) and Frank Peard (who married Sue Devlin, kept the tang in Guinness, and long represented Ireland in tandem with irrepressible Jim Fitzgibbon).

Scotland showed England the way when it converted a disused paint factory into its SBU Cockburn Centre, Glasgow. The BA of E took the hint and turned a farm on the outskirts of new town Milton Keynes into its National Centre.

2000-seaters Queen's Hall, Preston, and Kelvin Hall, Glasgow, both hosted unforgettable first Thomas Cup Inter-Zone ties and finals. But queen of all perhaps is London's Royal Albert Hall around whose arena rise tier upon tier of gold and crimson boxes.

There, Miss World has paraded her manifest charms—and the Salvation Army played out its soul; lawn tennis has vied with all-in wrestling; youngsters have danced in the aisles to Frank Zappa; and promenaders swayed to the fervent rhythm of 'Land of Hope and Glory' under the baton of the immaculate Sir Malcolm Sargent. There, too, the world's greatest have played in Friends' Provident Masters tournaments and in the 1982 Thomas Cup finals before the Queen.

Ideal conditions are still all too rare. The hazards of such lesser halls have led to the emergence of few orthodox champions. But it has undoubtedly bred strength of character and given the game charisma at club level.

Two/**Equipment**

Rackets

The laws of badminton are meticulously precise when prescribing the acceptable net ('. . . of fine natural cord or artificial fibre of a dark colour and even thickness not less than $\frac{5}{8}$ in *15 mm* and not more than $\frac{3}{4}$ in *20 mm* mesh'). But it is gloriously vague as to rackets. In fact, although a shuttle's vital statistics are as firmly laid down as those for Miss World, nothing, nothing at all, is said of rackets. For all the BA of E care, you could, if you wished to, play with a shaft as long as a broom-handle and a racket-head as big as a dustbin lid. Or, for that matter, with a racket in each hand!

Despite this licence, rackets have changed only superficially in general design. But they have taken full advantage of modern technology's wild gallop in the last half century. Today's rackets undoubtedly give players of the '80s several lengths' start as compared with the 'old-timers'.

As far back as medieval times, battledores were no more than roughly shaped pieces of wood. Seventeenth and eighteenth-century prints show how the battledore had progressed as part of the 'jeu de volant' played by the elegant nobility. At this period, the head was roughly of table tennis bat size, covered with vellum, and the shaft-cum-handle just a little longer. A portrait in the Chateau Amboise-sur-Loire by Phillipe de Champaigne (1602–74) of the young Louis XIV shows him with just such a racket.

Those used at Badminton House in the 1840s had rather larger, almost circular heads on shafts about 18 in *46 cm* long. The frame was of light wood covered with a velvet material which was also wound round the length of the shaft: vellum or parchment stretched across the frame gave rise to a drum-like boom that would have delighted childish ears—and driven adults frantic.

However, a portrait, *c* 1740, of the young Earl of Dysart, and Chardin's delightful picture 'Jeune Fille Jouant Au Volant' depict much more conventional if solidly built rackets probably strung

with raw kid-hide. In 1877, Ayres supplied another advance: gut strung rackets, but they still advertised 'drum-bats' and even a racket strung with gut on one side and vellum on the other!

Early rackets—3/6d *17½p*—were doubtless imported from Sealkot in India where badminton flourished. But it is recorded that the first English rackets were made by a chairmaker, H Day, Racket Master at Kennington Oval who published a set of Laws in 1878.

Frames

Early rackets were undoubtedly built for durability rather than flexibility. Advertisements constantly stressed not only the strengthening of the frame's shoulders but also of the shaft with celluloid, silk or gut binding. In the early 1900's the head was losing its pronounced egg shape.

Pride of racket too was on the move. Prosser's made fittingly high claims for their 'Phenomenon': 'Scientifically built' and 'absolutely perfect in every detail'. And in 1913 the 'ADP (rebble)' was boosted by the strain of advertising that still flourishes today: 'for the last six seasons almost every Open event was won with an ADP racket'. At Harrods, you could have bought the 'Perfect Bat' for—6/6d *32½p*. Ayres advertised, 'Our "Olympic" bat is very highly strung'. Obviously a thoroughbred!

But just before the First World War the frame was thickened to withstand the extra tension now being demanded. The 'ideal' weight was now between 5½ and 5¾ oz *156 and 163 g*. But it was noted that in the Scottish Championships 'two lads were playing with rackets of 7½ and 9 oz weight *213 and 255 g*'. Their smashing was very effective but, not surprisingly, the rest of their game was distinctly sluggish. Yet it was claimed by F A Davis that 'Hexagon' and 'Spartan' were 'light as a feather' as 'the modern game demands a well-balanced racket'. All things are comparative!

In 1923 there was a glimpse of the shape of things to come. 'H C Farrell's No 1', with a rent

Early rackets were little more than table-tennis bat size, shuttlecocks enormous.

ash frame, was strung 'at enormously high tension and with a maximum weight of 5 oz *142 g*'. ('Crux criticorum' was their trademark). And the 'Swallow' was 'balanced like a bird'.

A year later, the 'Birmal All-Metal' of aluminium alloy made its bow with appropriate ballyhoo: 'complete lack of wind resistance' optimistically heralded streamlining. Despite its not ill-founded claim to last three or four seasons (shuttles hit by it certainly did not) one must surely take with a pinch of salt that 'it throws itself heart and soul into your game to give you utter pleasure'!

Of endorsed rackets, the 'GAT(homas)' had 'its handle specially reinforced by a strip of material built into the centre and running the whole length of the shaft' (1924). MRT(ragett's) double ash-bend reduced warping to a minimum (1926). The Slazenger 'Queen' had a raw-hide insertion down the shaft (1927).

Theories differed. The 'Eltra' had a concave sycamore wedge: the 'Barrier Superb', an 'extra strong wedge'. But the Dunlop was 'Wedgeless' and Spalding's 'Top Flite' had an open throat as had the tennis rackets used by that mighty hitter 'Big Bill' Tilden.

As well as innovations there were offers. 'Dimid' carried a 6-month guarantee; Adams and Prosser's were selling direct 'at a saving of up to $33\frac{1}{3}$ per cent. And another firm even offered to take used rackets (but not shuttles!) in part exchange.

In 1936, things really began to move. Hazell's 'Streamline', with thin shaft but 'supports' on each side of it from frame to shaft, gave 'effortless

> *The head of Ray Stevens' racket crumpled in a single against Svend Pri; undeterred he still managed two further returns.*

follow through'. Ayres in their 'Silvershaft' produced at last a steel-shafted racket. Dunlop with its famous Maxply method countered that its wood gave 'the strength and resilience of tempered steel'. (Their lightweight 'Under 5' did not emerge until early in the 1960s).

Possibly a product of wartime technological advances, the 'Silver Fox' was made 'of steel strips of razor-blade thinness welded together'; it had an open throat and shock absorbers in the frame. Slazengers, taking over from Ayres, gave 'Silvershaft' an oval shaft to give whip from dead centre and later introduced the 'All White' with a tapered one. Carlton later experimented with the 'squeeze' to the same end.

Fibreglass too came into its own. It was used by Slazengers to armour 'Silvershaft's' shoulders; by Mullers to make 'Resilite's' shaft 'tougher than steel and more responsive'. Indeed a County Captain (male doubtless) was moved to write: 'The answer to a Maiden's Prayer'.

In 1967, Carlton really went to town with the new technology: a frame, weighing less than $1\frac{1}{2}$ oz *43 g* unstrung, of steel of a type 'used in rockets' and with a greater strength to weight ratio even than that of the 'miracle metal' titanium with resultant tighter stringing, faster strokes, and less air resistance.

Other firms moved with the times. Their more pointed racket-head, Yonex claimed, gave 'still better tension, an enlarged sweet spot, better impact absorption, and longer life' (for the racket, not necessarily the wielder!). And they threw in 'the slenderest shaft in the world' for good measure. Suggiyama brought out a twin-shaft with a strengthening bar; Sondico also had twin shafts, ribbed for strength (which they said gave 'directional stability') to say nothing of an extruded lightweight frame.

The John Mott 'Feather', all-English and expensive, offered a unique aluminium T-piece, a 100 per cent carbon-graphite shaft, recessed strings passing through self-locking grommets, and a claim to be the lightest in the world. And two years later—stringing suspended on loops! Carbon-graphite, an aerospace spin-off, is made of hair-like fibres of polyacrylonitrile which have five times the strength of fibre-glass together with an 80 per cent density saving.

The badminton racket has travelled far!

Stringing

In 1911 S M Massey (England) was doubtless fully entitled to his scornful: 'Rackets from India too frequently suffer in their stringing from Eastern

Hazell's 'Streamline' caused a stir in 1937 but never really caught on.

Nicky Goode played a delicate net-shot, only for the shuttle to remain suspended on the net-cord. (See p 57.)

lassitude'. But only a little later the ADP, probably the first of the endorsed rackets and one made by the craftsmen of J and S Sheffield, who were long to produce beautiful hand-made rackets from their tiny Hackney workrooms, were to boast 'stringing specially designed by Mr Prebble'. Then the 'Referee' had 'double centre-strings in red and white gut', whilst the oval faced 'FHA(yres)' and others started a vogue for 'close centre-strings both across and down'.

In the 1920s appeared the shuttle's greatest-ever scourge, the 'Birmal'—strung with single strand steel wire. To redress the balance, 'Merrie England' rackets were strung in 'artistic colours' with Sta-tite gut! More practically the MRT boasted of 'high tension stringing'.

In 1928, Eltra was among the first to use synthetic gut but the eight close centre mains were 'interlaced diagonally to prevent slipping'. Queens riposted with 'extra trebling in both directions that ensures minimum displacement of mains and cross'. Dimid pushed ahead with 'the scientific principle of diagonal stringing' which, with Carpando gut, gave 'extra devil'. And, such was their faith, they were first in the field with a 6-month guarantee of string and frame. Arena countered with 'split gut responsiveness'.

After the War, 'Silver Fox', a stainless steel racket appropriately made in Sheffield, was one of the first designed to prevent the abrasion of strings. These were led through nickel-plated eyelets with rubber cushions and they were 'protected everywhere from contact with the court'. Carlton in 1967 aimed to overcome the fraying of strings by radiusing the eyelets on both sides and coating them with nylon.

In the 1950s, ICI had returned to the fray with nylon strings, 'resilient, do not fray or split, and are unaffected by damp'. Carlton were in favour of synthetic gut because it could be strung 'at tensions beyond the limits of natural gut'. But it was another matter whether synthetic *maintained* its tension as well as natural did. Bow Brand, however, were sure that the split intestines of sheep had greater responsiveness and impact strength. Pacific also backed 'split lamb gut rather than that of cow or pig'. More, it produced it in nine colours and guaranteed it against premature breakage. 'Black Wedge' went one better by adding to the racket a pack of re-string gut.

Seeking greater resilience, the gut manufacturers have come up with a wide variety of new approaches: the hollow core, centred with solid substructures, oil, or floating nylon threads (the best). And each may be carbon or graphite coated.

A Racket is Made

Lengths of perforated stainless steel strip are carefully shaped into a head . . .

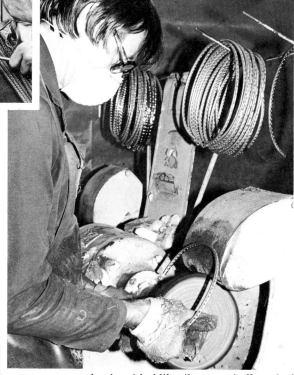

. . . then burnished like silver on a buffing wheel

. . . having first been tempered in a blazing oil-bath and then . . .

. . . plastic coating (4.3's only) before being oven-baked.

Only a man has a strong enough wrist to ensure the leather grip stays put on the hollowed wooden handle.

Clean-up and inspection before being passed into good hands . . .

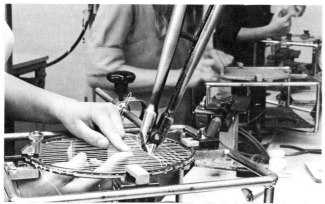

. . . where lightning fingers weave cross strings deftly under and over the verticals.

. . . even for England's Jane Webster—and a galaxy of other stars.

One last check and then a Carlton racket is good enough . . .

Despite all this, Nature is still a stride ahead of Science in that natural gut has a far greater area of effective response.

Handles

Originally rackets had no handles—they were simply held by the unshaped shaft. Slowly this was thickened to give a better grip but it was not until the 1900s that further improvement followed. The 'Sirdar's' mahogany handle smacked of India and solidity. Prosser's 'Phenomenon' boasted 'a cane insert for spring' whilst the 'Olympic Bat' was 'deeply scored'. In 1921, Prosser were again to the fore with a 'pneumatic handle that is not only comfortable but improves the grip and avoids tired fingers'.

Although the Fulford leather grip was introduced in the 1920s, many rackets were advertised gripless into the mid-1930s. In 1933, the 'Barrier Superb' with its 'aerogrip handle' was advertised. This green calf skin gave 'increased grip control, resiliency—and aeration'. Advances indeed! To supplement such grips, some handles had a thong attached. 'Slippery customers' put their hand through this and, with the racket now securely anchored, opponents were grateful that they were no longer on the receiving end of a potential knife-throwing act.

For many, the overlapping spiral of chamfered leather with its aeration holes was sufficient. But in 1970 the 'Maxply' appeared with a towelling grip, initially soft but tending gradually to become matted and hardened. In 1978 a racket was even named after its new type handle, the 'Black Wedge' so designed to prevent slip.

Another advance in that year was the Gauze Grip, fixed over worn leather or towelling and, since it adhered to itself, quickly changed. With it, handles could easily be built up to exact grip size to prevent possibility of tennis elbow. In 1980 came the coloured 'Cresta' grip—'no swet'. The pack consisted of two absorbent, stretch cotton towelling grips and strips of adhesive backed 'Velcro'. Other palliatives were 'Surgrip', an anti-perspirant liquid gel that dried to adhesive powder, and the Nadim Safety Glove of white leather with Velcro hooks and loops on the glove and the grip respectively. Neither, hopefully, impeding smooth change of grip.

> *As Roy Wallace smashed, his racket slipped from his hand, hit the taut net-cord, and bounced straight back to the base-line.*

The most revolutionary change came in the same year—the brainchild of English international Derek Talbot—the Grip Shaft. This was a plastic foam or cork grip of consistent weight that could easily be made to a player's own specifications. Into this was fully inserted a 15.74 in *400 mm* shaft —cf usual 11.41 in *290 mm*—so 'giving greater flexibility, balance, feel and recoil whilst lessening metal fatigue'.

Shuttles

Unique amongst sporting missiles the shuttle has too often been villified for its feminine qualities of expensive fragility and wayward flightiness as well as for being 'hard to get'. Too infrequently praised for its beauty and delicacy, for its aerodynamic marvels, for its responsiveness to touch and its consistency.

A shuttle is a minor miracle! Weighing a mere 80 grains *5.18 g* it is hammered from the racket-face at an estimated 310 km/h—or so said a surely optimistic Yonex racket advertisement. And yet, such are its powers of deceleration, it lands smoothly on a runway only 44 ft *13.42 m* long. Unflinchingly it faces execution by the sharp edges of the racket-frames of the unco-ordinated. Featherweight v heavyweight indeed!

The shuttle is a prima donna and has long had a tempestuous love-hate relationship with her public. Yes, her, for the shuttle is a lady—and should be treated as such.

They have always consisted of a cork base into which have been inserted feathers. Clumsy at first, as evidenced by Chardin's delightful picture; streamlined later. The little French girl's shuttle had seven feathers, red, white and blue, and was probably twice the size of today's $3\frac{1}{2}$ in *89 mm* tall miniature.

Indeed it is recorded that shuttles of this size were in use at a club in Lymm, Cheshire, which was still, in 1903, sublimely unaware of the Badminton Association's recently imposed size regulations. Recorded too that 'fluffy' shuttles were obtainable from the Army and Navy Stores in 1893. And that the 'spreadeagle' was in use in 1900.

In India, in the late 19th century, balls of wool, worsted or even chicken feathers were used. And legend has it that the first shuttles at Badminton House were merely champagne corks bedecked with such feathers. A rich but perhaps unlikely story, for that cradle of badminton can actually show you much less crude shuttles. (So too can

Blair Castle, seat of the Duke of Atholl, the only person in the country allowed to have his own personal army, the Atholl Highlanders).

J H E Hart, one of badminton's founding fathers and RSL's representative Ken Matlock's counterpart, 'indefatigable in handing out shuttles to competitors at the All-England', tells a delightful story of his Poona (Pune) days. A young Maratha became so keen and expert in making shuttles from champagne corks and fowl feathers that he was also promoted to Club Treasurer. 'Alas for perfidy of human nature he became confused as to rightful

The Second World War brought brown, black or speckled feathers in its train: 'excellent against white walls' but apparently inclined unpredictably to veer from slow to fast like a learner-driver. But it wasn't the blackout that caused the conception of a short-lived West German luminous shuttle in 1970. In 1949 Ian Maconachie of RSL introduced the plasticized middle-binding which undoubtedly lengthened an ephemeral life. And in 1950 they introduced for practice the aptly named 'Hercules' that had only eight feathers—but each was very sturdy and almost square cut. The 1970s saw the

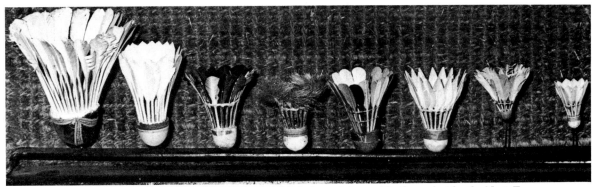

A row of early shuttles in the museum at RSL's factory, birthplace of the world's finest shuttle, the No 1 Tourney.

ownership'—and languished in gaol. When urged to continue the good work there, he replied with Hindoo cunning that such work was not demanded by Prison Regulations. That even should the latter be amended—he could not now recall his craft.

Early shuttles were inconsistent in both size and length of flight. Players frequently resorted to inserting tacks or drawing pins to make up their weight. Bussey's shuttles of 1911 were an improvement on this in that the base was of cork ('Regulation' shuttles had one of hard rubber) 'accurately turned'. Today, this is done to a tolerance of one five-thousandth of an inch *0.127 mm*.

The base was covered in *one* piece of leather or velvet, white, buff or red, so no covering tape was needed over the seam. And a leather disc secured the base of the feathers so 'rendering the bottom binding thread unnecessary', though the latter was used by other makers.

Feathered shuttles have changed comparatively little in basic construction. In 1911 the *Gazette* categorically stated 'the straight feathered variety completely holds the field!' And so the 'barrel' shuttle (recently tested to a length of 59 ft *18 m*), though still preferred by some, passed, after a 'Battle of the Bulge', into limbo. Colonel Deane advocated fourteen feathers as it gave less 'hang' in drop- and net-shots; and the BA amended the Law to fourteen–sixteen feathers.

decease of the rounded feather, one speed slower than the pointed (6 in–8 in *15 cm–20 cm*).

To give economical longevity both care and repair are needed. As far back as 1913 players were censured for 'ruthlessly hitting shuttles along the floor'. They still do so today. And as late as 1955 at least one Club Secretary handed out shuttles only after they had been warmed for an hour in front of a gas fire! This in complete contravention of course of RSL advice to wrap badly stored tubes in a damp towel to restore some of the loss of the feathers' 9.8 per cent of natural oil. And in times of economic crisis the *Gazette* printed DIY letters on the cannibalistic art of removing ('by biting off the quills'), and replacing damaged feathers, a skill still practised by ex-international Warwick Shute.

And yet for all this, reports of sturdy shuttles *did* filter through. In 1924 Ayres shot down critics of their English-made All-England shuttles: their life had averaged one per game as compared with the previous foreign shuttles of five per game! (The latter, first used in 1908, were probably of French or Indian descent). A Northern Club

Frank Rugani drove a shuttle 79 ft 8¼ in 24.30 m at San José, California, on 29 February 1964.

A Shuttle is Made

Mountains of feathers, having been washed and dried, are sorted into grades.

The operator poses with natural feathers in her right hand; those cut to shape by her machine in her left.

The shaped feathers are fed into a machine which deftly slots them into the ready-drilled and revolving cork-base inside.

No machine can improve on human fingers when the knot is tied. Now the threads can be sprayed with strengthening adhesive.

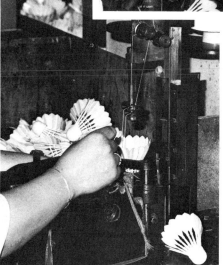

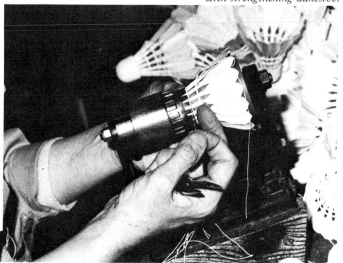

Correct spread, and therefore speed, is achieved by means of two binding-threads magically woven around the quills.

Now for the green ribbon, or lute, to add a touch of distinction.

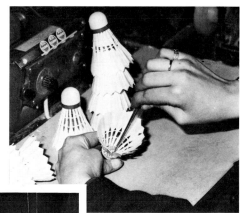

Surgical tweezers are needed to insert and secure the finishing RSL label.

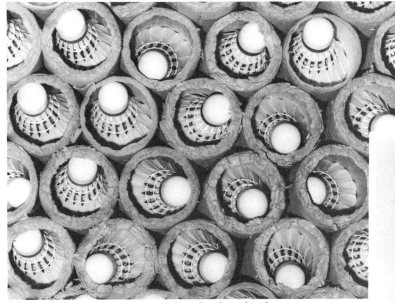

Each shuttle is precisely weighted with a tiny lead slug firmly secured in the cork; it ensures the requisite speed.

The finished article and its liveried tube—to say nothing of its synthetic cousin.

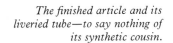

Everywhere you look, in factory tubes, shuttles galore!

miraculously kept one shuttle in full use for a month! Was 'Northern', Scotland, one wonders? In 1950 when Eddy Choong beat David 15–12, 10–15, 15–10 only two RSL shuttles were used— and the second was far from dead. (A useful economy as, together with cousin Amy, they won four of the five titles!)

But shuttle carnage grew. In 1929 Ayres admitted a scarcity. More and more people were taking up the game. In 1938 the first All-England Danes were 'staggered by the astronomical number of shuttles used and the wealth of the BA of E that could supply them'. 'Wood' shots were legalised: one such damaging shot so often led to another. Metal frames were almost as lethal as Glasgow razor-gangs. Top players in the quest for ever-growing prestige and prize money grew correspondingly more fastidious and shuttle-conscious. Dead birds littered the court-side like the aftermath of an Edwardian grouse shoot. Even in 30 years Danish views had somersaulted: Kobbero used 45 shuttles in one 75-minute match. And in the '70s came cut-smashes closely followed by the '80s 'Sidek Slice Serve' banned in 1982 by the IBF partly because its effectiveness was in direct proportion to the shuttle's pristine crispness.

Not surprisingly, the world's geese did not sportingly rally round to save the situation. 1936's 'Export or Starve' crisis forced RSL to send its shuttles overseas. War added its quota of difficulties. The Spanish Civil War led to a shortage of cork; the Second World War saw only a meagre supply of feathers available. After the War RSL were pleading, like any dairyman, for the return of its essential containers—shuttle tubes. After sundry wars, treaties and rebellions, the greater part of the world's supplies were behind the Iron and Bamboo Curtains. Prices for feathers rose from 4/6d $22\frac{1}{2}$p per lb *50p per kg* in 1938–9 to £7.50 per lb *£16.50 per kg* in 1979.

Shuttle manufacturers were never as numerous as racket-makers. First Ayres No 1 was supreme; it held the accolade of supplier to the All-England from 1910 to 1939. Then, after the War, the palm passed to RSL which had been set up only in 1930, first in South Norwood, where it received bomb damage, and then, in 1946, just outside the ancient Cinque Port of Sandwich. The reign of their

A 2 ft 'golden' shuttle was presented by RSL to club-player Vic West when he announced that in a lifetime's badminton he had put paid to some 15 000 shuttles.

superb 'No 1 Tourney' with its thirteen different speeds, lasted from 1947 to 1982 when inflation and ever-growing floods of cheap Asiatic shuttles made their production in this country no longer a viable business proposition. Fortunately a compromise was found: specialised English machinery was sent to China to complement the latter's supply of first-class feathers and cheaper skilled labour.

Of the smaller fry, Bussey's could never quite rival Ayres. In 1928, Eltra, at 12/6d $62\frac{1}{2}$p per dozen, boasted sixteen feathers and 'strongly cemented double-ties'. Battle's claimed 'without false pride' (or modesty!)—'the World's Finest Shuttle'. In 1932 came the fittingly named 'Beaufort' whilst in 1935 the Lynn Precision Shuttle waxed lyrical—'lovely, lively birds with a scandalously long life'. In 1937, En Tout Cas packed its five grades of 'matured' shuttles in tubes with metal, flush-fitting lids.

Ever rising costs and demand, and diminishing supplies of feathers ended the feathered shuttles' long, unchallenged rule. In 1950, Carlton presented modern technology's reply to Nature—the plastic or synthetic shuttle. The *Gazette* was unimpressed: 'Most ingenious but unlikely to be the last word'.

So it proved, for Carlton laboured for the next 30 years to overcome the difficulties of bettering Nature and overcoming players' innate conservatism. They certainly won the day on durability and cheapness—but, despite all their claims—never quite matched the feather's flight or 'feel'. Nevertheless Carlton became as synonymous for plastic shuttles as Hoover for vacuum cleaners. Their sales quickly rocketed to over a million in a single year.

With brash enthusiasm they advertised: 'Goose feathers are as archaic as hickory-shafted golf clubs' and 'We do not believe a feather can do what a plastic cannot'. In 1952 they claimed: 'They rise like a feather' but even in 1982, despite 'It is not non-U to play with a plastic' skilled players were still unconvinced. But 'Guaranteed to last five times as long as a feather even if badly hit' had appealed to beginner and club player alike. So too must have 'after seasoning, they may be hit with a hammer without breaking'.

Eddy and David Choong hurriedly dissociated themselves from an advertisement that claimed they had switched from feather to plastic without noticing it. Other advertisements claimed that two shuttles had sufficed for a nine match Men's Doubles tie, and that a single shuttle had survived 32 games in one session at a 'Recreational Institute'. Surely the 'Golden Age' was at hand!

A smaller Carlton was devised with a thinner skirt 'that will make your strings last twice as long'. A challenge was offered to the 'giants of the game' to 'tune up their muscles' to see if their smashes could collapse it. In a Copenhagen tournament 237 matches were played with only eighteen shuttles. And in 1958 they got the IBF's seal of approval—but still not that of top players.

Meantime, in 1957, RSL had joined in the hunt for the ever-growing market with its 'Nash Plastic' which after much experiment in their USA factory at Altoona 'spins like a feather'.

But not until 1974 did the real break-throughs start. The RSL 'Nash' graduated to a cork base that replaced the 'puddingy' rubber generally used. At last a synthetic had 'touch' and 'feel'. Its successor, the 'Viktor' had a special 'inner support'. The 'Competition' came in 13 exact speeds and not just the hitherto prevailing general guides of 'Slow', 'Medium' and 'Fast'; this helped to prolong a shuttle's life. It came too in 'Gold', for better-sighting, and 'Cold', for greater resistance to winter-created brittleness. In the Wiltshire Open in 1980, 144 shuttles sufficed for 360 games and about £400 was saved. Persistent scientific research with spin-gauges and wind-tunnels brought its flight much nearer that of the feathered shuttle.

The battle was on. Carlton 'goosed up its nylon' and also provided a cork base and a gold skirt. It went one further and produced a skirt moulded to resemble feathers. (Adam Wilson, Middlesex, had indeed been a prophet before his time when in 1955 he had urged experiment with cork base and plastic feathers).

The criticism of the Carlton had long been its slowness. And from the earliest days 'speed' has been a dirty word in connection with shuttles. (Blessed indeed is the tennis ball that needs only an easily measurable bounce test). Until 1900 there had been no stipulated speed or test. In 1911 a shuttle struck from over one back boundary line by that mythical "player of average strength" had to fall within a foot of the other. In 1913 it was

Stuart Debnam worked with shuttles, first for F H Ayres (1912–38), then for RSL (1938–72)—60 years in all.

revised to 'between back boundary line and an imaginary line 2 ft *0.61 m* short of it'. Today of course it is anything up to 18 in *0.46 m* beyond the doubles long service line.

Even with that length immutably fixed, the problem was far from solved. Players tended to want a slower than regulation shuttle—it was easier to control. Few players knew how to test. And of those who did, no two tested a shuttle similarly or with identical strength, or even from the clearly laid down 'above the back boundary line'. (Frank Hodge tested them backhanded!) Every hall varied in size, temperature, humidity and even altitude, all of which affected length of flight.

The Danes always preferred 'slow' shuttles which have long been a whipping boy. Herbert Scheele attributed English defeats in part to them —and was soundly castigated for such heresy. David Bloomer wrote 'Danish post-war shuttles were a remarkable achievement in aerodynamics. They left the racket at the speed of sound, crossed the net like aged waiters fighting an uphill battle with rheumatism, and arrived at the speed of a horse-drawn hearse'. And got away with it!

Complaints about slow shuttles by old-timers have long been the stock-in-trade of the *Gazette*'s 'Letters to the Editor'.

Today the battle still rages unabated. Can modern badminton import sufficient feathered shuttles of quality, consistency and reasonable price from the Far East? Or will it have to turn to the slightly less perfect but cheaper and more durable synthetics? Even the IBF thinks it may well be so.

Clothing

Ladies' dress has run the gamut from maximum coverage to 'le minimum'; from Victorian prudery to modern Naturist nudity where over-developed girls are joyously 'snapped' using under-developed techniques.

Basic fashion on court changed little up to the First World War. Ladies with only two hands must have been sorely impeded by 'drag'. They were often caught in two minds as to whether to employ the free hand to lift floor-skimming skirts or desperately to hold on to sturdily constructed

---

Shuttle Care

Use the correct speed.

Take advantage of life prolonging 'Gold' and 'Cold' synthetics.

Store correctly: feathers away from dry heat; synthetics in gentle warmth.

Never half-volley.

Smooth ruffled feather-plumes.

Remove carefully from uncrushed containers.

hats, pinned but precarious on high-piled coiffures. R C Robertson-Glasgow, more famous perhaps for amusing cricket reports, once delightfully described the plight of a mixed pair when the man's skimming drives all too frequently went to roost in his partner's cherry-decked hat.

Blouses were white with choker collars and bow or short black ties, denying any ventilation. Puffed shoulders, worthy of 200 lb *90 kg* all-

What the well-dressed lady wore in 1914! (Mrs Bottomley, All-England Singles runner-up).

American footballers, and leg of mutton sleeves drawn in at the wrist gave no licence to streamlining. The sole concessions in that respect were tightly corsetted waists encircled by black belts which helped to keep voluminous skirts just above foot level.

Some hint as to the more liberated dress of the 1920s may be garnered from the following items left at the 1923 All-England Championships (and still unclaimed 6 months later): one pleated and one piqué dress, one crêpe de Chine blouse, one pair doeskin gloves and three undergarments

(unspecified). Photos of that period show bandeau, open-neck blouses, badge emblazoned V-neck sweaters and calf-length skirts.

In the 1930s things were looking up: divided skirts just above the knee (such flightiness often compensated for by knee-length socks), and short-sleeved shirts and sweaters rivalled dresses. And as a final fling, Bervic Patent Corset Garters were advertised in 1938 'for all sportswomen who prefer to discard stockings'. Without the latter 'they prevented corsets riding up'; with them, 'stopped ladders and twisted seams'. (At the same time it was remarked that Danish men had progressed to zip 'flies'—with all their attendant problems).

In the early '50s, 'Velma', (Herbert Scheele's wife and P.A., Betty) remarked on 'severely cut shorts like those favoured by US Wimbledon star Helen Jacob's and 'pleated skirts and yellow sweaters ranging from palest primrose to deepest ochre'. White and pastel-hued cardigans were also much in vogue. Lillywhites, one of the first *Gazette* fashion advertisers, offered 'trim flannel skirt gored with a fly front fastening and cellular cotton shirt with your own initials on the pocket'.

As ever, men's fashions varied comparatively little. Indeed, at the Bournemouth Club in 1900 the men didn't change at all—merely threw off their jackets. Though even that social gaffe is recorded as having been sufficient reason to black-ball the perpetrator in the élite New York BC of the 1890s.

Early All-England champions played in white shirts and black ties with sleeves sometimes daringly rolled back to the elbow. Trousers, short and tight, were held up by narrow, coloured, buckled belts. Black socks in light sandshoes provided the finishing touches. Slowly, long-sleeved sweaters and blazers brought more dignity to the turnout. Some, including Sir George Thomas, favoured cardigans.

It was only just before the Second World War that international Bill White daringly took to the court in shorts. Post-war, the Choongs' knee-length ones, with sweat-towels dangling from the pocket, were steadily replaced by ever shorter ones. John Best's 'arousers' of the 1960s would cause no comment or eyelid flicker today in this age of unisex shorts as tight and brief as nature permits. Judy Hashman felt urged to write: 'Much persuasion is needed in both dressing-rooms before the body can be eased in; back seams surely being insured by Hearts of Oak' (sponsors). And 'Old Timer' wrote in the *Gazette* 'Shorts are so unbecoming as to be ludicrous; they should never be worn at greater tension than 10 lb to the sq inch'.

Cheeky but charming! A Dutch firm advertises the sports-girl's all-essential bra.

No wonder Litesome's Gallic gentleman says 'Oh, la, la!' when he spots track-suited, Ireland's broth-of-a-girl Barbara Beckett (left) *and Yorkshire's pretty Paula Kilvington.*

But many ladies retained their feminine charm not merely by 'buttons on shorts pockets' but by wearing well tailored shorts or divided, flared, or pleated skirts together with the almost ubiquitous (non-iron) shirts. In 1959 Fred Perry Sportswear boasted '95 per cent of All-England competitors wore our clothing'. Tonny Petersen (D) and Amy Heah (M) looked as attractive in white trousers then as Barbara Carpenter does now.

In the 1930s, blazers were the male order of the day at all levels. They lent colour and distinction to the scene. Especially the famous and eye-catching England and All-England Championship blazers now, sadly, seen only on ceremonial occasions. Slowly but surely they were replaced by the more practical tracksuits which helped to prevent pulled muscles as well as add peacock colour to the courts.

Their advent roused the ire of Herbert Scheele (rightly a stickler for etiquette) if worn on court and 'not where their name implied they should be worn'. To Herbert, a tracksuit worn during play was anathema, tantamount to Gower wearing his overcoat whilst fielding at cover-point during a Lord's Test. They were a break with tradition, a rainbow-hued eye-sore, and an impediment to fluent movement.

Earlier, 'Knock-knees' (vowing no connection with the textile industry) had made an epistolatory plea to the All-England Committee to revoke its ban and not to legislate against the tracksuit with the same disapprobation that the All-England Lawn Tennis and Croquet Club had once bestowed upon frills, fancy pants and broderie anglaise.

Even worse in Mr Scheele's eyes was the growing trend of players virtually changing from their workaday clothes (braces and all!) by the umpire's chair. He begged club secretaries 'to eradicate this awful blot on the game: a horrible sight and monstrous offence to spectators'. To which Chief Coach Ken Crossley was moved to riposte: 'If men may not bring jackets courtside, they will be forced to carry handbags'. With the advent of the all-seeing television eye the worst excesses of scattered equipment and clothing have been banished to unobtrusive, designated areas.

Ladies had long breached the 'all-white' edict. But to this Herbert was prepared to turn an avuncular, Nelsonian eye 'rather than deny ladies their attractive pale blue and pink cardigans'.

Man's only on-court concession to colour had been round the neck, cuffs, and bottoms of sweaters. Now shirts and shorts alike have collars, plackets, panels and stripes to add a dash of not unwelcome colour. In mixed, unisex clothing and colour is often the order of the day.

Black is beautiful! And so is today's badminton girl's brief white dress with scarlet and black panels by Litesome.

All-colour shorts and shirts (the blue and yellow of Sweden) may be worn if they are a team's national colours and both players in a pair and all players in a team wear them. Apart from that 'predominantly white' is still the watchword: a touch of harmonising colours not a clashing hotchpotch.

Shoes

In days of old, seven league boots were mandatory dress for earth-shaking giants. Today, just as essential for players and especially those hell-bent for the top, are shoes, the springboard to all-essential speed, agility and 'the early take'. Too often, uncleaned and unloved, they are taken for granted with no thought spared for their lineage. But their badminton story does leave an intriguing trail.

In the 1890s, sandshoes (black or brown) were dress of the day. By 1910, S M Massey, sternly against plimsolls, was advocating buckskin shoes with $\frac{1}{4}$ in *6 mm* rubber soles or—seemingly dangerous—chrome leather soles for concrete floors.

Ladies often wore heavy tennis boots—a legacy perhaps of the button-up days—which together with voluminous skirts can have done little for speed off the mark. Margaret Tragett herself was photographed with such boots peeping daringly from beneath her skirt.

Refinements were slow to follow. In 1912 however, Dr Hoggyes' 'Air Spring' asbestos socks (sponge-rubber impregnated with asbestos, the latter not as a fire-fighting precaution but rather as a cooling agent) were enthusiastically recommended—by Dr Hoggyes himself. And in the early 1920s, the quaintly named firm 'Pioneers of Crepe-Soled Footwear' offered crepe soles 'from the largest stock in the world' for 'better grip' and three times the wear', a quest still eagerly pursued today.

The 1930s were more adventurous. 'Scotia' soles were 'moulded like a tyre for greater flexibility'; 'Garagard' offered orthopaedic lasts, heel shock absorber, instep-to-toe lacing and, better still, a challenging 6-month guarantee. (How well the author remembers desperately pounding the courts in the last few days to beat that deadline!). 'North British' side-strap for extra support did not catch on; 'Dunlop' brought in toe-cap reinforcement.

In 1955, Canadian champion Marjorie Shedd put the clock back by playing in light boots. 'Greengate' got things moving again with non-marking honeycomb soles and nylon ventilation panels, whilst 'Keds' put a ribbed bumper strip on the toe. In the '60s, cushion socks became an added extra and cartoonist Syd Robinson depicted the delectable Danish Rasmussen sisters in 'original shin-length ribbed socks'. Herbert Scheele pertinently and pithily commented that 'last season's off-white shoes are now off-black—but old-fashioned white is still stocked in shops'.

In the '70s came today's taken-for-granted refinements. Vulcanised side strengthening by 'Spring Court'; zig-zag soles and suede toe-caps by 'Relum'; cushioning round instep, pressure-free foot-form tongue, and lightweight nylon uppers by 'Adidas'; extended heel for better grip, micro-soles, and even pull-proof eyelets by 'Rucanor'; padded collars and towelling insoles by 'Inter'.

Everybody went for colour and logos—but no-one invented an unsnappable lace.

'Un Lapin' in Round One was shown as 'Un Lupin' in Round Two on the umpire's score sheet. Just a game of Animal, Vegetable or ...?

Three/**Badminton and the Media**

Press and Television

In England, badminton has never had its just deserts! A strenuous, exciting and skilful game played by millions the world over. And yet always the wallflower as far as publicity has been concerned. In its early days, its very lineage was against it. Battledore and shuttlecock indeed!

More recently, McEnroe's tantrums, pot-bellied darts hot-shots, Giant Haystacks with the other freaks of all-in wrestling, and the punters' racing paradises: all have held the television screen whilst badminton languished on the side-lines.

So too in the dailies. A half column in the *Telegraph* is as much to be rejoiced over as 'the one sheep that was lost and is found'. The 'popular Press' turns a Beaverbrook or Murdoch blind eye.

And yet in Indonesia, badminton banner head-lines scream from the front page. Twenty-four page supplements are issued. So too in Malaysia where every shot in Thomas Cup Inter-Zone ties was televised. Admittedly in that context their records gave them a lot more to screen than did England's.

In the early 1900s, the *Field* was badminton's main hope. *Lawn Tennis and Croquet* too, gener-ously gave it *some* space, amongst the reports of its presumably more strenuous contemporaries. *Sporting Life* promised critical reports on the All-England in 1912 and *Lawn Tennis and Badminton* was hailed as a capital 6d *5p* worth! But, in 1947, the latter was taken to task for sparing no more than five columns in 368 pages of thirteen past issues for the 'junior partner'!

Even when mention of badminton was made, it was all too often derogatory. *Fry's Magazine* (1911) commented 'From a 100 yards sprint at one end to badminton and bridge at the other'. Even croquet ranked higher!

In 1924, the Press still had no clue: 'Can be played in summer frocks, tweeds or evening dress'. The Handicap Mixed winners were proudly proclaimed as All-England champions; S M Massey was hailed as 'a promising beginner'—11 years after winning his first All-England title! And later: 'Fast drop-shots were played to the back of the court' wrote one reporter—not alto-gether surprisingly, Irish. The *Daily Mail* sports artist faced with a photo of Daphne Young playing a shuttle-less clear, neatly drew in—a tennis ball.

And even as late as 1947 John Oliff, *Mail* tennis reporter, 'stuck his chin out' when he wrote: 'There is something medieval and wholesomely amateur about badminton. Toy-like rackets and a miniature net are reminiscent of the nursery. Styles and strokes so similar that it palls'. And he finally damned the game completely with: 'A poetic pastime for the Parish Hall: ideal for a wet Sunday afternoon'.

Let's hope that now his face is suitably crimson and much of the egg removed.

Nevertheless, badminton had its moments. The *Daily News* (1913) hailed it as 'one of the most popular winter games in London'; a Rugby inter-national was quoted (1926): 'A ten-minute single is worse than 30 minutes in the scrum'; and Grape Nuts breakfast cereal advertised itself as: 'Takes the "bad" out of badminton'.

As a result of this paucity of cover (though 'locals' were never as purblind as the 'nationals') counties produced their own magazines. Yorkshire BA were among the first; Portsmouth and District followed with *Cackle* and Herts BA with *Bad News*. Worse atrocities were committed in America: 'Bird-droppings' was featured in *Bird-chatter*! The Commonwealth was little better: Victoria BA in Australia printed the *Feathered Pill*; South Africa BU, *Goose Feather Gossip*. Nevertheless these enthusiastic amateurs did a great publicity job. Even if the *New York Herald* wrote in 1936: 'Can be played over a table and is fast ousting ping-pong'.

Films too were being made. In 1935 Jess Wil-lard, a professional champion, featured in *Good Badminton* whose humour and zip and slow motion were seen in some 6000 cinemas across the USA.

Badminton seldom got its fair share of time 'on the box'. But here the TV eye is firmly on England's Ray Stevens.

This was closely followed by the inimitable Ken Davidson's *Gladminton*—trick shots and all. Coaching loops too were being advertised.

Radio did not seem a likely medium for so fast a game as badminton. In 1928 Sir George (surprisingly shy) declined an invitation to talk on badminton. Ireland's B L Bisgood stepped in: 'How does that great cricketer Jack Hobbs keep fit in the winter? By playing badminton with Andy Sandham (Surrey's No 2) and Herbert Strudwick (England's wicket-keeper)'. No bad opening!

In 1936, Wales' E Trevor-Williams broadcast an eye-witness report on the Welsh Championships. A year later Bernard R Taylor gave a running commentary on the All-England Men's Doubles final: 'Despite the pace, gave a good idea of the game' was contradicted by 'Non-players could make nothing of it'. 1950 saw, or rather heard, champions Wong Peng Soon and Tonny Ahm being interviewed whilst Sir George was prevailed upon at last to make his radio debut.

The BA of E were only too keenly aware of the problem. In 1934, they had formed a publicity committee and appointed a Press Agent at the princely salary of £25 per annum. Little more, apart from fervent pleas or saddened diatribes, was done until the late '70s when full-timer Nick Budibent was appointed as Development and Publicity Officer.

Even then, despite a mountain of handouts, only the quality papers had their own specialist reporters: Dickie Rutnagur (*Daily Telegraph*), Christina Wood (*Guardian*), Richard Streeton (*The Times*) and Richard Eaton (*Sunday Times*). On great occasions the *Daily Mail* press-ganged their distinguished tennis correspondent Laurie Pignon into action. Nevertheless, in 1981, a Badminton Writers' Association was formed of reporters and regular badminton contributors.

In 1948, a Middlesex BA exhibition match was the first to be televised. Queenie Allen, Betty Uber, Donald Hume and Tom Wingfield, ill-advised, played in an amazing miscellany of coloured clothing—only to find that Noel Radford showed up far better in conventional whites. In 1951, the first part of the All-England was televised by the BBC. Three years later, the commentator, on a similar occasion, was taken to task in the *Gazette*: 'That ill-informed chatterer who gives false information and explanations during the rallies should be suppressed'. It turned out to be knowledgeable ex-international Harold Morland who explained that he was catering for non-badminton viewers.

Sadly, over the years it was the latter who were not impressed by what they saw and heard—and badminton paid the penalty. Television camera angles did the game scant justice. Its whirlwind speed, its subtle deception, its pinpoint accuracy were never captured. Nor was found a really effective commentator, a John Arlott, an Eddy Waring, or a Geordie Sid Waddell, the man who makes darts bricks with very little straw.

Nevertheless, major badminton events did receive a slowly growing viewing time until 1981. Then the axe fell with disconcerting suddenness. The BBC, having provisionally agreed coverage, backed out at the last minute from a prestigious event, the Friends' Provident Masters, in which the eagerly awaited Chinese were playing for the *first time ever*. Only an estimated 800 000 viewers switched on for badminton. Anything under 3 000 000 didn't warrant coverage explained the BBC. After all snooker could pull in 6 000 000 and darts go better still with 10 000 000. Repeated entreaties to clubs to write to the BBC had fallen on deaf ears; the general public hadn't been thrilled.

Worse still followed in 1982. For the first time in nearly 35 years the Thomas Cup Inter-Zone ties were allotted to England. As a signal honour the Queen and Prince Philip attended the Royal Albert Hall final: the BBC did not! A cliffhanger China v Indonesia final was beamed out to millions in the Far East. But not a single screen in the UK so much as flickered into badminton life!

Top *Who better to coach Britain's up and coming generation on TV than England's Gillian Gilks?*

Above *Barry Davies and Lincoln 'Imp' Roddy McCrimmon put badminton on the air when commentating on the Friends' Provident Masters Championships at the Albert Hall.*

But badminton did have one television triumph. A *Better Badminton* series was devised: this was partly historical, including interviews with 'greats' of the past such as Betty Uber and Frank Devlin, and partly, basic coaching under the direction of National Coach Jake Downey. The former section included a charming re-enactment of the first games in Badminton Hall itself, with Champions Judy Hashman and very spry octogenarian Kitty Godfree and others all in period costume (see p 10).

Badminton's publicity future looks far from bright. The game is in the centre of a vicious circle. Until it receives big-time prize money sponsorship, it will not appear on television; and until it appears on television to earn viewing figures commensurate with those for darts or snooker, advertisers will not sponsor it.

With hope seemingly lost, the Cinderella Chan-

nel 4 has given a gleam of hope. Not only has it covered the 1983 World Championships but also it has discovered new camera angles that do much more justice to the game.

The Badminton Gazette

The *Gazette*, as it has long been affectionately known, pioneered the way for the current crop of international publications. Through its columns, the wider joys of badminton were offered over a span of 72 years to its world-wide circle of readers by a succession of dedicated editors and business managers who were amateurs—but only in the best sense of that word.

The first issue was published as far back as November 1907 under the editorship of S M Massey (England), largely at the instigation of C Dudfield Willis and A D Prebble who had tired of badminton being very much the junior partner in 'Lawn Tennis and Croquet'. The outside cover was a Slazenger advertisement; the inside, one for F H Ayres; firms who valiantly backed the *Gazette* in every issue over some 40 years.

Its 12 pages, which increased within the year to 16 and then to 20, cost 2d (less than 1p) or, for six issues, 1/- *5p* post free. In these, shuttles were advertised at 5/6d *27½p* per dozen and rackets ranged from 5/9 *29p* (Sirdar) to 15/- *75p* (GAT). Much space was devoted to printing club match scores in full. For this a 3d *1p* fee was charged 'to keep down their numbers'. Photos were slow to appear as they were considered 'extravagant'.

The editorship after just two issues passed to no lesser person than Sir George Thomas whose aims were a '*weekly* magazine avoiding personalities and biassed criticism'. Although receiving from time to time, from disoriented contributors, articles on varied subjects ranging from horsemanship to big-game shooting and from veterinary matters to poultry-keeping, he frequently had to appeal for badminton contributions. (Which editor hasn't?)

Misprints :

Robin Denton was the New Zealand tripe *champion.*

The shuttle must be below the watsit.

There was heatfelt *sympathy for the perspiring loser.*

It's an Ooopen *tournament.*

Men's ararfw arfawyY-ludb TSHR *beat P Gardner 15–12, 15–5.*

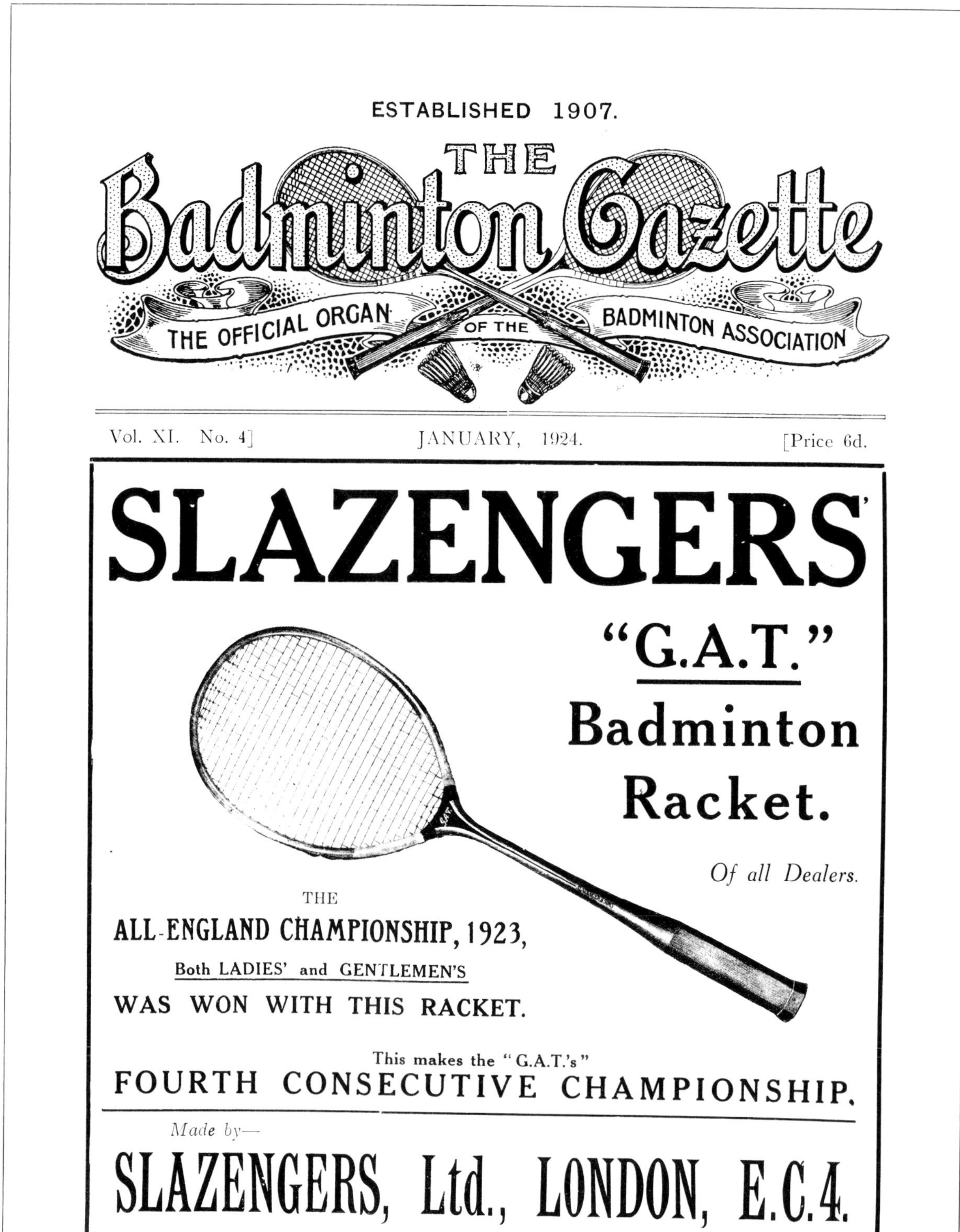

ESTABLISHED 1907.

THE Badminton Gazette

THE OFFICIAL ORGAN OF THE BADMINTON ASSOCIATION

Vol. XI. No. 4]   JANUARY, 1924.   [Price 6d.

SLAZENGERS'

"G.A.T."

Badminton Racket.

Of all Dealers.

THE
ALL-ENGLAND CHAMPIONSHIP, 1923,
Both LADIES' and GENTLEMEN'S
WAS WON WITH THIS RACKET.

This makes the "G.A.T.'s"
FOURTH CONSECUTIVE CHAMPIONSHIP.

Made by—

SLAZENGERS, Ltd., LONDON, E.C.4.

The Gazette *logo for many years : and a typical advertisement by Slazengers who held the cover for over 30 years.*

The Badminton Gazette *in 1907 cost*
2d 1p; *postage was 1d.*

The Badminton Gazette

The Official Organ of the Badminton Association of England

Edited by H. A. E. Scheele

For years the Gazette *contents page featured, chauvinistically, a lively men's doubles. Here airborne Tan Joe Hok (with Ferry Sonneville) attacks Hammergaard Hansen (partnered by Finn Kobbero).*

From 1912 to April 1915, Miss Lavinia Radeglia who won the All-England singles in 1913 and 1914, partnered first S M Massey and then Sir George in the editorship. The War brought publication to a halt for 6 years until October, 1921. Then the feminine touch continued until 1930. Margaret Tragett, one of England's greatest lady players and a very successful novelist, took over in 1921 and again in 1926 until another book intervened. The reins were taken up by Miss H E D Pocock between 1922 and 1926 while Miss Radeglia stepped into the breach again, when Mrs Tragett was in the throes of yet another novel, from 1927 to 1930. Then, for a year, all-conquering Frank Devlin wielded pen as well as racket.

Margaret Tragett had been paid £75 and the first £25 of any net profits (whether there were any was never revealed). Devlin's honorarium was reduced to £50 but with the added incentive of 37½ per cent of the profits. Obviously not a lucrative enough proposition for he soon turned to coaching. That indefatigable sportsman of many parts, D L H Mercer, who could never refuse a job, took over from 1931 until the outbreak of war by which time the subscription was 3/6d *17½p*.

The *Gazette* returned from the First World War in October 1921 still in its pre-War format—but with its price trebled to 6d *2½p* and with the match reports fee quadrupled at 1/- *5p*. In 1935, as a result of a two guinea *£2.10* prize competition, the crossed-rackets and shuttles cover-motif disappeared to be replaced by court-markings and net with a coloured background. But the old appeals for articles, and reminders to Secretaries that the *Gazette* was a club, and not a personal, 'perk' continued.

After the Second World War, the *Gazette* reappeared in November 1946 under the editorship of the BA of E's newly appointed Secretary, Herbert Scheele. And for 25 years both as editor and as 'Invicta', he and his wife Betty ('Velma') did a sterling job. From 1944–6, Frank Henley of RSL had miraculously brought out ten issues of the *Badminton News Bulletin*. In 1951, clubs were asked to contribute 2/6d *12½p* towards mounting costs. And 2 years later, the *Gazette* also became the official outlet for IBF news and notices.

Photographers were at last getting to grips with the problems of taking action photos under the Stygian conditions of Wembley Arena. Pioneers were R W Butler (Surrey), John Newland (Kent) and a lady, Pat M Turner. Over the years there was to follow a succession of generous photographers which culminated in those artists Graham Habbin and 'Mr Lens' himself, the omnipresent, indefatigable Louis Ross who crouches by the net for hours on his tiny stool.

One small but delightful feature of the *Gazette*

New version Gazette *on sale at Wembley Arena. Cover photos of England's top players of the '70s were taken on a TV set.*

was the action photo at the head of the Contents page. Initially, it showed Sir George wrong-footing Frank Devlin with a low backhand cross-court net-shot. This was followed by those lively Irish characters Jim Fitzgibbon, in full cry at the back, and Frank Peard against the eager defence of the little Malayans, Eddy and David Choong, towels dangling from pockets. Male chauvinism was the order of the day with further photos of Denmark's Poul Erik Nielsen and Finn Kobbero against Teh Kew San and Lim Say Hup; then Finn again, this time with Hammergaard Hansen against a bounding Tan Joe Hok and Ferry Sonneville; and England's All-England finalists, Bob Powell and David Eddy.

On the other hand, the editor had made it clear that though 'Progressive papers are omitting the courtesy titles Mrs and Miss, the *Gazette* does not intend to follow this practice'. But he had aban-

doned the use of Mr though 'refraining from overuse of Christian names'.

In November 1970, the author had the onerous but vastly enjoyable task of following 'Mr Badminton', (Herbert Scheele). Coloured covers and larger photos, publicity displays and Sales Officers, prize competitions and cartoons, charm photos and humour were added to the old formula. Circulation and advertising steadily mushroomed.

But it was not enough. The BA of E decided that with the advent of Open badminton a glossier, more professional image must appear on the bookstalls to gather a wider public. And so the *Gazette* made its swan song in February 1979 after a life spanning 72 years.

Phoenix-like from its ashes arose *Badminton*, produced amongst other titles by Marsh Publications, ably edited by an old Fleet Street hand, Ron Willis, generously illustrated, incorporating colour, and sustained by much advertising. But shortly after, now with *twelve* issues a year to pay for and clubs reluctant to pay increased affiliation fees, the BA of E decided that, after over 70 years, they could no longer afford to give their 'Official Journal' to every affiliated club. Many of them, all too parochial in outlook, were unwilling to subscribe privately. The BA of E's optimistic dreams of *Badminton* in every W H Smith's never materialised. The number of readers sadly declined; Marsh went into liquidation. After a year's lapse the BA of E went back to *Gazette* days by producing their own magazine *Badminton Now* under the editorship of Tommy Marrs.

Editors tend to get the few bouquets but on the other hand they are certainly the target for the more numerous brickbats. But the rock bottom foundation of any magazine is its Business Manager. Prior to the First World War, Mr and Mrs Dudfield Willis and the indefatigable Colonel Dolby

Badminton Gazette Editors

1907	S M Massey
1907–12	G A Thomas
1912–13	S Massey and Miss L C Radeglia
1913–15	G A Thomas and Miss L C Radeglia
1921–22	Mrs R C Tragett
1922–26	Miss H E D Pocock
1926–27	Mrs R C Tragett
1927–30	Miss L C Radeglia
1930–31	J F Devlin
1931–39	D L H Mercer
1946–70	H A E Scheele
1970–79	P R Davis

BA of E's high hopes of a glossy commercial Badminton *to replace 'old faithful'* Gazette *came to nothing, through reader apathy, despite glamorous sales-girls.*

gave yeoman service. A memorable trio followed. All-England title winner S M Massey ran affairs from 1922–34. Then K L (Ken) Livingstone was in charge. An employee of RSL, a hard-hitting English international, and a dedicated founder of the Badminton Umpires' Association of England, he gave the *Gazette* unstinting service for 30 years before he retired to Spain where he died 2 days after his wife (a descendant of William Wordsworth). Mrs Dorothy Lodge, also an RSL employee, unstintingly gave time and care to *Gazette* affairs almost up to its demise.

It was dedicated enthusiasts such as these who helped the *Gazette*, if not 'to all parts of the Universe' as Herbert Scheele once wrote, then at least to all the badminton playing nations of the world. There to interest and entertain. To spread badminton's own story in its own way.

Woodley BC (Berks) made the staggering claim of having thirty National Coaches in their club! They played in a bus depot.

Letters to the Editor

The number, or dearth, of 'Letters to the Editor' is generally a fair reflection of a game's health. In this respect the *Gazette* always sounded a very steady heartbeat. 'Wood-shots and Slings', 'Foul Serving', 'Slow Shuttles' and 'Slippery Floors' were hardy perennials. Other subjects ranged from the sublime ('Maestro's Magic' or 'Is Pronation Power?') to the ridiculous ('Shorter Shorts' or 'Two Left Hands') by 'Well-wisher' or 'Disgusted Veteran'.

They were written in prose and verse; in righteous wrath and cool seriousness; with tongue in cheek and with unconscious humour.

*   *   *   *   *

The formation in the mid-fifties of the Badminton Umpires' Association of England roused the wrath of those who had delighted in the fact that badminton even at county and tournament level had long been played in the best amateur tradition without gaggles of official linesmen and umpires. Ex-international and Scots administrator David Bloomer clashed with English international John Best in a scintillating, good-humoured singles.

Dear Sir,

Umpiring and the BUA of E

I have read with tolerance—and very little interest—the several letters in your correspondence columns on the subject of umpiring.

I must assume that this highly organised cure, the BUA of E, is the result of disease. Truly, is the cure worse than the disease?

The agitated machinations of this well-meaning body doubtless provide occupation and, perhaps, even relaxation for some whose interest in the game has outgrown their physical capacity for too active participation. It is sad to observe, however, that this old country, in common with the rest of our world, succumbs rapidly to the uncontrollable urge of the few to associate, amalgamate, legislate, harass, bedevil, and eventually dictate to its unsuspecting hordes of simple people even unto how to live, eat, think, act, play and now—umpire play.

Little did I think, when I first fell in love with badminton, some 30 years ago, that, in 1954, solemnly elected, examined and approved members of a high-sounding body like the BUA of E would glue their anxious optics to the floor, concentrating assiduously on that reprehensible eighth-of-an-inch of daylight between the floor and the foot to bawl a triumphant and self-important 'fault'. This is one of the lesser inanities I have observed.

I have had some experience of badminton at every level, and have yet to experience insurmountable difficulty in obtaining adequate umpires and responsible and articulate linesmen who are efficient, co-operative, and—bless their modest hearts—unobtrusive.

I look forward, without pleasure, to the foundation of the Honolulu Linesmen's Association to which will be affiliated the Amalgamated Federation of Service Judges and the Anti-Track Suits Union of Spitzbergen whose representatives on the controlling international body will inevitably be residents of Kingston, Kensington and Kew. I will *not* be a founder member.

Yours faithfully,

D L Bloomer

Glasgow.
6 January 1955

Dear Sir,

In Defence of the BUA of E

While I do not advocate the rebuilding of Hadrian's Wall, I feel it is time some resistance was offered to the Celtic interference in matters purely Anglo-Saxon, which I have noticed recently in the correspondence columns of your excellent magazine. Mr Bloomer is justly famed for his defence on the court, and his attack off it, but I feel that this time he has carried his acerbity too far.

The Badminton Umpires' Association of England, in the short time since its inception, has done a great deal of good work in this country, and I write as a player with some experience of bad and indifferent umpiring (some of it in Scotland). I am sure that Mr Bloomer, clad as he is in the mantle of eternal youth, would really agree that it is a good thing for players to put back into the game what they have gained from it. What better direction for their energies than the improved organisation of tournaments and matches, of which the BUA of E has already shown itself capable?

He warns of the dangers of regimentation and over-enthusiasm, but I can assure him that the members of the Association are themselves fully alive to this problem, although I know they would wish to thank Mr Bloomer for his concern.

It is significant, I think, that there have been requests from all over the world for information about the work of the Association, and Mr Bloomer's attention might be drawn to the renegade behaviour of a Scottish official, who requested an Association umpire to run a successful course in Aberdeen.

No cries of protest have been heard in Kingston, Kensington or Kew over Mr Bloomer's dignified refusal to join any such organisation whether invited or no.

In fact, he might just as well go toss a caber.

Yours faithfully,

John Best

Beckenham, Kent.
February, 1955

Dear Sir,

Riposte!

Mr Best is amusing, and tenders have been invited for supplying a caber. The traditional repository for balancing that perilous projectile is there in amplitude, and, in this connection, I have sought quotations for a smaller model for Mr Best's personal recreation.

I feel, however, that he is better temporarily adapted to the muscular effort required, and that success is his in any Highland Gathering by tossing the caber in roughly the same trajectory as that employed in his service. He is at least assured that no competing Highlander will smash it at his feet.

Yours faithfully,

D L Bloomer
April, 1955

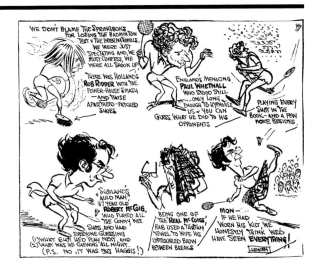

United Nations,
New York.
6 November 1975

UN Rebuke

Sir,

We were intrigued to read on Page 15 of your October issue a heading '*England* Wins Tests'. We assume that the authoress, Miss Webster, is of English descent although Webster is an old Pictish name.

On reading the article we find that three members of the Test team came from England but were hindered by two Nederlanders, one Deutschlander, one Danishlander and one Scottishlander, who, we were pleased to see, was nominated as captain by virtue of his good looks and command of the English language. We notice that the team was accompanied by Mr and Mrs Scheele, who we assume are Internationalanders.

We trust the above explanation clarifies the position of the team for all your many readers, particularly those in South Africa.

Yours faithfully,

Kurt Waldheim

Editor's Note: It is not Miss Webster's face that is red but the Editor's. He alone is responsible for the heading. His only plea in mitigation of this heinous crime against good international relations is that it was committed at 2 am in a fit of 'mock-up' madness! However, philosophical to the last, he can only plead, 'out of evil comes good'; from a careless heading, a delightful letter. He is tempted to commit more such errors. January, 1976.

Irish international 'Chick' Doyle makes a spirited reply to a suggestion that the Home Countries should amalgamate to form a single United Kingdom team.

Dear Sir,

Irish Independence

By all means let us have the McCoigs and Jordans, Sullivans and Findlays, Kellys and MacHendersons playing together in tournaments. Also let us have a British and Irish touring team going on safari to Africa (this is long overdue).

But Mr Reedie presumes too much if he expects the Irish, at any rate, to lose their national identities and characteristics, and be neatly wrapped up and labelled MADE IN ENGLAND.

Anyway, 'I'm shure 'twould be a mortal sin'.

Yours respectfully,

James Patrick Doyle
Dublin.

A charming letter of encouragement from Japan to severely injured English international Margaret Lockwood. Sadly, it was to no avail. She never played again.

615-2-212, Noba-machi
Konan-ku, Yokohama 233,
Japan.

Dear Sir,

Cheer up, Maggie!

I've read 'That knee . . .' in the October *Badminton Gazette*. I feel terribly sorry to hear that the condition of Mrs Margaret Lockwood's knee is not well.

I can't help remembering her enchanting play of last year in Japan. We were deeply impressed by her elegant court manner which must be a typical English way, and her calm behaviour.

By the way, Miss Hiroe Yuki who stays in the top representative player in Japan was blowed by a big accident which cut down her Achilles tendon in 1970. In spite of this fact, she has recovered perfectly, after having persisted in her treatment.

I guess Maggie's suffering must be beyond our imagination. But we wish she would do her best therefore she's got such strong back-up in Japan as a million of fans are sending her a great support. We are looking forward to seeing her when she's recovered.

Sincerely yours,

T Seto
Editor 'Badminton World'

Ex-international and England Team Manager Jack McColl takes a novel look at the hoary 'Foul Serve' chestnut.

Dear Sir,

Foul Serving

I used to liken the service rule to the start of a sailing race, where it is vital to get as near to the starting line as possible without actually crossing it before the gun goes. Experienced sailors always said 'If you're not called back once in five starts, you're not trying'. The service could be similar.

Yours faithfully,

Jack McColl

The Editor's hastily scrawled letter to National Coach Frank Smith evoked this shattering all-too-well-deserved reply.

Sir,

Illegible Imitation

I took your letter down to the chemist, who, after some minutes asked, 'Is this prescription for a very big horse?' When I said I thought it was a letter from a very dear friend of mine he turned quite pale, invoked the name of the Deity —and muttered something under his breath about

my being a poor piece of turf. However, after translating it from its original Sanscrit we got the hang of it (as the public executioner said).

Yours faithfully,

Frank Smith
February, 1976

Dear Sir,

Pseudonymous Correspondence

May I make a plea for a higher criterion of editorial selection of letters to be printed than you have recently seen fit to adopt? I refer not, as you may think, to the wrangling match which has gone on at such length in your columns between various umpires, whose Association reminds me more and more of a Labour Party Conference; although their letters might be faulted by a more severe arbiter on inadequacies in style, logic, and sense of values.

My main complaint, however, stems from certain recent letters which, over pseudonymous signatures, mention the names of current personalities in the badminton world, often adversely. As there is no way for the reader to judge the standard of the complainant, this amounts to little more than scandal-mongering. From the plaintiff's point of view, there are better and less cowardly ways of venting antagonism; from your point of view, there are better and more respectable ways of maintaining circulation.

Lest anyone should think that I am sheltering behind a pseudonym myself, which I have often maintained cannot be beaten for its just and accurate description, let me say that it is by an accident of birth that I am able to sign myself,

Yours truly,

J R Best
20 March, 1961

Your caption, Sir,
will cause a stir;
Master *Freud*
is quite annoyed.

Poetic comment after Clement Freud's long-haired son had been 'Mis-sexed' in a photo caption.

Laughter in Court

Badminton has always had its lighter side. A game with no humour is no game. Bridge's accusing post-mortems, football's violent fanaticism, and tennis tantrums, are happily not for badminton.

The game in its amateur days was brimming over with larger than life character internationals. Jovial Warwick Shute and genial giant Ian Maconachie; Ireland's broth of a boy 'Chick' Doyle and Scotland's cryptic MacHenderson; practical joker Tony Jordan and urbane wit David Bloomer; perky Maurice Field and impressionist Maurice Robinson would have made a comedy team hard to beat.

With greater prestige and prize money at stake some of the champagne sparkle has gone. But, thank heavens, there's still a lot of 'Laughter in Court'—and always will be!

A Dicey Game

Apart from crossing city streets against the traffic lights, reminiscing is as dicey a game as the elderly can enjoy. It is played cosily with fellow ancients, fretfully with middle-aged sceptics, and on sufferance with unlucky youngsters trapped in a bar, and too thirsty or too well-mannered to contrive escape. It can also be enjoyed solo, lightening the dull chores of morning ablution, chatting to the bathroom mirror in that last bastion of privacy in this intrusive world.

David Bloomer

Nothing by Halves!

Extrovert Warwick Shute, BA of E National Coach and ex-international, never one to do things by halves, has been struck down by housemaid's knee—in his ankle—and quadriceps torn while starting his 500 cc motor bike (rumoured to be fitted with a 30 mph governor). To remedy these defects he installed a static cycling machine in his sitting-room—so that he could watch television while he pedalled.

The only point our correspondent has not been able to clear up is whether the appearance of a

Ken Davidson, Scottish badminton international and Yorkshire county cricketer, put badminton on stage with Royal Command and other Palladium performances.

particularly nubile young starlet on the screen causes him to free-wheel or set off in even hotter pursuit.

Pat Davis

Grunt Play

The loser, McCoig, however reigned supreme in one aspect of the game, namely advanced grunt play. This is a superior and extremely difficult type of deception and occurs when one is caught flat-footed by a skilful drop-shot or fast clear. One emits a grunt as if to concede the point, and then just manages to scrape a return over the head of the opponent, who has stopped, thinking the point won. Robert has a fine selection of grunts, from a lamenting 'Och' to a pained, mournful 'Ah', with a few other expletives capable of taking care of

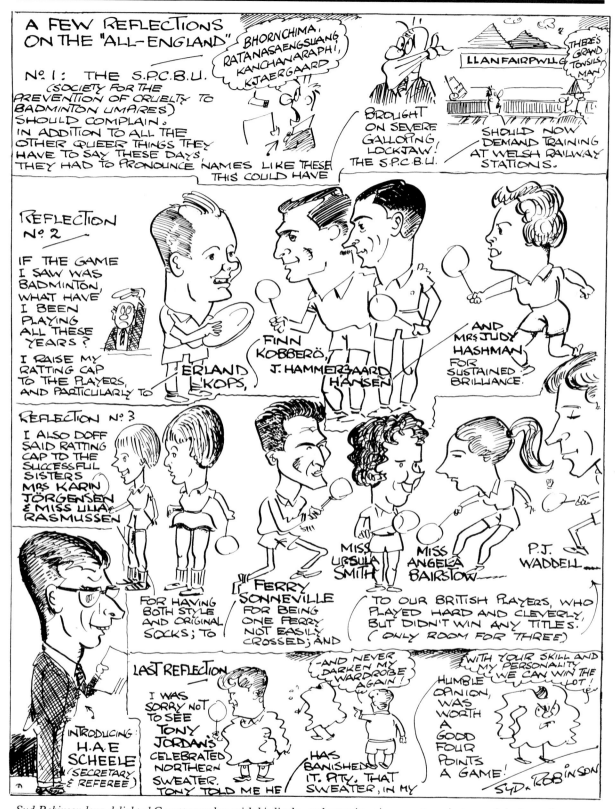

Syd Robinson long delighted Gazette *readers with his lively, and sometimes irreverent, caricatures of the 'greats'.*

any situation. Talbot's mighty snort every time he completed a smash, commendable though it was, served only to label him the apprentice in the presence of the master.

Douglas Hendry
'Cock o' the North'

The Ne'er-Do-Wells of Vagabonds' IV

Even before the first session he'd been christened 'Greyhound'. Something to do with an American coach, I believe, but then I never really understood the fourth team's jokes. When he arrived, I had to admit that his nickname seemed appropriate; he was lean, close-cropped, built for speed and immaculately turned out, with more badges on his tracksuit than a Butlin Redcoat.

I was not altogether sure that this admiration was mutual as he surveyed the assembly of mis-shapen and geriatric 'humanity' that constituted his new class. Nor did I quite hear what he muttered as his lower jaw dropped but Theresa O'Dooley, standing next to him, became convinced from that point in time that her new coach was a devout Catholic.

A Anderson

Like Income Tax and the Titanic, I suppose, it *had* seemed a good idea at the time. England were due to play West Germany at the nearby Sports Centre: my scheme was to procure tickets for our Fourth Team squad and let them see how the game should and could be played. To some of them it would undoubtedly come as a revelation that players actually moved their feet during the course of a rally, and seldom uprooted the net in the course of delicate net-play. A glimmer of the brilliance might be absorbed by some form of osmosis. Pityingly, the Committee members informed me that, as an optimist, I was seeded second-only to the President of the Flat-Earth Society.

A Anderson

Le Sport

It is the dream of my life to see badminton played by some of the more expressive races, those French housewives, for instance, who pour out a couple of Rostand's dramas over every egg they buy in the market place, or Spanish senoritas each in half-a-dozen petticoats and with flower-bedecked hair.

Fearing such a joyous drama could never be realised, I did the next best thing. I took a young Frenchman of my acquaintance to my club, as I warned him, 'to see the English play'.

All the drill halls I have ever seen wear an expression of 'abandon hope all ye who enter here' but ours does its best. Everything is painted in a shade of murky grey. Grey guns stand against grey walls. A length of grey corrugated iron screens the rifle range. If the eye can pierce the gloom above, it discovers at last a dirty glass roof where the rain comes through from a grey sky and forms in pools on a concrete floor, grey with dust and oil.

There is no doubt our members have drunk deep of the spirit of the place—unless they were drawn to it by the natural attraction of like to like. Anyway new and shy members have been known to shrivel up and fade away under the heavy frost of a first night.

Unfortunately, just as I led Henri into the hall a vicious crackle of rifle fire broke out, and I had to race through the village to catch him. On my assurance that it was 'le sport', and nothing but 'le sport', and that one amused oneself—tiens! how one amused oneself!—he allowed me to lead him back. He seemed happier when I placed our stools under the muzzle of a big gun.

Three courts were occupied, the distant one by four men, very blue about the legs and grim about the face, getting in some hard smashes. Near at hand the women had disposed themselves on two courts according to their generations, four fortyish virgins in white and four young, hard things in slaughterhouse lips, nails and socks with a spot of navy shorts between. A few of Madame Defarge's daughters sat around silently knitting the ever-lasting jumper.

I explained nothing to Henri. I just let it soak in: swift running of feet, violent action of wrist, ever-changing position and never-changing expression,

At a Cork badminton exhibition, play was held up half-way through to allow a complete change of spectators. Twice as many tickets had been sold as there were seats!

World Pro champions Hugh Forgie and talented son Reg, with glamorous Shirley Marie, put 'Badminton on Ice' for millions.

shuttle being hurled aloft into impenetrable gloom then smashed like barbs of lightning into the opposing midriff; bodies apparently galvanised by electricity: faces obviously frozen in the refrigerator. We know our worth.

Henri's face was a joy to watch: so quick with intelligence, frankly puzzled, then amazed but diligently searching for a clue. Then by a curious coincidence there came another burst of rifle fire just as one of the men on the far court collapsed with a sprained muscle. I caught Henri at the door!

One backward glance at the silent women encircling the supine figure and nothing would persuade him to return. Saturation point was reached, however, and weeks of watching would not have improved his explanation of the game of badminton. Over a flagon of wine, with a running commentary of adjectives ending in 'able', he delivered himself enthusiastically in this vein:

'But yes! I know it! I understand it! (C'est incroyable!). It is the game. It is the sport. Yes! But it is the ritual also—always with the English it is the ritual (jmpitoyable!). It is like the Freemasons, the cult, yes? (imperturbable!). I regard very well and I see the virgins in white; they are the virtues (impérissable!); and the others in red (impermeable!), they represent the vices. What terrible vices! (indebrouillable!). Then they play for the soul of the man—the little soul with

Overheard as two diminutive Scots laddies left the court after a 15–0, 15–0 hammering: 'Aye but ye ken what it would ha'e been like if we hadna' been playing well'.

feathers. The virtues fly it up to heaven, and the vices knock it down to earth (inevitable!). I do not discover how the points go, but sometime the virtues win and the man live to play tomorrow, but tonight the red ladies win and the man die! (Incontestable!) Hein? Yes?'

All I desire now is to take Henri to a baseball match.

P P

International Idiosyncrasies

In a perfect example of from the sublime to the ridiculous the Portuguese party left sunny Portugal only to find themselves stranded in rain-lashed Wigan when Rugby League 'fans' wrecked their train.

I could not finish without mentioning the charming Russian interpreter who looked the part right down to the Stalin moustache and the black leather belted coat. However, his tough exterior did not convey the true image which changed when you discovered that his name was Valerie and that he addressed everyone in a broad American accent as 'You'se guys' regardless of their sex.

Amongst gems such as 'Toilet paper is plentiful and of good quality' the Tour Information Sheet told us that 'Rape carries the death penalty' and that 'Spring is very dry and can give rise to powerful static electricity. Care should be taken in wearing nylon'. The moral therefore was clear—do not wear nylon when committing rape in China in Spring.

One result of this banquet was that we lost Peter Birtwistle for most of the following day. Something (could it have been over-indulgence in food and/or wine despite his heated denials?) caused him to suffer from what is commonly known as 'a severe loosening' and he spent the night and most of the following day doing what does not come easily to him—sitting still—where he would have preferred not to have been sitting at all.

Tommy Marrs
BA of E Promotions Manager

Women's Lib

The Executive of the Ottawa District Badminton Association, a group of hairy, wild-eyed, sometimes ne'er do well, always trouble-making (so it seems) left-wing pinko (we all attended a reception at the Chinese Embassy in 1971) bird-bashers, took Miss Tinline's words to their collective heretical hearts and hoary heads—and acted. Our motto is 'never look when you can leap', and the breach put before us in the inspired words of Miss Tinline's liberal lecture just seemed to match the stride of our seven league boots.

So, feckless Frank Carr ('Funky Frank' to his friends), a gleam in his eye, a spring in his step, a frog in his throat, eager to nurture novelty, put it to the Directors. And they found 5 (two females) to 3 (two females) in favour of the proposition.

The Westminster Spring Meeting—Form and Fancies

A long and interesting programme is assured for this forthcoming five days' meeting, and a few notes on prospective runners and possible winners are appended.

The course is in good order, and though the going may be hard it will undoubtedly be light. I have numbered the various events as they appear in the card printed on another page, but will take

   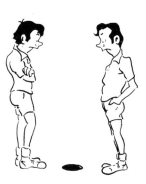

That modern Women, being as fit as Men, can well play 15 up and be entered in the Men's Singles (hereinafter known as 'Singles').

Ms O'Brien had drawn with wily Dhan Khare, a devious Oriental and Pediatrician to boot, whose stoic, ruthless approach to the game has forced many a hard-hearted, tournament-toughened competitor to wilt in the heat of combat.

The doctor wielded deceptive drops and attacking clears with the precision and finesse of a surgeon tying sutures during open heart surgery to take the first game 15–9. The second game was similar to the first, except that Barb got into the swing of things and gave the good Doctor some of his own medicine. It was reported that Dhan was seen reviving himself with some potion from a small vial between the second and third games (can you get high on a bottle of Johnson's Baby Lotion?). But all to no avail! Superior conditioning and shuttle control retired the infant specialist to the sidelines where he performed auto-artificial respiration and heart massage.

The other female contestant, Ms Lynn Goudie, Ontario Junior Ladies' Doubles Champion in 1973, took the court against sturdy Steve Joncas. Steve, who is reputed to hold many skirt-chasing titles in Ontario and Quebec, found the tables turned as his opponent pushed him from corner to corner with great authority. Only a series of untimely errors cost Lynn the match, 15–12 in the third game.

Alan Baird

the Singles Stakes first.

Event No 5—The issue appears to lie between that ever-popular chestnut, The Baronet, and the Irish crack, Evelyn. They have met several times this season, and The Baronet has usually won, Evelyn not being a stayer, three furlongs seeming to be fatal to him, whereas over the shorter distance he won at Ealing. The Baronet has also been beaten this season by some of the other runners— by Burberry (I am writing these notes immediately after a Dublin meeting), Day's Partner (at Glasgow), and Bloomsbury Lass (at Paisley). Owing to his recent illness Farmer will not be competing, otherwise he would have to be reckoned with, whilst Tart Sue is abroad again. That heavy but effective galloper, Wine End, after his victory at Glasgow, must not be forgotten; but I fancy The Baronet, with Burberry most dangerous.

Event No 4—Last year's winner—Make Hay— being absent, the issue of this—the equivalent of the Oaks—is very doubtful. Regalia, Barter, and the stylish Target are all worth watching, and I vote for the last named.

Vital details of all-important handicaps for the other events have not yet been published. However, Sweet Seventeen, Set up and Clear

> *From the official rules—'If a tournament entry is made under an assumed name, that same assumed name must be used all the season'.*

Well (if he doesn't drop) should all go far, and both 'On the Line' and 'Bird from the Wood' want watching. I do not fancy Smasher (out of Court, by Yards), Always Mine Partner, or Mr Gain (whose Dam, The Light, was to the fore in recent years at this meeting).

PUN-TER

Author's Note: *Octogenarians will need little help to identify the runners: others may find the BA of E Handbook 'List of All-England Championship Winners' more help than 'Ruff's Guide to the Turf'.*

Murder on Court

For the aching curse of every badminton club is the member who 'comes just to enjoy herself'. In a game that requires the wit of Ulysses, the speed of Atalanta, and the grace of a Ranji, she plants herself like a six-foot windmill (she is always six feet high and has arms to match) down the centre line and roars with delight as she booms about backwards and forwards, right and left, missing everything but the net, the walls and the roof. Scoring nothing but her partner's scalp.

P P

No MOT Test Needed!

What the London to Brighton run is to antique cars, the All-England Veterans' Championship is to our vintage players: the highlight of the season; a chance to renew past glories and to compare notes on present running-order with old friends. And all this without the deflating and noisy intrusion of the modern, streamlined jobs with souped-up engines.

By 11 o'clock a fair array of pre-war models had panted into the Ebbisham BC lounge. The filling station for the higher octane fuel (so necessary to put 'a tiger in the tank') unfortunately didn't open till a little later—much too much later for some. It required all Herbert and Betty Scheele's long refereeing guile and experience and Brian Bisseker's geniality to persuade them to back out for a quick service before they clanked to the starting line.

One or two of the more modern models (mainly from Derby, home of the Rolls Royce) got off to a flying start; others needed a generous touch of the choke before they were on the move. Even so, acceleration was distinctly sluggish, and braking left much to be desired. After only a few points, piston slap could be clearly heard and slack fan-belts were evidenced as competitors left the courts in clouds of steam.

Collisions too were not infrequent. The Middle-sex Morgan Special sustained damage a little above the radiator cap as the result of an intuitive but unsignalled right turn by her lady partner. The Pidgley Poulton two-seater crashed so spectacularly that blood was drawn, a windscreen shattered and, worst of all, the match lost at 16–17!

It was good to see there such very long service vehicles as the 1902 Adam Wilson and the 1903 Gerald Tautz of the Equipe Middlesex. Admittedly not taking part but still in regular weekly going order, chrome gleaming and upholstery in very good shape.

Pat Davis

Author's Note: *Just a scrap of yellowing paper found in a cupboard. But maybe it epitomises both the play—and the players.*

Goofs Increase. No one immune!

'G'wan laugh. Can I help it if I'm crazy about badminton?'

From which, readers will quite rightly gather that they are 'Goofs'.

The writer proclaims badminton is the fastest and most skilful of games: 'it sure is no cissy!' The democratic features of the game too have touched his heart. Its appeal is 'to the ordinary guy'—not 'the Society mob'. And under the delightful sub-title of 'No High Hats' he mentions the finals of his State tournament being played before 1500 people 'scarcely any of whom wore tall hats or ermine wraps'. Not only the players but also the fans were apparently members of the great proletariat.

If you would like to read the article in full you will find it on the reverse side of advertisements for 'Tovarich', 'The Trudi Schoop Comic Ballet', a Symphony Concert conducted by Stravinsky, and

> *In a Ladbroke Trophy final David Eddy (England) shamefacedly apologised for a winner off the wood— then won the next two points with net-cord shots.*

Nicky Goode says, 'You can't do better than that!'

'Modern Motherhood—the Forbidden Secrets are Daringly Revealed', but the place and issue of the paper are unknown.

Shuttle Bait!

The Garrison Theatre, Canterbury, used by the Pilgrims BC is notorious throughout East Kent, and possibly East Siberia for that matter, for its bitter cold and for the colander-like ease with which its aged roof admits driving rain or drifting snow. Anyone who knows it well will scarcely be surprised that the Pilgrims' Secretary, Ron Broadway, should dream—or have nightmares!

One Monday night, with the car park rendered inaccessible by deep drifts, he trudged knee-deep through snow to the entrance. At the mercy of the bitter wind, the door banged eerily to and fro.

Inside burnt a single light. By its dim rays he observed, without undue surprise, that the floor was covered with snow and ice—and that by the umpire's chair there stood an igloo. In front of it, swathed in layer upon layer of sweaters, looking like some monstrous Polar Bear, was one staunch club member. In her numbed fingers she grasped a fishing rod; at the end of her line dangled—a feathered shuttle, a vintage RSL Tourney.

Only now were his emotions stirred. He strode forward, shouting angrily, 'Marjorie! Marjorie!

What are you doing! You know perfectly well that on Mondays we use plastic shuttles, not feathered!'

Pat Davis

Verse – or Worse

The poetry of badminton itself has sometimes evoked outpourings in verse. But that there are no Poet Laureates on court is self-evident. The following examples, however, do show some lively footwork and deftness of touch.

The All-England Championships were held from 1911 to 1939 in that Mecca of Flower Shows, the Horticultural Hall, Vincent Square, Westminster.

THE 'HORTICULTURAL SHOW'
I sing the silk-clad foot that scuttles
Swift in pursuit of fragile shuttles,
The pretty maids of haughty culture,
Who in expensive chocolates mulct yer,
    But give a rare All-England air
        To Vincent Square!

I own, of course, that Monsieur Paquin
Might consider something lacking
In their plain white piqué kirtle,
But *I* do think a six-inch skirt'll
    Lend a most sweet All-England air
        To Vincent Square!

The FHS, who patronises
Rose and carnation paradises,
Here held with regularity,
Might hint at a disparity
    'Twixt these and other bloomers fair
        At Vincent Square!

Myself, I think these Champion Roses,
With their pretty powdered noses,
Would tempt the late Saint Anthony—
They've scored a 'Double Hit' on me—
    These lovelier flowers that take the air
        At Vincent Square!

Bach E Law

Fellow of the Horticultural Society

'Ruthless Rhymes' and Limericks featured prominently in the '20s and '30s.

Thomas, playing Hodge one day,
Caused his death—which hindered play.
Smiling, as they picked Hodge up:
'My fault' cried George, 'but mine the Cup!'

Devlin gave his partner, Mack,
In the eye a fearful crack!
'Pooh' quoth he, 'the pain soon passes—
Praise the pigs, ye don't wear glasses!'

There was a young man who said 'Dash!
I really must learn how to smash.'
The housemaid said, 'Pooh!
You should do as I do:
Just drop—and wait for the crash!'

There was a young man who said, 'Sir,
I will play any shot you prefer:
Off the strings or the wood
They are equally good—
But off both my best strokes occur!'

Miss Gowenlock had a very bad fall:
Broke both her legs and couldn't move at all.
Mrs Harvey, her partner, (absolve me from
    malice)
Continued the rally, exclaiming, 'Up, Alice!'

Rita Heywood, Lancashire, has a winning smile and non-stop feet which earned her the nickname of 'Miss Perpetual Motion'.

A Poulter deftly captured the image of Club badminton—and later submitted unusual match reports in similar metrical vein.

Dear kind and noble Editor
Of *Shuttlecock and Battledore*,
Or is it *Badminton* these days?
Excuse our antiquated ways—
A learned scribe we would not vex
But here in ancient Middlesex
We tend to be a bit 'old hat',
And feel we're none the worse for that!
So please accept (and here's the nub)
Fond greetings from the HILLSIDE CLUB.
For small and humble we may be,
In League Division 7B,
With ill-marked court and low ceiling—
I'm sure you know the sort of thing—
And some who come to knit and chat
And talk at length of this and that,
A few infirm, and too few men—
At best we number nine or ten;
And yet, how many clubs find time
To give their match reports in rhyme?
Mind you, I think it must be said
Results like ours are better read
In verse, for, though the game's the thing,
They are a bit disheartening.
So, two I now enclose, dear Sir,
And hope they'll pass as 'literature'!

Gillian Clark, hard-hitting, lively and acrobatic on court, could become England's leading ladies' doubles player.

Hampshire's Peter Pennekett and Brian Keeling bring a heroic dash to the 1976 French Championship Veterans' Doubles between J R Beal and Ivan Stouse, and Bill Rickard and M Vallet, played in Le Havre's glass-sided Salle Beauville.

Rickard in for the kill; from the crowd came
   'Shot, Bill'
'Yes, he should be' said Ivan intensely.
Such wit and asides were enjoyed by both
   sides,
And amused the spectators immensely.

Amidst cries of despair and much rending of
   hair,
The game crept to thirteen points each.
They set, both got four, missing chances
   galore—
The game is within both pairs' reach!
'Is it in? Yes or no? O God, what a blow!
On the line—it came right out of the sun!'
The applause thundered out to acknowledge
   the clout
That made the set-score one-one.

But at last the end came—fifteen-twelve,
   final game
Goodness knows it was lengthy and hard.
To the French crowd's elation, 'midst
   a standing ovation
The match went to Vallet and Rickard.

In 1963, All-England Ladies' Singles proceedings were held up for some time when reigning champion Judy Hashman decreed that water on the court be mopped up before play commenced. England's Angela Bairstow showed her displeasure with actions that spoke far louder than any words.

VERSE-ATILITY AT WEMBLEY
'They also serve who only stand and wait'
The singles final's stage was set
when, almost underneath the net,
the lady champion found a spot;
though whether it was there or not
I could not tell, because to me
there was not anything to see.

Thereafter there was some delay
and so, in hope of starting play,
officials had to search about
for means to wipe the damn thing out.

A mop, made wetter than it 'oughter'
by former player's casual water
was then applied on champion's order
to middle court as well as border.

Mikiko Takada (above) *and Atsuko Tokuda were labelled T'NT because of their explosive play.*

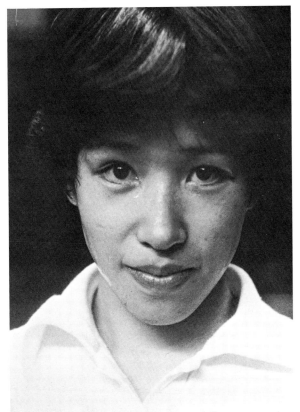

Tiny Yoshiko Yonekura, Japan, delights crowds with her fierce smashing, last-ditch defence and quicksilver footwork.

The consequence, as you may guess
was merely to produce a mess,
which made the lady champion cry
'I cannot play until it be dry'.

Miss Bairstow then essayed relief
by getting out her handkerchief
and hands and knees upon the floor
rubbed hard, as on a homely chore,
but not enough; and I must state
that some grew tired of this long wait.

Now, showing little signs of nerves,
Miss Bairstow tries some practice serves
and to and fro her way she wends
continually changing ends,
as if she'd solve her rival's troubles
by partnering her in ladies' doubles.

When all the champions who appear
produce the same results each year
and none are English, let's take pride
that we can see the funny side.

C H C

---

*In 1973, Chinese players emerged from behind the
Bamboo Curtain. By their speed and power they
swept England aside like chaff in singles matches.
Good losers ever, the England team composed and
sang the following lament at a farewell party.*

ENGLAND'S LAMENT
We'd like to learn to play the game
The way the Chinese do:
To smash and bang like Fang and Tang,
And drop like Hou and Liu.

We'd like to win a men's event,
To even up the score,
But when we count up all our points
We find we've averaged four!

Our boys are getting desperate
As you will soon detect;
If only Gill would lose a match
They'd save their self-respect.

We've trained as hard as we know how;
There's no more we can do!
Unless we steal their super coach—
And kidnap Doctor Who.

We thought that we knew badminton
Until the Chinese came
But now we think we'll learn Mah Johng
And play them at their game.

But if we are to win a match
We must do more than sing;

We'll use our Captain's favourite shots—
The double hit and sling!

Jack McColl

Action Snaps

Modern photography offers us superb studies of
the great in action—for a hundredth of a second
the human frame is frozen in full flight like a
pinned butterfly.

Modern journalism does more. It softens the
edges by showing not only the full flow of strokes
but by revealing character and charisma as well.

The following vignettes show some of the greats
on court—and off.

Succinct Malaysian Summary
Of particular importance to the committee, the
games have shown that *Tan Aik Huang, Tan Aik
Mong*, and their education together pose eternal
problems with no easy solution in sight. *Gunalan's*
play was superb but his lack of stamina stuck out
uncomfortably prominent. *Ng Boon Bee*, ever so
slightly slower, will continue to be a menace to any
doubles opponents. *Abdul Rahman's* sporadic
brilliance is offset by patches of endemic mediocrity.
Tan Yee Khan and his back are enigmas yet.
Yew Cheng Hoe's expanding equator causes concern. His adiposity and avoirdupois will have to be
whittled down considerably. *Ng Tat Wai* is effective, not ebullient, and, with a little more staying
power built in, will become a welcome striking
force in our armoury. *Teh Kew San*, participant
in four Thomas Cup contests, has decided to call
it a day.

The committee has hard work to do in the
coming months, the players harder. And time?
Time flies; and lo, the bird is on the wing.

'Omega'

Contrasting Styles
Their appearance and style of play was so very
different. *Donald Smythe*, a strong, sturdy, somewhat stocky figure played a hustling and bustling
sort of game. He has a heavy but rather horizontal
smash, and I got the impression that he never
really quite managed to time it as well as usual,
owing perhaps to the immense size of the hall. He
looked to me rather like an association football
player; he certainly worked as hard, and ran as far.
He was never beaten until the shuttle was on the
ground.

Johnnie Heah, on the other hand, looked like a
small slight schoolboy, and bounced gently on his

feet the whole time the shuttle was in play. Holding his racket rather in front of his face, he hit his clears most beautifully to the corners of the court, and dropped with amazing accuracy just over the tape. Heah seemed to occupy the centre of the court, and forced his adversary to run all round the other side of the net.

Betty Uber

Lancashire Lass

The English were invited in large numbers mainly due to the cheapness of the standby, off-peak air fare. *Margaret Barrand* (Lancs and England) provided the very necessary comic relief. Only a player of the highest order could play so many shots the difficult way, including a few from a seated position in the middle of the court, entertain the crowd with a running commentary in a dialect none of them could understand anyway, and still win.

Also in this group was the lady with the Scandinavian name from South Africa who plays for England referred to by an Indonesian fan as 'the tremendous, sporting, Mrs Heather Nielsen'.

'Scotia'

One of those Days!

Angela Bairstow took the court brimming with confidence against Miss Imre Rietveld in the top match. She had beaten her twice before. She tested 'birds' *ad nauseam* and then won the knock-up conclusively! Even when she was love-5 down we did not think things were going too wrong. She collected three points and then promptly lost three, and finally the game at 7–11. In the second she was being continually caught on her backhand. At love–8 even she began to be worried . . .

Jack McColl

Game and Gallant

The match of the meet, however, was the Ng Boon Bee/Tan Soon Hooi v Abdul Rahman/Ng Takt Wai semi-final encounter, all four of them Thomas Cup trainees. Thrills and spills came fast and furious right through the 90 minutes of the three action-packed games and there was a terrific applause at the end. But what pleased one most was the spontaneous ovation which burst out for *Ng Boon Bee*, the Malaysian Sportsman of 1968, as bag in hand, beaten but in no wise humbled, his lone, tired figure marched out of the hall. He was a game and gallant fighter right to the very last point in one of the grandest doubles ever seen in Malaysia

and richly deserved the homage that was paid to him.

'Omega'

Badminton on Ice

Shirley Marie's first appearance abroad was at Wembley. Tall, with a warm personality and bright eyes, she has the hair style and piquant looks of a Julie Andrews—but long legs all her own. Dressed—or should it be sheathed—in perfectly tailored, leg-clinging trousers and red shirt she is an eye-catching figure with a vivacity to match. And to Shirley Marie, 66-year-old Hugh Forgie is still tops. 'As a youngster, I didn't believe anyone could play better—I still don't. He's my idol.'

Pat Davis

Gillian Intercepts

Gillian Gilks served short and low. The reply was tight, accurate and way across court. Gillian assumed the dimensions of Jack the Beanstalk, hurtled sideways, proving that spines do have vertebrae, and from a horrifying horizontal position hammered an interception between Joké van Beusekom and Marjan Leusken.

Roddy MacCrimmon

Quite Unruffled

Flemming Delfs, in a way, was reminiscent of Frank Devlin in the versatility of his backhand. Although, unlike Devlin, he never allowed the shuttle to fall below shoulder height and, whereas Devlin was always best (which was all the time) when steaming like mother's copper, Delfs somehow managed to keep his cool. This unruffled physical economy, not to be confused with any lack of effort, coupled with supreme confidence as to the final issue, rode the waves and saw him safely home.

A Rare Miss

Only once did this sporting, diminutive Indonesian falter. Whether because of an unwelcome ray of light or unkindly displacement of air affecting flight, *Swie King*, registering dismay and astonishment, completely missed a descending clear and looked round, almost furtively, for some sign of conspiracy.

Whatever his thoughts and his speculations he responded with the agility of a polished gymnast. He leaped high into the air whence he delivered a series of devastating smashes, acutely angled, which plugged the floor like bolts of Jupiter.

John Vincent

Awesome Power

. . . and *Flemming*'s shots began to flow. One could only admire the exquisite spinning net-shots to dig out which you need a bucket and spade so tight to the net does he play them—the fluency and awesome power of that superb backhand, both overhead and on defence—and the final, crunching kill coming down so steeply from that enormous reach. 15–10 to Delfs.

David Eddy

Chinese Cracker

As *Chen* himself put it in a nutshell after the match, 'It is necessary to be as fast back as forward'. And he was. The conventional fast lift to the backhand corner was tantamount to signing one's own death warrant. A jump, round-the-head smash of extraordinary speed was the lethal riposte, often cross-court, but occasionally, and more disconcertingly, straight. And at the feet rather than the belly!

'It's the hardest smash I've ever met—and I've met a few in my time' admitted a shattered but admiring Kevin Jolly after his 15–3, 15–2 defeat.

Confident of his speed backward, Chen set up base camp only a couple of feet behind the front service line. One from which, restlessly, he made continual eager forays to the net for the early, very early, take—and the decisive kill.

Pat Davis

Inimitable Indonesian Vignettes

'While in drop shots they were even, the quicker-moving young man had an advantage over the tall, gracious Sture. *Johnsson* was not expecting *Nunung*'s liveliness in jumping high in the air for taking his powerful smashes.'

'In the third set, Sri Wiyantit led 9–3 with much luck and sudden smashes, placings as sharp as knife-edges.'

'This lean boy Tjun Tjun had the skill to halt a too dynamic tempo and bring it back to the easy and slow game of drop shots and placing but sometimes with sudden and deadly smashes.'

Indonesia Times

Ready for Adventure

The final was a classic! *Miss Köppen*'s action-packed style, full of energetic running and 'front-on' overhead shots, so very reminiscent of Mrs Stuart was a joy to watch. She doesn't worry over much if she gets out of position, falling over backwards after an overhead shot or unwinding herself after manufacturing a clear from the deep backhand corner; she just runs faster for the next one. Her big assets are, apart from this, that she keeps the shuttle in play and is always ready to try an adventurous shot.

John Woolhouse

Ice Cold and Angry

In the midst of a caterwauling atmosphere of anti-sportsmanship (Thomas Cup Final played in Tokyo with a large section of Indonesian students in the audience), *Knud Aage Nielsen*, determined and ice-cold angry, won the first game against Tan Joe Hok amid spectator frenzy and player fussiness that did nothing to ease tension.

Shuttle speeds were disputed, tested and re-tested, accepted and discarded for apparently puerile reasons. Shuttles that Tan Joe Hok could not test to length were nonchalantly proven adequate by Nielsen who crossed the net to his opponent's side to do so; and having done so, bowed ironically.

The spectator furore heightened but Nielsen having reconciled himself to the intended distractions, concentrated totally and, playing like the All-England champion he is, won 15–9 in the third game to close the margin to Denmark 3—Indonesia 4.

David Bloomer

Confidence

Martin Dew, after replacing Ray Stevens at an hour's notice as Mike Tredgett's partner and winning the prestigious Friends' Provident Masters Championships: 'Nervous? Of course not! It's your chance so you've got to take it.'

Charm

Pat Assinder added delicate touches at the net—and considerable charm over a much wider area.

No emotion!

Impassive *Teh* was comprehensively 'flicked' by inscrutable *Tredgett*.

Sex Equality

Too often *Lene Köppen* sank to her haunches at the net as if both to give Skovgaard unobstructed sight of the shuttle, and firmly to dis-associate herself from the sex-equality nonsense on the other side of the net by sides-pair Kartono and Teh Soo Gwan.

Pat Davis

Four/Coaching and Training

The Development of Coaching

Before the First World War, coaching in the British Isles was a dead-letter. Pitched in at the deep end, players learned—or did not learn—by hard experience. Doubtless, old stagers were, as today, only too ready to give advice—and were as infrequently asked. There was just one instructional book on the market, S M Massey's *Badminton* (1911).

Immediately after the War, coaching provisions improved a little. Coaches—all seemingly high-class—did advertise regularly in the *Gazette*. Colonel C de V Duff, CBE of Caterham 'recommended by six County Associations and over 100 clubs and colleges' charged a guinea for three 45-minute lessons. Subordinate in rank, Captain H C Evans nevertheless outdid the Colonel by boasting 'Winner of five Open Championships; recommended by English Internationals'. But coaching was not a male prerogative for double-barrelled Miss Ida Plomer-Walker and Mrs Ferrers-Nicholson were also eager to help. So too was no less a player than pre-War All-England Singles Champion, Miss L C Radeglia. Unfortunately, however, within a few years coaching slowly ground to a halt: hamstrung perhaps by a dearth of courts, the added extra of their hire and of shuttles, and the difficulties of effective follow-up.

In the '30s, it even slid into reverse—with a Trans-Atlantic brain-drain. Canada and America boasted luxurious clubs with large memberships and excellent facilities in Montreal, Toronto and other big cities as far west as Winnipeg and Calgary. They skimmed the cream of British Isles badminton. Ireland lost both her greats, 'Curly' Mack and Frank Devlin; England, B P Cook; Wales, W Basil Jones, and Scotland, James Barr, who 'gave 65 lessons in a week in Canada'. Cruellest blow of all was the loss of Scotland's brilliant Ken Davidson who emigrated to America just before the War. In England, still no signs of activity.

Nothing was heard but a plaintive cry in the *Gazette*. It bewailed the fact that, without coaching, improvement was slow, and faults became ineradicable. Sadly, it contrasted the boom of coaching in golf: every club with its pro—and players queuing up for instruction.

Badminton remained unmoved. And not surprisingly so since R C F (Ralph) Nichols, its No 1 player, had trumpeted, 'Coaching is definitely detrimental to playing ability'. For him, anything other than match play was so much wasted time. Frank Devlin at least had left a valuable coaching book behind, *Badminton for All*. Betty Uber, on the other hand, wisely urged the appointment of a BA of E Coach.

In the '50s there was a rustling of action, stirred perhaps by the parlous plight of the English game engendered by a virtual eight year lay-off. And yet it was left to Ireland to make the first move—a farsighted, three-pronged one at that.

First, a third of Dublin's clubs accepted coaching on their own court. Unfortunately, this could be done only once in the season, as a majority of members resented the loss of actual playing time involved.

Then came the tricky business of selection ('talent was invariably blonde'). For 1/- *5p* a night 55 pupils from 28 clubs were coached in separate grades by two men and two ladies (the latter only if other ladies were in the group) in a central Dublin hall—at a total cost of £11. Later, matches were arranged with the coach as non-playing captain, empowered to give advice both between games and at the change. So, whilst the trainees might lose the first game, they often won the match. And a compulsory tournament schedule was insisted on in the following season. Only one nominee, disenchanted with the coach's own playing ability, resigned.

> *'If you get to 14—all in the third and your legs have turned to jelly, do you decide to set?'*

With such glamorous leaders no wonder Ken Woolcott's Popmobility fitness groups worked till they dropped!

In 1949–50, Lancashire and Cheshire BA set the ball rolling in England. County players took 40 students but 'were unable to teach any advanced play because many pupils could hit the shuttle only a short distance'. But things progressed: promising Juniors were coached by County players; club players by lesser lights who had themselves gladly paid 7/6 *37½p* (later free) to receive four 2-hour courses on the art of coaching, and then be tested and graded.

The BA of E pricked up its ears. Rhona Barlow (Staffs) and Ken Gregory (Lancs) were recruited together with Ian Palmer (Surrey) to run their first ever 12-hour courses for coaches at Hunter-combe (near Henley) and at Harrogate. Other courses followed at Southdean near Littlehampton and the CCPR's HQ at Lilleshall Hall near Staf-ford. A slender booklet of coaching instruction (later to become known as the 'Little Red Book'—not to be confused with Chairman Mao's tactical dicta) was published. And in 1956 the BA of E listed its first National Coaches.

In that year, England turned for help as Honorary Coaching Secretary to a charming, effective and talented international, modest Nancy Horner—a Scot! She overcame prejudice ('*We* had no coach-ing!'), fears ('They'll stifle all flair'), and organisa-tional chaos. Counties were encouraged to build up their own schemes. Surrey were particularly successful. This together with the presence of Ian Palmer, a talented and forthright coach who poured

time and money into producing a string of English international girls from Iris Cooley to Gillian Gilks, must have been the foundation of their incredible run of Inter-County Championship successes.

From then on, 'Coaching Notices' featured regularly in the *Gazette* listing strings of courses and exams to be held throughout the season and the country. And Lilleshall coaches presented Nancy with a frying-pan!

Coaching mushroomed! To such an extent that in 1961 Nancy Horner (71 Middlesex 'caps') reluctantly dropped out of the team because 'coaching takes up so many of my weekends'. And they continued to do so until 1966 when her administrative assistant, Olive Johnson, became Coaching Secretary.

In tandem had come exhibition demonstrations by groups of talented (but unpaid) internationals. In England, the Central Council of Physical Recreation organised 'Focus on Badminton'. In Ireland, Morton's Male Circus was a less conven-tional means of coaching: audience participation; knock-about contrast of the right and the wrong way; and a climactic Mixed Doubles with the 'help' of two hairy-legged 'colleens' of Junoesque and highly inflated proportions.

1968 saw the appointment by the BA of E of its first professional Chief Coach, Ken Crossley, a Middlesex and Surrey county player and former RAF PTI. At the end of his three-year contract they parted without apparent regret on either side.

Crossley's successor was Roger Mills at the peak of a brilliant career that had brought him 44 'caps', 1 All-England and 91 other titles, and 5 Com-monwealth and European medals. His drive and originality were undoubtedly establishing him as a leading figure in the coaching world; he toured European and Asian badminton strongholds on a Churchill Scholarship.

Sadly, in 1975, he and the BA of E fell foul of each other. His contract was terminated on the grounds that he 'had entered into endorsement agreements in contravention of it'.

Mills fought his dismissal before the Industrial Tribunal, maintaining that his original contract, never signed, had allowed such endorsements and that a later one did not clearly disallow them. The Court found that the BA of E had acted too precipitately but commented that Mills' 'evasive and intransigent attitude had exacerbated the

Sally Leadbeater practised in near darkness—to improve her concentration.

Above *Roger Mills, England's best-known Chief Coach, caught bending—by Strobe lighting as he lunges to play a tight net-shot.*

Right *With a quick-fire shuttle barrage Chinese coach speeds up student's net reflexes.*

situation'. Consequently the damages awarded of £3549 were reduced by 30 per cent to £2484.

During his reign, there had been innovations. Les Wright was appointed as his Assistant and did (still does) a cheerful and enthusiastic job at County level. Ken Woolcott's 'Popmobility', originating from Butlin's Camps and Robinson's Barley Water, featured at numerous courses. To its lively strains, players exercised happily and nearly painlessly to undreamt of limits.

Ollie Cussen, a former RAF Coaching Secretary who sported DFCs, and who had enticed into the RAF many badminton-talented youngsters due for National Service, was appointed Coaching Secretary to succeed Olive Johnson on her retirement. An English Youth Squad to bridge the tricky 'after under-18 honours' gap was formed under Nev MacFarlane. Regional co-ordinators were appointed. Coaching courses no longer terminated in a formal traumatic exam but were assessed throughout their 20 hours. 'Sit-ins' under international tutelage were organised at the All-England. The *Daily Express* ran a coaching strip. Breweries Vaux and Guinness sponsored top-flight courses much sought after by coaches—for obvious reasons —as well as players.

Mills' departure was followed for a time by a return to conventional England team manager and selection committee system. These were replaced in 1977 by a single Supremo, Canadian-born, American-qualified Judy Hashman, perhaps the greatest woman player ever. For a brief 8 months, aided only by her self-chosen assistant, Maurice Robinson, a talented Glamorgan cricketer and unconventional badminton coach, she planned English badminton's long-term future.

Then, with unbelievably bad timing, the BA of E handed her her dismissal 4 months before the expiry of her contract—on the very day England won the European Team Championship! Never one to take defeat easily, Mrs Hashman, in defiance of the BA of E, outgunned the newly appointed selectors by handing her Commonwealth Games nominations to the Press in the teeth of BA of E instructions. No official reason was ever given for the dismissal but the grapevine suggested that Mrs Hashman's forthright approach abroad had not endeared her to the BA of E's badminton neighbours.

Today coaching is very much a going concern. Coaches range wide from the English Schools' Badminton Association to the BA of E, and from Club to National. Many counties have their own Coaches' Association; the BA of E its Coaches' Register which, like the Scottish Badminton Union, issues its own coaching bulletins. International Coaching Conferences are arranged to coincide with major international events.

Every conceivable type of enthusiast is catered for: the under-12's and the veterans who regularly turn out for Senior Citizen morning; the harassed, unco-ordinated housewife who seeks domestic respite at Adult Evening Classes and the aspiring under-18 champion still fighting his way up the ladder; the ambitious teacher eager for another qualification and the English international seeking world-class status. Venues are equally varied: dusty church halls; equipment-festooned gyms; multi-million civic Sports Halls; famous National Centres such as Bisham Abbey, Lilleshall and Scotland's Inverclyde, each in its own superb setting.

At the top of the pyramid is recently appointed Ciro Ciniglio, England Coaching and Team Manager who with Cheshire's Barbara Wadsworth, Coaching Secretary, has got off to a flying start. (Far East Tour, under-18 visit to Malaysia; Denmark-England interchanges).

All that is lacking are coaching giants. Capable county and national coaches abound but there have been few coaches of real stature to whom top players can confidently turn. Only Ian Palmer and Maurice Robinson, Jake Downey and Roger Mills, Paul Whetnall and Mike Harvey, have stood out head and shoulders above the ever-growing army of volunteer enthusiasts.

Books

Badminton players through the generations seem to have been men of action rather than words for the number of books published has been comparatively small. And of those, the large majority have been instructional with only a handful devoted to histories of the game itself or to its 'greats'.

Apart from a few leaflets often incorporating the rules, the first real book, *Badminton*, was written in 1911 by S M Massey, an international and thrice winner of the All-England Men's Doubles. Not

Harry Jennings of St Andrews BC, Cheam, played for over 60 years and was going strong until he was 79 running junior clubs four days a week, and coaching on two.

unnaturally it received a warm welcome 'from good, bad and indifferent players'! Massey, obviously no male chauvinist, farmed out ladies' singles and doubles to experts Margaret Tragett and Lavinia Radeglia, and men's singles and mixed to one G A Thomas. He himself covered the men's doubles, explained how to run clubs and tournaments, reminisced and described leading players' favourite strokes. A mine of information that breathes life into badminton's early days.

The First World War was doubtless responsible for no other book appearing until 1922. And then only a slim paperback entitled *How to Play Badminton* by J H C Prior, Honorary Secretary of the London League; the *Gazette*, censoriously, 'was not altogether in agreement with some of his dicta'.

A year later followed the first classic, *The Art of Badminton* by the master, Sir George Thomas, written as crisply as he played. It was later incorporated in Vol 16 (Racket Games) of the handsome and comprehensive Lonsdale Library. Next, well ahead of its time, appeared the *Magpie Badminton Instructor*, a chart issued by sports manufacturers Jacques and written by professional coach Miss I Plomer-Walker.

Not to be outdone, Sir George's female counterpart, Margaret Tragett, international and All-England winner, produced *Badminton for Beginners* —2/6d 12½p. It received high praise from Frank Devlin in his preface: 'The almost Roman road to the coveted position of a star' and from Sir George 'Instruction in full without being prolix . . . never dogmatic!' Not surprising as Mrs Tragett under her maiden name Margaret Rivers Larminie, as stylish with pen as with racket, was a best-selling novelist (*Deep Meadows, Search, Soames Green, Dr Sam*), a *Gazette* editor, and an eager writer of coaching articles in it.

Mrs N Ferrers-Nicholson, another of the few professional coaches, collaborated with swimming expert Sid G Hedges to produce another *Art of Badminton* (with two diagrams!). Two years later a second classic, *Badminton for All*, by J F Devlin, dealt fully with 'fundamentals, strokes and tactics' but raised a mild reproof from reviewer Ken Livingston by advocating left foot forward in serving because 'leading players all use the right'. It was, surprisingly, published at the end of the season in April—in time to accompany the author on a coaching tour of Australia, New Zealand and Malaysia.

As competitive off-court as on, H S Uber and Elizabeth(!) Uber produced—for half-a-crown $12\frac{1}{2}p$—the 'eminently sensible' *Badminton*, the first book to use ciné photos 'to serve the purpose of a slow motion film'. (And Margaret Larminie rounded off the era with *Gory Knight*, a skit on the current flood of detective novels, written 'as subtly as she plays her drop-shots').

With the world nearly back to normal in 1949 a solo effort by Mrs Uber, now Betty, was her neatly named *That Badminton Racket*. It was unique in that the greater part was reminiscences and opinions and dealt with badminton world-wide. Then there was F W Last's *Introduction to Badminton*, a book of frequent glimpses of the obvious ('in doubles you have two opponents') and very dubious tactics (as my partner excelled at the

back, he chose to play at the net'); the reviewer most certainly did not feel it would enable its readers 'to step into the international limelight'. It also advocated 'a serve that causes the shuttle to swerve': a statement which after a 'vitriolic' review' engendered a running battle in the *Gazette*'s correspondence columns. During this it appeared that some of Mr Last's experience had been acquired in an act at the London Coliseum.

'It is clearly impossible to spin a shuttle' was the critic's parting shot. Little did he know!

A year later, Canadian Doug Grant, a former World Professional Champion, produced the lavishly illustrated *Badminton : International Textbook of the Game*, serialised in the *Gazette*. Also from North America came that classic of all time, on which this author teethed, *Winning Badminton* by the inimitable Ken Davidson, a brilliant Scottish international and coach who had put badminton on the stage. Noel Radford, a Canadian

Author and National Coach Pat Davis might well look pleased—with four Kent internationals (Ray Sharp, Maggie Boxall, and Sue and Paul Whetnall) to help him illustrate one of his six books. Note the England blazers.

who crossed the Atlantic to join up—and stayed, wrote *Badminton* which, in addition to strokes and strategy, dealt with players of the past. And yet another foreigner (though England took him to its heart) the ebullient Eddy Choong, together with Fred Brundle, followed much the same line in the *Phoenix Book of Badminton* but was smartly rapped by the *Gazette*'s reviewer for the 20 years' ahead-of-its-time suggestion that top players might be allowed to make money out of the game.

Lightweight books followed in 1961 after a 5-year dearth. C G Rangecroft in the *Right Way to Badminton* came into dispute in the *Gazette*'s columns with I Witness as to whether or not the wayward genius Finn Kobbero played deliberate 'bounce' shots off the net-cord. And Ken Davidson wrote *Badminton*, a slender book for absolute beginners, which contained the odd statement that players 'can swing and miss as many times as they like during rallies'. Again a 5-year gap until England's No 1 Singles player Roger Mills (later BA of E Chief Coach) and ghost writer Eric Butler produced *Modern Badminton*.

In the late 60s, Civil Servant Eric Brown in *Badminton* 'gave experienced players a detailed basis for critical examination'. Ken Brock with *Simply Badminton* neatly bridged the gap between the latter's complexity and *Know the Game*'s simplicity. D R Gregory and G A Webb produced a useful loose-leaf *Teaching Badminton* for novice Evening Class instructors. Ken Crossley, the BA of E's first professional coach, wrote *Progressive Badminton*, labelled 'a book for a player' by Margaret Lockwood.

For the next decade, publishers, eager for books on a fast booming game, found willing authors among the top coaches. Jake Downey, a PE lecturer deprived of international colours only by a serious car crash, produced detailed academic studies of the game (based on war strategy) and its concomitant fitness: *Better Badminton for All* and *Badminton for Schools*. The legendary Judy Hashman wrote three books: *Badminton : A Champion's Way* was a blend of interesting experience and shrewd instruction; *Winning Badminton* was a slender treatise on psychology, tactics and anticipation, for top tournament players; whilst *Starting Badminton*, rather oddly in conjunction with former Davis Cup player and leading tennis coach,

Two teams of four from the RAF Badminton Association played doubles for 74 hours 1 minute at Rheindahlen, Germany on 25–28 June 1981.

Jimmy Jones, was for youngsters and beginners.

Meantime (1967), *Badminton Complete* (Kaye & Ward) by Pat Davis, the most prolific writer of them all, had been hailed as 'the best book for a decade'. This was followed by *Badminton Coach*, the only book ever written for the whole strata of coaches; *Better Badminton* for schools and clubs had 'the readability look and marvellous photographic coverage'—thanks to Louis Ross; *Badminton is Fun* ('one of the best books ever . . .') lived up to its title with pointed, humorous drawings and a light-hearted approach to serious instructions which, strangely perhaps, appealed to the Japanese who translated it in a sumptuous edition; *How to Play Badminton* (Hamlyn), with readers actually on court with young marrieds Sam and Samantha, was 'thoroughly recommended' as it brought coaching right into the home; and finally a lavishly illustrated and definitive *Badminton : The Complete Practical Guide* (David & Charles) appeared in 1982. (All quotes from the game's official publication the *Gazette*).

Lending admirable variety were: a succinct 72 pages for the young, *Your Book of Badminton* by ESBA founder Len Wright; an exhaustively illustrated *Badminton* by Roger Mills (then BA of E Chief Coach): a regrettably slender *Badminton* by the talented internationals Sue and Paul Whetnall; an equally concise *Badminton at the Top* backed by experience of 83 times capped Derek Talbot (1981); a purely photographic bonanza, *Louis Ross Picture Book*, and BA of E's Staff Coach Les Wright's *Successful Badminton*.

And as a welcome relief from such a spate of instruction, BBC producer Bernard Adams' *Badminton Story* was based on his television series and intriguingly illustrated with a wealth of contemporary photos as well as modern Ross action ones. Different, too, was *Gillian Gilks* by *Observer* reporter David Hunn, the first book devoted to a single player.

'A book by every badminton bedside' is the cry. A cut-price coach on hand 24 hours a day to give better and more enjoyable play is surely a worthwhile investment.

Tips from the Top

J D EDDY (*Staffs and England*) : The time to be deceptive is when you are in position early—not when you are struggling to meet the shuttle.

LEW HOAD (*Australian Tennis Champion*) : Concentration! Great players never give away a

Svend Pri (Denmark) shows the straight arm and wrist-whip essential for power.

Cecil Whittaker (Derbyshire and England) was so keen he played seven days a week. To save time, he bored holes in his case so that his kit could be aired without removal.

point, never take ridiculous chances, never think of anything but how to win the match.

JUDY HASHMAN *(USA and England. Ten times winner of All-England Singles)* : Those last 10 minutes before going on court are the most vital part of the match preparation. A mental run-through of your opponent's game and your own. Mentally rehearse the shots he dislikes—and those which in set patterns are his favourites. Think of the importance to you of starting well, of serving well, of keeping the shuttle in play, and of going safely, not violently, for winners.

GILLIAN GILKS *(All-England Triple Champion)* : In mixed doubles, an incredible percentage of shots can be cut off at the net if only you *anticipate* intelligently and have a go; provided always that your partner is ready to back up when you guess wrong and that you are not over-ambitious if it happens to be an off-day.

MIKE TREDGETT *(Three times All-England Champion)* : *In defence*, take the shuttle early and drive it away from the front player before the back player has recovered. *In attack*, use the jump smash but look to your timing and be on balance for instant recovery.

JIM POOLE *(USA)* : For power, forearm rotation is more important than wrist snap. The forearm is rotated strongly to the left in the forehand action (pronation), to the right in the backhand action (supination).

DAVID HUNT *(England 'B' Team Coach)* : The more you play, the faster you become; the faster you become, the earlier you take the shuttle; the earlier you take the shuttle, the more alternatives are open to you, the more winners are on.

KAREN BRIDGE *(All-England Junior Triple Champion and England)* : By accuracy and consistency keep the rally alive, then the points will come. Round-the-head cross-court drops and steeply angled half-smashes can be very effective in singles.

JANE WEBSTER *(Ladies' Doubles World Champion)* : Increase your variety of strokes—but only if you can play them consistently. That way you keep your opponents on tenterhooks and so slow them down.

BRIAN WALLWORK *(Lancashire)* : Fitness is a matter of dedication: you get back only what you put into it. Club, league, tournaments, county matches: five nights a week!

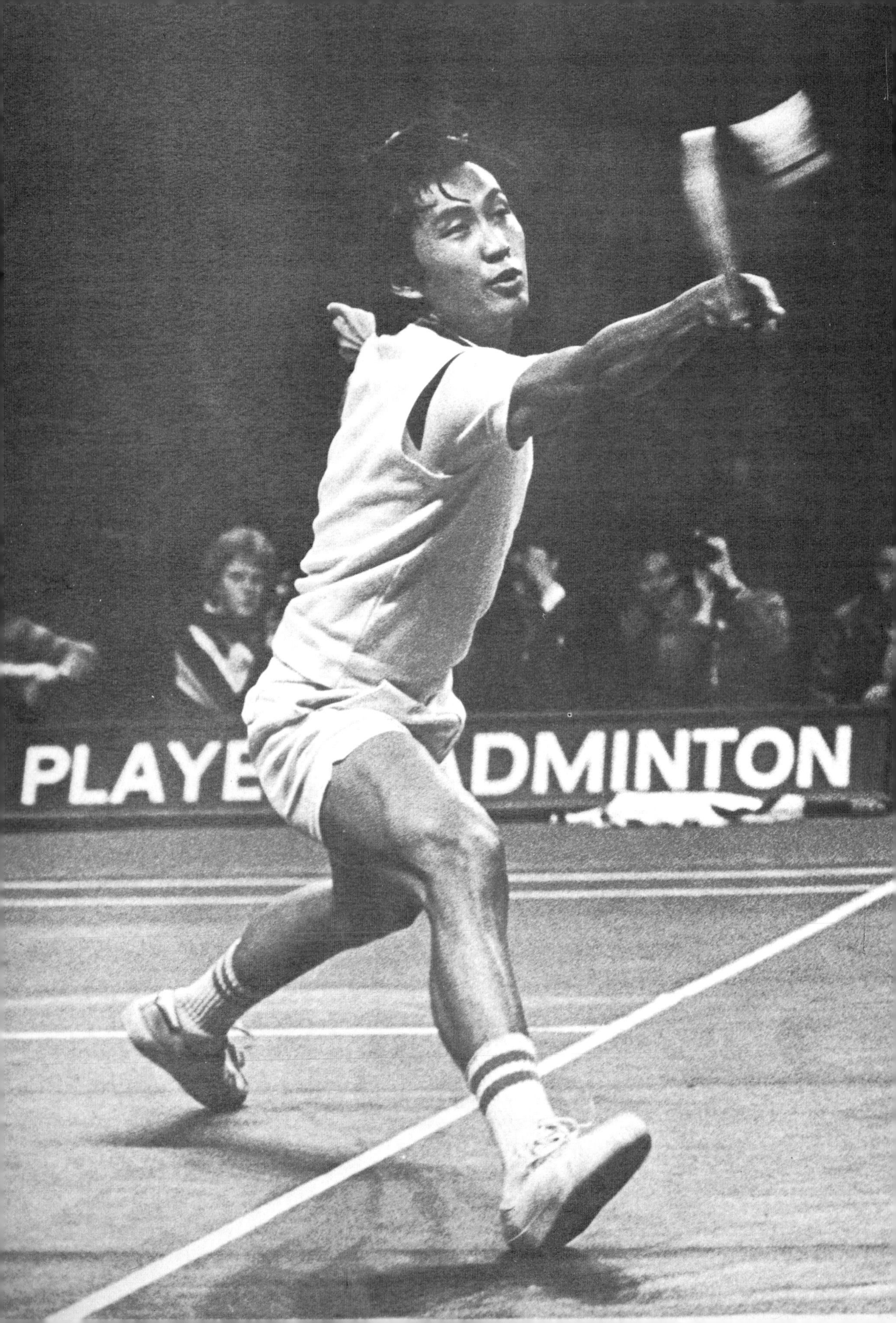
PLAYE ADMINTON

Top *Grace, reach and balance as Japanese star Hiroe Yuki makes a very long lunge and so stays virtually 'on base'.*

Above *Why play backhands when you are as supple as Sally Podger? Take them round-the-head!*

Left *Liem Swie King shows that vital dash to 'take the shuttle early'.*

Pertinent Proverbs

When you are losing, wear a winning face (France)

The man on the wall is the best player (Holland)

Make your feet your best friends (Scotland)

Every couple is not a pair (England)

When the head doesn't work, the legs suffer (Romania)

When the heart undertakes, the body is its slave (Hausa)

It is not enough to run, one must set out in time (France)

The mourner is not listened to (Bechuana)

The vulgar keeps no account of your hits, only of your misses (England)

NORA PERRY (*Five times Winner of All-England Mixed Doubles*): Even at the net, I use a lot of deception. To that end I do a lot of wrist-roll exercises so I can now hold shots and play fast attacking lobs and clears as well as split second deflections.

DEREK TALBOT (*England*): Mental fitness is as important as physical fitness. You must be able to read the game, spot strengths as well as weaknesses, see patterns of play, know when to change tactics.

Singles can be won and lost on the net so you must be able to play cut shots—very, very tight.

JOHN HAVERS (*England Team Manager*): Length is still a singles fundamental; so too is accuracy of smash down the side-lines.

JOHN VINCENT: Self belief, unbounded confidence that 'I am the Greatest' sustains champions under pressure. Play hard; play often; never walk when you can run in daily life. Go in and be beaten: come out and be wiser.

BJORN BORG (*Five times Wimbledon Tennis Champion*): Play one point at a time. When exhausted, winning the next point must become the most important thing you have ever done in your life. Then you start all over again with the next point.

ERLAND KOPS (*Seven times All-England Singles Champion*): Play against opponents better than yourself—but you must be physically fit enough to benefit from it. Strong legs and ankles are absolutely essential.

Always be aggressive; kill the rally at the first opportunity.

PAUL WHETNALL (*England*): It's the three D's: dedication, discipline, determination. In singles, maintain pressure with smashes and half-smashes: be ever ready to follow in to the net to maintain the attack.

SVEND PRI (*Denmark*): In singles, vary your pace. All-out attack can leave you out of position.

SIR GEORGE THOMAS (*England*): To deceive to deceive to deceive is the art of badminton. For beginners: Hit downward; at every opportunity hit hard!

THOMAS KIHLSTROM (*Sweden*): You must forget the receiver; see only the tape—and skim it. And still be ready to cut off the pushes through you or to the side-lines that such a serve forces.

You must vary your returns so that your opponents cannot anticipate.

It is essential to keep calm under pressure.

Pushes are more effective if you follow them in.

LENE KÖPPEN (*Denmark. Twice All-England Singles Champion*): It is not good to argue—besides you only lose concentration.

RAY STEVENS (*England*): You must smash tight into the body if you want a kill at the net by your partner.

I'm still learning!

MORTEN FROST HANSEN (*Denmark*): Only with practice do chances become certainties.

A little defence—then sudden attack.

You must have fight, have determination! You must never know when you are beaten!

PAT DAVIS (*BA of E National Coach*): Anticipation gives time to make a decisive stroke instead of a rescue operation.

'You never made a mistake!' is the greatest compliment that can be paid to care and concentration. Look after the points; the games will look after themselves.

IAN MACONACHIE (*Ireland*): Winning is a matter of inches—between the ears.

FERRY SONNEVILLE (*Indonesia*): It is essential to have ambition. Without it there is no fire to drive you on through the pain-barrier or when all seems lost.

Enthusiastic Douglas Fairbanks, Hollywood screen idol, met stiff resistance when trying to inveigle comedian Jack Oakie to play. 'Badminton? Why that's only shrivelled-up tennis!'

Five/**Junior Badminton**

With the Juniors

Junior badminton, unlike juniors themselves, took a long time to mature. But once growth started (after the Second World War) it was fast.

In 1912, it was reported that 'Miss Musgrave runs a children's club (girls only) in North Kensington Hall'. And the Engineers BC (Scotland) ran 'an Infant School where faults are early corrected by adults'. It was even whispered that one of the leading Edinburgh schools was considering taking up badminton, and that Surbiton BC were coaching boys from Westminster, Clifton and Oundle in the Christmas holidays. Unfortunately badminton has never had sufficient cachet to be taken seriously in Public Schools and has limped along a very poor third in the shadow of tennis and squash.

Until the '30s, children's events were neither seen nor heard very much and then only fleetingly. Though a tournament is recorded at Ealing in which amongst others IBF President-to-be Humphrey Chilton was playing. In 1934, Surrey BA, with National Coach Ian Palmer ever to the fore in Junior coaching, ran a Junior Tournament. B P Cook and three other internationals gave a demonstration at Marlborough School—in a classroom! In 1938, Eastbourne also ran a Junior Tournament in which a certain T Bowker (now President of the English Schools' Badminton Association) beat the unfortunately named J Pine Coffin!

The author himself learned his trade at this time in the icy Nottingham Drill Hall by remorselessly battering already battered shuttles against the wall when weary adults left the courts for a sit-down 9d *4p* cream-cake tea. A few kind hearts—among whom was unassuming international Cecil Whittaker—put stars in his eyes with an occasional snatched knock-up. Eventually, he was old enough to join the Junior Christmas Holiday club where his brother, W A M, used to beat him left-handed; the tournament booby prize was inevitably his; and a very Senior Citizen, Herbert Sansom, earned his undying hatred (later turned to gratitude) by serving side-line drives up his eggshell-frail backhand.

In 1947, *Gazette* correspondent 'Old Player' suggested that each county should pick one Under-20 player and his coach, and hold a national knock-out tournament. 'Hopeful Junior' pleaded for 'just one or two junior tournaments'. But things *were* starting to stir. Shenley Hospital BC demanded 'Has the BA of E a policy to coach juniors?' Leicestershire BA gave them a dusty answer by forming a Junior Club with County players as coaches. And Surrey (yes, Surrey again) ran a teenage tournament and held a first ever Junior County match in which, with a youthful June White 'head and shoulders above the others' they beat Middlesex 9–5. And Brian Grozier, 15, was chosen for Kent 'A'.

Only a year later, 1950, the first All-England Junior Championships were held at Wimbledon Squash and Badminton Club. And, because of an 118 strong entry—by charabanc-borne youngsters —at Ebbisham BC as well. A fine array of cups had been given by Sir George, Mrs Barrett, Donald Hume, Ralph Nichols, Margaret Tragett, Betty Uber and other 'greats'. What an incentive! John Shaw (Notts) was a triple winner (and again in 1951) but a fifteen year old, Tony Jordan, was already hailed as 'incredibly sound and good'.

Ten-year-old Kath Redhead (later to play for England), a spectator at the Lancashire Junior Championships, stepped into the breach when Alan Harkness' partner didn't turn up. Using borrowed racket and shoes, in ordinary clothes, but quite unperturbed, she helped clinch the title at 11 pm—two hours after her usual bed-time.

Which title? The Under 18!

Gorm and Anders Nielsen, all packed up—and somewhere to go. Not surprising when Mum is ex-All-England champion Heather Ward.

In 1954, 3 ft 11 in, 11-year-old Roger Mills started his meteoric rise to fame by flooring a six-footer. A year later Heather Ward was described as 'the best ever fourteen year old': in all she won the Singles four times and was thrice Triple Champion! And in 1963, first year of the transfer of the Under-15 singles from the Wimbledon Junior to the All-England Junior, a 12-year-old with matchstick legs, weighing in at under 6 stone *40 kg*, took the title from a field of five—Gillian Perrin, England's 'Golden Girl' to be! (Between 1963 and 1968 she was to win the Under-15 singles three times, the Under-18 four times; and *both* in 1964–65!) NB: All three were Surrey players.

1951 had seen a successful first Northern Junior Championships. And that despite a flu epidemic and a blizzard that caused eighteen last minute withdrawals. 1958 saw the inauguration of the South of England Junior Championships. Two years later the main Junior circuit was neatly completed by the Midland Counties Championships so long and happily held at the Central Council for Physical Recreation's lovely Lilleshall Centre, under Warden Jim Lane's sternly paternal eye.

In 1954, the BA of E formed a Youth Players' Fund to help with tournament fees and expenses. And, in 1963, a Youth Committee was elected. Bill Wiltshire, another Surrey stalwart, died in 1968. He left sufficient money to provide an annual place on a top adult Lilleshall course for a promising junior who 'would benefit from more coaching'.

So vast, over 300, had become the entries for the All-England Junior, that qualifying rounds had to be held in 1977. And in 1978 the venue was changed from Wimbledon, which had for 28 years given it so homely a background, first to Woking then to the excellent but rather inaccessible Watford Leisure Centre north of London.

In 1978, it was Surrey again. Karen Bridge gained her second triple crown as had other Surreyites Roger Mills, Oon Chong Hau (only Paul Whetnall in the Mixed had prevented his being a triple 'triple'!) and Angela Bairstow (later Palmer) before her!

1979 saw a Hearts of Oak Benefit Society sponsored scheme to encourage badminton in Youth Clubs. And 1980, a newly titled Friends' Provident English National Junior Championship replaced the familiar All-England Junior. Thanks to financial backing from that Life Office, this was a useful piece of sponsorship which tied in with their Friends' Provident English National Under-21 Championship. And in 1980, to keep young talent on the boil, an England Under-23 team was formed.

From 1964 much of this development had taken place in conjunction with the growth of the English Schools' Badminton Association (see page 79). Together they have produced a wealth of talent, matches, tournaments and foreign tours. In 1981, an unfulfilled dream, a tour of Ceylon in 1971, was partially fulfilled by an Under-18 tour of Malaysia. And since then Under-18 teams have toured Indonesia and China!

Sally Leadbeater won the Guernsey U12, U15 and U18 Singles titles in one tournament.

English National Junior Championships

(Restricted to competitors under 18 at midnight on the preceding 31 August/1 September and currently eligible to play for England. Up to 1979–80 known as All-England Junior Championships.)

Boys' Singles

1949–50	F J Shaw (Notts.)
1950–51	F J Shaw (Notts.)
1951–52	A D Jordan (Cheshire)
1952–53	G H King (Kent)
1953–54	D Jones (Isle of Man)
1954–55	A P Billingham (Northants)
1955–56	P J Waddell (Sussex)
1956–57	Oon Chong Jin (Cambs.)
1957–58	R J Mills (Surrey)
1958–59	R J Mills (Surrey)
1959–60	R J Mills (Surrey)
1960–61	Oon Chong Hau (Surrey)
1961–62	R J Westmorland (Cheshire)
1962–63	Oon Chong Hau (Surrey)
1963–64	Oon Chong Hau (Surrey)
1964–65	Oon Chong Hau (Surrey)
1965–66	C J Kirk (Notts.)
1966–67	C J Kirk (Notts.)
1967–68	C J Kirk (Notts.)
1968–69	R P Stevens (Essex)
1969–70	K P Arthur (Essex)
1970–71	P J Gardner (Surrey)
1971–72	J C Stretch (Essex)
1972–73	P H Wood (Lancashire)
1973–74	P H Wood (Lancashire)
1974–75	G J Scott (Lancashire)
1975–76	G J Scott (Lancashire)
1976–77	K R Jolly (Essex)
1977–78	A B Goode (Hertfordshire)
1978–79	N Yates (Kent)
1979–80	S D Wassell (Hampshire)
1980–81	D P Tailor (Middlesex)
1981–82	S Butler (Warwickshire)
1982–83	D J Hall (Essex)

Girls' Singles

1949–50	M W Glassborow (Essex)
1950–51	U H Smith (11) (Kent)
1951–52	U H Smith (11) (Kent)
1952–53	M Semple (3) (Lancashire)
1953–54	H M Ward (4) (Surrey)
1954–55	H M Ward (4) (Surrey)
1955–56	H M Ward (4) (Surrey)
1956–57	H M Ward (4) (Surrey)
1957–58	A M Bairstow (12) (Surrey)
1958–59	A M Bairstow (12) (Surrey)
1959–60	A M Bairstow (12) (Surrey)
1960–61	A C Price (7) (Essex)
1961–62	A J Swinstead (15) (Surrey)
1962–63	M B Boxall (22) (Hampshire)
1963–64	S Jones (Essex)
1964–65	G M Perrin (18) (Surrey)
1965–66	G M Perrin (18) (Surrey)
1966–67	G M Perrin (18) (Surrey)
1967–68	G M Perrin (18) (Surrey)
1968–69	M Beck (23) (Cumberland)
1969–70	M Beck (23) (Middlesex)
1970–71	N C Gardner (25) (Essex)
1971–72	N C Gardner (25) (Essex)
1972–73	A E Forrest (21) (Hampshire)
1973–74	J A Webster (Suffolk)
1974–75	P M Kilvington (Yorkshire)
1975–76	K S Bridge (Surrey)
1976–77	K S Bridge (Surrey)
1977–78	K S Bridge (Surrey)
1978–79	S J Leadbeater (Guernsey)
1979–80	S J Leadbeater (Guernsey)
1980–81	M A Leeves (Kent)
1981–82	H S Troke (Hampshire)
1982–83	B V Blair (Devon)

Boys' Doubles

1949–50	F J Shaw (Notts.) and B T Grozier (Kent)
1950–51	F J Shaw (Notts.) and B T Grozier (Kent)
1951–52	A D Jordan (Cheshire) and H T Findlay (Hertfordshire)
1952–53	G H King (Kent) and B E Fletcher (Warwickshire)
1953–54	D Jones (Isle of Man) and E J R Stanford (Hertfordshire)
1954–55	G Bell (Surrey) and L Ellwood (Yorkshire)
1955–56	P J Waddell (Sussex) and A E Flashman (Surrey)

Something to laugh about! Gary Scott (Lancs), All-England Junior Triple Champion in 1976. Now a full international.

1956–57	P J Waddell (Kent) and D Winthrop (Westmorland)
1957–58	D Curtis (Hampshire) and K Paul (Hampshire)
1958–59	R J Mills (Surrey) and D J Minton (Surrey)
1959–60	R J Mills (Surrey) and D J Minton (Surrey)
1960–61	J Gisborne (Notts.) and D J Smith (Notts.)
1961–62	P A Seaman (Gloucestershire) and P R Falle (Jersey)
1962–63	Oon Chong Hau (Surrey) and M J Boutle (Surrey)
1963–64	Oon Chong Hau (Surrey) and B E Jones (Lancashire)
1964–65	Oon Chong Hau (Surrey) and B E Jones (Lancashire)
1965–66	C J Kirk (Notts.) and P Wing (Notts.)
1966–67	M Beck (Cumberland) and G A Connor (Cumberland)
1967–68	C J Kirk (Notts.) and I P Clark (Derbyshire)
1968–69	T A Goode (Hertfordshire) and J F Walter (Surrey)
1969–70	D E Hounslow (Essex) and D R M Pither (Essex)
1970–71	J C Stretch (Essex) and J K H Woodgate (Essex)
1971–72	J C Stretch (Essex) and J K H Woodgate (Essex)
1972–73	R A Rofe (Kent) and D S Whitfield (Berkshire)
1973–74	R A Rofe (Kent) and D S Whitfield (Berkshire)
1974–75	D P B Bridge (Surrey) and S R Stranks (Essex)
1975–76	G J Scott (Lancashire) and S R Stranks (Essex)
1976–77	K R Jolly (Essex) and N G Tier (Hampshire)
1977–78	C J Fetherston (Derbyshire) and D L Roebuck (Derbyshire)
1978–79	S J Baddeley (Sussex) and D Burden (Yorkshire)
1979–80	E J Outterside (Essex) and N S Sargent (Essex)
1980–81	D P Tailor (Middlesex) and A Wood (Derbyshire)
1981–82	C C Dobson (Worcestershire) and D P Tailor (Middlesex)
1982–83	D J Hall and S A Spurling (Essex)

Girls' Doubles

1949–50	J R White (1) (Surrey) and L M Cash (Surrey)
1950–51	I A Kenningham (2) (Yorkshire) and U H Smith (11) (Kent)
1951–52	I A Kenningham (2) (Yorkshire) and U H Smith (11) (Kent)
1952–53	M Semple (3) (Lancashire) and K Parr (5) (Lancashire)

1953–54	M Semple (3) (Lancashire) and K Parr (5) (Lancashire)
1954–55	H M Ward (4) (Surrey) and S A Hole (Surrey)
1955–56	H M Ward (4) (Surrey) and H J Pritchard (6) (Surrey)
1956–57	H M Ward (4) (Surrey) and M A Bonney (Surrey)
1957–58	G H Lawrence (Bedfordshire) and P S Wheating (9) (Bedfordshire)
1958–59	A M Bairstow (12) (Surrey) and P S Wheating (9) (Bedfordshire)
1959–60	A M Bairstow (12) (Surrey) and C E Lindsay (Yorkshire)
1960–61	A C Price (7) (Essex) and S D Pound (10) (Kent)
1961–62	S Jones (Essex) and A J Swinstead (15) (Surrey)
1962–63	S Jones (Essex) and M B Boxall (22) (Hampshire)
1963–64	M Bridge (19) (Derbyshire) and L M Veasey (28) (Middlesex)
1964–65	P Protheroe (Yorkshire) and L M Veasey (28) (Middlesex)
1965–66	W J Wilson (Cheshire) and L M Veasey (28) (Middlesex)
1966–67	G M Perrin (18) (Surrey) and J S Colman (17) (Surrey)
1967–68	M Beck (23) (Cumberland) and C M Wightman (Westmorland)
1968–69	M Beck (23) (Cumberland) and C M Wightman (Westmorland)
1969–70	B Giles (29) (Essex) and S B Ringshall (Essex)
1970–71	B Giles (29) (Essex) and N C Gardner (25) (Essex)
1971–72	M J A Brewer (24) (Surrey) and Miss N C Gardner (25) (Essex)
1972–73	A E Forrest (21) (Hampshire) and K Redhead (Lancashire)
1973–74	A Gardner (Surrey) and K Redhead (Lancashire)
1974–75	K T Puttick (30) (Sussex) and A G Tuckett (26) (Essex)
1975–76	K S Bridge (Surrey) and R Heywood (32) (Lancashire)
1976–77	K S Bridge (Surrey) and K T Puttick (30) (Sussex)
1977–78	K S Bridge (Surrey) and G M Clark (Kent)
1978–79	G M Clark (Kent) and S J Leadbeater (Guernsey)
1979–80	S J Leadbeater (Guernsey) and G M Clark (Kent)
1980–81	M A Leeves (Kent) and S J Leeves (Kent)
1981–82	J A Edwards (Sussex) and G C Gowers (Sussex)
1982–83	L J Chapman (Derbyshire) and J A Shipman (Essex)

Mixed Doubles

1949–50	F J Shaw (Notts.) and L M Cash (Surrey)
1950–51	F J Shaw (Notts.) and D Pratt (Hertfordshire)

The England team, all with well-earned bouquets, who won the European Junior Team event in Malta in 1977.

1951–52	A D Jordan (Cheshire) and I A Kenningham (2) (Yorkshire)	1967–68	I P Clark (Derbyshire) and G M Perrin (18) (Surrey)
1952–53	G H King (Kent) and G A Smith (13) (Essex)	1968–69	P Bullivant (Lancashire) and C Barron (Lancashire)
1953–54	D Jones (Isle of Man) and J Quilliam (Isle of Man)	1969–70	D R M Pither (Essex) and B Giles (29) (Essex)
1954–55	A P Billingham (Northants) and H M Ward (4) (Surrey)	1970–71	P J Gardner (Surrey) and B Giles (29) (Essex)
1955–56	A E Flashman (Surrey) and H M Ward (4) (Surrey)	1971–72	J C Stretch (Essex) and N C Gardner (25) (Essex)
1956–57	P J Waddell (Kent) and H M Ward (4) (Surrey)	1972–73	R A Rofe (Kent) and D J Kirby (Kent)
1957–58	R J Mills (Surrey) and M K Bishop (14) (Essex)	1973–74	R A Rofe (Kent) and D J Kirby (Kent)
1958–59	R J Mills (Surrey) and A M Bairstow (12) (Surrey)	1974–75	T B Stokes (Somerset) and K T Puttick (30) (Sussex)
1959–60	R J Mills (Surrey) and A M Bairstow (12) (Surrey)	1975–76	G J Scott (Lancashire) and K T Puttick (30) (Sussex)
1960–61	L Brown (Cheshire) and C E Lindsay (Yorkshire)	1976–77	K R Jolly (Essex) and K S Bridge (Surrey)
1961–62	R J Westmorland (Cheshire) and J McDonald (8) (Cheshire)	1977–78	A B Goode (Hertfordshire) and K S Bridge (Surrey)
1962–63	Oon Chong Hau (Surrey) and J McDonald (8) (Cheshire)	1978–79	C V Back (Kent) and G M Clark (Kent)
1963–64	Oon Chong Hau (Surrey) and C E Bird (16) (Cheshire)	1979–80	D P Tailor (Middlesex) and M A Leeves (Kent)
1964–65	P E Whetnall (Warwickshire) and L M Veasey (28) (Middlesex)	1980–81	D P Tailor (Middlesex) and M A Leeves (Kent)
1965–66	A I Morton (Cheshire) and G M Perrin (18) (Surrey)	1981–82	D P Tailor (Middlesex) and G C Gowers (Sussex)
1966–67	I P Clark (Derbyshire) and G M Perrin (18) (Surrey)	1982–83	M D Lawrence (Essex) and N S Roope (Surrey)

English National Junior Under-15 Championships

(Restricted to competitors under 15 at midnight on the preceding 31 August/1 September and currently eligible to play for England up to 1979/80 known as All-England Junior Under-15 Championships.)

Boys' Singles (Under 15)

1962–63	J P Farmer (Bucks.)
1963–64	S Aylmer (Essex)
1964–65	C J Kirk (Notts.)
1965–66	J F Walter (Surrey)
1966–67	K P Arthur (Essex)
1967–68	P J Gardner (Surrey)
1968–69	J C Stretch (Essex)
1969–70	R D Wallace (Warwickshire)
1970–71	P G Kidger (Yorkshire)
1971–72	G J Scott (Lancashire)
1972–73	S R Stranks (Essex)
1973–74	K R Jolly (Essex)
1974–75	A B Goode (Hertfordshire)
1975–76	C V Back (Kent)
1976–77	S D Wassell (Hampshire)
1977–78	C R Wood (Lancashire)
1978–79	S P Butler (Warwickshire)
1979–80	N J Fraser (Essex)
1980–81	D J Hall (Essex)
1981–82	M A Smith (Hampshire)
1982–83	Event discontinued

Girls' Singles (Under 15)

1962–63	G M Perrin (18) (Surrey)
1963–64	G M Perrin (18) (Surrey)
1964–65	G M Perrin (18) (Surrey)
1965–66	M Beck (23) (Cumberland)
1966–67	M Beck (23) (Cumberland)
1967–68	B Giles (29) (Essex)
1968–69	S Storey (20) (Cumberland)
1969–70	K Whiting (31) (Glos.)
1970–71	K Redhead (Lancashire)
1971–72	S E Coates (27) (Surrey)
1972–73	K S Bridge (Surrey)
1973–74	K S Bridge (Surrey)
1974–75	K S Bridge (Surrey)
1975–76	S J Leadbeater (Guernsey)
1976–77	G M Clark (Kent)
1977–78	W J Poulton (Surrey)
1978–79	W J Poulton (Surrey)
1979–80	H S Troke (Hampshire)
1980–81	S Louis (Devon)
1981–82	D Hore (Hampshire)
1982–83	Event discontinued

Boys' Doubles (Under 15)

1969–70	A P Fish (Notts.) and I Loten (Notts.)
1970–71	G J Scott (Lancashire) and P H Wood (Lancashire)
1971–72	S R Stranks (Essex) and J Virdee (Essex)
1972–73	S R Stranks (Essex) and D P B Bridge (Surrey)
1973–74	G M Reeves (Warwickshire) and N G Tier (Hampshire)
1974–75	A B Goode (Hertfordshire) and S J Perry (Hertfordshire)
1975–76	C V Back (Kent) and N Yates (Kent)
1976–77	M J Cattermole (Avon & Somerset) and A G Plater (Derbyshire)
1977–78	M P Methven (Buckinghamshire) and P J Scott (Sussex)
1978–79	M D Parker (Middlesex) and D Tailor (Middlesex)
1979–80	P N Goddard (Kent) and P J Walden (Kent)
1980–81	A J Downes (Essex) and D J Hall (Essex)
1981–82	A Nielsen (Surrey) and M A Smith (Hampshire)
1982–83	Event discontinued

Girls' Doubles (Under 15)

1969–70	S A Martin (Surrey) and K Whiting (31) (Glos.)
1970–71	S Parker (Lancashire) and K Redhead (Lancashire)
1971–72	S E Coates (27) (Surrey) and A B Maine (33) (Surrey)
1972–73	K S Bridge (Surrey) and K T Puttick (30) (Sussex)
1973–74	K S Bridge (Surrey) and K T Puttick (30) (Sussex)
1974–75	K S Bridge (Surrey) and L P Bunday (Hampshire)
1975–76	N A Rollason (Worcestershire) and R Wardle (Derbyshire)
1976–77	S J Leadbeater (Guernsey) and S R Tardif (Guernsey)
1977–78	W J Poulton (Surrey) and C T Sanders (Sussex)
1978–79	W J Poulton (Surrey) and R M Rollason (Worcestershire)
1979–80	D Simpson (Yorkshire) and H S Troke (Hampshire)
1980–81	A D Fisher (Essex) and N S Roope (Surrey)
1981–82	D Hore (Hampshire) and C Johnson (Essex)
1982–83	Event discontinued

Mixed Doubles (Under 15)

1975–76	A J Pryce (Worcestershire) and N A Rollason (Worcestershire)
1976–77	M J Cattermole (Avon & Somerset) and S J Leadbeater (Guernsey)
1977–78	C R Wood (Lancashire) and S J Leeves (Kent)
1978–79	D Tailor (Middlesex) and G L Gowers (Sussex)
1979–80	P J Walden (Kent) and D Simpson (Yorkshire)
1980–81	D J Hall (Essex) and A D Fisher (Essex)

'Let's all have a go!' : the cry of thousands of young enthusiasts nationwide.

1981–82	P Edevane (Hampshire) and C E Palmer (Hampshire)
1982–83	Event discontinued

(1) Later Mrs E J Timperley
(2) Later Mrs J A Turner
(3) Later Mrs G W Barrand
(4) Later Mrs E B Nielsen
(5) Later Mrs W L Hunter
(6) Later Mrs H J Horton
(7) Later Mrs F Darlington
(8) Later Mrs P Stephens
(9) Later Mrs Downs
(10) Later Mrs P E Whetnall
(11) Later Mrs L Oakley
(12) Later Mrs H I Palmer
(13) Later Mrs Primett
(14) Later Mrs J Soldan
(15) Later Mrs T Gower
(16) Later Mrs Cook
(17) Later Mrs M J Boutle
(18) Later Mrs M A Gilks
(19) Later Mrs J D Eddy
(20) Later Mrs M Beck
(21) Later Mrs A E Skovgaard
(22) Later Mrs E J Allen
(23) Later Mrs R J Lockwood
(24) Later Mrs S Ellison
(25) Later Mrs J P Perry
(26) Later Mrs J C Stretch
(27) Later Mrs C Martin
(28) Later Mrs L Bird
(29) Later Mrs E H Sutton
(30) Later Mrs K Chapman
(31) Later Mrs M G Tredgett
(32) Later Mrs R Durnian
(33) Later Mrs S C Jordan

English Schools' Badminton Association

No game will flourish without a constant in-flow of young players, both able and enthusiastic. The ESBA has been just such a reservoir.

Len Wright, a Cumbrian schoolmaster, was the driving force when, in 1964, he helped to organise a fixture between his Whitehaven school and a Nottingham one. This was quickly followed by a Cumberland v Lancashire match.

From that sprang an inaugural meeting at Manchester YMCA on 10 July 1965 which gave birth to the ESBA. A memorable date indeed because it gave youngsters (either not welcome in or not able enough for adult clubs) the chance of real competition, the spur of winning a coveted badge or a team place. It canalised the growing stream of schools' badminton.

Founder members Cumberland, Lancashire, Essex and Hertfordshire organised the first of many Inter-County Competitions. Unfortunately they forgot that 5 April 1966 was not a holiday for all schools. So Cumberland and Lancashire, with newly joined London Counties, fought it out alone. Birmingham and Sheffield Schools were the next to join, closely followed by regions as diverse and distant as West Hartlepool and Wiltshire. Today virtually every county in England sends a team at Easter to Nottingham University to fight for the Gannon Shield and Povey-Richards Trophy for the winners and runners-up respectively.

After an inter-regional trial match, a hoped for first 'international' in 1966 eventually boiled down to Lancashire and Cumberland v Isle of Man! But in 1968 English Schools Under-16 met and defeated Scottish Schools at Workington. And in 1969 they scored again against an overseas opponent, Denmark.

Meantime, essential coaching had not been overlooked. In 1967, each county had been briefed to make its own plans—with the help of BA of E grant-in-aids. Only a year later, Regional Co-ordinators were appointed. And a little later still a Teachers' Coaching Scheme, never meant to replace the BA of E Coach award, was organised to give even non-badminton playing teachers sufficient knowledge to start a club. Since then over 5000 Teacher Awards have been made.

In 1969, a Bronze, Silver and Gold Award Scheme was launched. Hearts of Oak Benefit Society later gave it financial support, a task taken over by Carlton Sports. Since then some 34 000 badges have been gained. And recently wise provision has been made for a Primary Award to

England Youth Squad under benign eyes of Nev McFarlane (left) *and Roger Mills* (right) *show a fine crop of internationals-to-be. Can you spot them? (Answer at foot of page).*

Pip Capon, ESBA Treasurer, not only looked after the shekels, but also enlivened international match programmes with these delightful drawings.

encourage still earlier participation.

Again, since 1969, like the ripples on a pond, the ESBA's scope has widened: National Individual Championships (today supported by National Girobank) at Under-12, Under-13, Under-14 and Under-16 levels; a 'Top Schools' competition; international matches at home and abroad for Under-14, Under-15, and Under-16; Under-14 and Under-18 Six Nations Championship, and Under-15 Triangular match; and a Home Countries Under-16 Quadrangular. A formidable list indeed. Players in such competitions all receive a stringent briefing on game ethics.

This plethora of voluntary work was pioneered by Honorary Secretary Len Wright and then largely taken on by chairman Nev MacFarlane. Finance (and delightful programme 'illustrations') have long been in the hands of P B Capon. Netta Capon, elected to the Executive two years before her husband, did much valuable work in connection with Awards. Ian Graham and Allon Horrocks gave invaluable coaching. Many other names could be mentioned if space permitted. But, as Nev MacFarlane emphasises, 'ESBA is no one-man band; it's a co-ordinated orchestra with everyone giving 100 per cent'.

English badminton owes it much. Few of today's top-flight players have not passed through its ranks. Young players, thanks to ESBA and BA of E, to dedicated coaches and devoted parents, play incredibly mature badminton.

Answer to query in caption above is: Kevin Jolly, Karen Bridge, Karen Puttick, and Paula Kilvington

Six/England's Major Events

Inter-County Championship

For many years the Inter-County Championship has been the backbone of English badminton. It gives the season an added tang of competitive play, one all the keener because county loyalties are involved. It is an initial proving-ground for those with international ambitions. And it is a yardstick by which counties can measure a part of their success: the prowess of their players; the enthusiasm and support of their affiliated clubs.

The first ever county match was arranged as far back as 1899 when Surrey, all unconsciously no doubt, presaged the shape of things to come with a 12–4 victory over neighbouring Hampshire. They won again in 1903 (at Southsea—Sir George Thomas's home club) and in 1904 (at the Crystal Palace).

Interest so far was mainly in the South but in 1905 the England team, landing at Liverpool after a crushing 8–1 defeat of Ireland in Dublin, were bravely challenged by Lancashire who not surprisingly lost 3–14. In 1911 Hampshire were equally ruthless when they beat Sussex, 14–2.

From then on there was a slow but steady increase in county matches. Lancashire and Cheshire happily recorded: 'We played for fun with never a cup at the end'. With the growth of County Associations in the '20s the pace quickened. It was not, however, until 1928 that an official Inter-County Championship was initially organised in ten regionalised groups but, oddly, without any provision for a play-off of winners. Two years later with 30 counties now whittled down into seven groups, group-winners played off and London, through Middlesex, began its crushing domination

of the Championship. Metropolitan Counties have won the event 33 times (and shared it once) in 44 years of actual competition.

The fact that in the early '30s the controlling organisation was the Badminton Association (not the BA of E) which controlled badminton worldwide, accounted for the inclusion of North and South Wales and East and West of Scotland. Later the Isle of Man and also Jersey and Guernsey joined in. Still later Leinster and Ulster entered the fray.

English counties at first enjoyed these trips 'overseas' but later, when transport costs became crippling, Irish and Scottish entrants were on occasion penalised by having to play all 'away'

Tom Wingfield (Kent) beat Harold Marsland (Yorks) 18–15, 17–18, 18–13—99 points out of a maximum 105.

ICC (Div I) semi-final 1933 : Middlesex (10) included internationals K G Livingstone, R C F and L Nichols (blazers, back row); Gloucestershire (4), R M White (blazer, second from right).

matches. Maybe occasional stories (in the *Gazette*) —of bumpy flights and stormy crossings of an unfriendly Irish Sea with a wealth of unhappy detail—also played their part in such demands from English counties.

In the '30s, Kent and Surrey pioneered 2nd team matches. And in 1937–8 an ICC Division II of four groups of 2nd teams, zoned regionally, was formed. This continued until 1948 when Berks, Bucks and Oxon's 1st team after becoming something of a chopping block entered for Division II. As other small counties, not surprisingly, also had 1st teams weaker than the big counties' 2nd teams, the Competition was reorganised. In 1948–9, 1st and 2nd teams were regraded into three divisions on past performance, and promotion and relegation rules put into operation.

1955 saw the entry of 3rd teams—often used as a nursery for promising youngsters but skippered and strengthened by a scattering of ex-1st team players who were becoming a little long in the tooth. As a result a Division IV and then a Division V were formed. Meantime cups had been presented: Division I a combined effort by famous Cheshire clubs, Claughton, Wallasey, Grosvenor and Chester; Division II by BA of E Vice-President (later President) Brigadier R Bruce Hay.

Brian White (Wilts) played 26 games in one day at the Wiltshire Open including two 3-game finals, both of which he won. Between 1964–82, he won 45 Wiltshire Restricted titles.

And records were emerging. Middlesex, mustering a star-studded team that included internationals such as Ralph and Leslie Nichols, Donald Hume and Geoff Fish, Marian Horsley, Jean Stewart and Nancy Horner, won seven of the nine pre-War finals. Cheshire, all too often on the receiving end, broke their losing run in 1933–4 with a narrow 9–7 victory over Middlesex. In 1937–8, Sussex, who had dethroned Middlesex in the semi-final, lost by the narrowest of margins in the final to Lancashire, 8–8 (19 games to 18). Sussex, however, had the consolation of also reaching the first Division II final—and winning. The following year Middlesex kept up the fashion for close finishes by beating Cheshire (for the fifth time) 8–8, 21 games to 18. (And in 1947 Hampshire and Surrey tied 6–6, 16–16, 406–406 in a Group match).

The first post-war Championship was something of a fiasco. Cheshire and Middlesex despite the intervening years, carried on where they had left off—but, unable to agree a date for the final, had to share the title.

In the following decade it was good to see Cheshire, so often the best man but never the groom, equalling Middlesex's record of seven consecutive final appearances—including three victories.

In 1955, Surrey, still licking their wounds from three successive defeats (1948–50) started their steam-roller run. In the 21 years from 1955 to 1975 they won the title no fewer than nineteen times. Kent and Essex were each allowed a first ever win—with West of Scotland, on each occasion, runners-up, as, tantalisingly, they were to be six times in all. In their second victory season, Surrey boasted four international ladies: Iris Cooley, June White, Barbara Carpenter and Heather Ward, to whom of course they later added Angela Bairstow and Gillian Perrin amongst others!

Since then Essex, winning the title in 1977 and 1978 with a powerful side, looked set fair for a long run had not their internationals Ray Stevens, Kevin Jolly and Nora Perry pleaded pressure of world-wide play and withdrawn; a practice fortunately not followed by other internationals. This defection let Lancashire in to make it three in a row. After five vain attempts they ended Surrey's marathon run in 1975, nearly 40 years after their first (Lancashire's) success. But in 1982, it was Surrey yet again with Yorkshire's White Rose unlucky for the third time in four years.

Division II honours were much more evenly and interestingly shared apart from a six-year run by— Surrey II!—1958 to 1963. Cheshire II and Kent II are the only other 2nd teams to have won the Championship against the might of 1st teams.

The Middlesex 1930–47 record makes astounding reading. They won the title seven times and shared it once. Their two losses were both by 7–9 margins only. They played 56 matches, won 54, lost two; and scored 605 points to 168. Eighteen of their 33 players were internationals. After the War they shared once and won twice but since 1953 have never been in serious contention.

Cheshire too had a great record. Six pre-war

Aggressive Yorkshireman: 'Yon chap 'ld mek a reet good musician. 'E's damned near as good on t'wood as on t'strings!'

final appearances out of nine (W1:L5). And in the immediate post-war decade, a further eight appearances, seven of which were in succession (W3:L4:Divided 1). In 1950, both Cheshire teams, who obviously enjoyed a 'close-run thing' reached their respective finals: Cheshire I beat Surrey 8–8 (21 games to 17); Cheshire II lost to Essex 8–8 (19 games to 21).

In 1952 they did the 'double'. The 1st team gave their old tormentors Middlesex an 11–4 trouncing; the 2nd team nearly whitewashed hapless Gloucestershire (who did not raise their heads again until 1978) 14–1. The 2nd team never lost a group match in nine seasons.

Alan Titherley, a left hander of great deception, made 90 appearances. Tony Jordan, who, despite 100 caps for England, was always a most loyal county player, received his national colours before his Cheshire ones.

Titherley's was a record rivalled only by that of Ralph Nichols. The latter first played for Middlesex in 1930. The last of his ten appearances as a winning finalist was in 1953 when he helped regain the cup from rivals Cheshire. On one occasion Middlesex chartered a three-seater plane to whisk Nichols and Hume from work in London

Happy Lancashire took the Division I trophy North three years in succession (1979–81).

to play in Birkenhead. Conditions were so bad that the pilot refused to take off. Undeterred, the pair then hired a better equipped twenty-seater. And had to sit one in the back and one in the front to keep it in trim! Nevertheless, they won 13–3.

The format of County matches changed over the years. Until 1950 it consisted solely of doubles—four men's, four ladies', and with the accent on eight mixed. A draw was 8–all though not in knock-out stages when games and even points had to be taken into consideration; a state of affairs that occurred no fewer than five times.

A letter in the *Gazette* from H W Ruffle advocated putting an end to this and improving our standard of singles. And in 1950–1 the format was officially changed by reducing the mixed to four games (England had long excelled in this branch of the game) and including two men's and one ladies' singles. Too often counties found it difficult to dragoon even one lady into playing singles. 'Walkovers' became so frequent that preventive legislation had to be drafted. And in 1970–1 it was considered wise to blood yet more singles players by raising the tally to three men's singles and two ladies' singles, an overall total of seventeen matches per tie.

In the same year, Division I was reduced to two groups of four (North and South) with the winner of one group playing the runner-up in the other in semi-finals. And a 5th Division was added, divided into four basic zones, sub-divided again where necessary.

In 1963, the Isle of Man BA had appealed for umpires and scoreboards in particular and better presentation in general to encourage spectators. Slowly this came about. Even Supporters' Clubs were formed. In the '60s costs escalated and sponsorship was welcomed. Bowring Shipton Insurances first gave much needed help; then, when they pulled out, Friends' Provident Life Office stepped into the breach. Tracksuited teams sporting county badges—the white horse of Kent, the martlets of Sussex, the red and white roses of Lancashire and Yorkshire, the scimitars of Essex and Middlesex that 'Velma', the *Gazette*'s columnist, had hoped for in 1953, were presented to a growing number of spectators.

Today no fewer than 115 teams play the snakes and ladders of challenge, relegation and promotion. It is a competition that gives inspiration and practice to top players and great enjoyment and badminton education to those club players who watch.

Generally played on a Sunday—so try it for yourself!

The Inter-County Championships

Division One
Results of Final Ties

1930–31 at York
MIDDLESEX beat Northumberland, 13–2

1931–32 at Birkenhead
MIDDLESEX beat Cheshire, 11–5

1932–33 at Newcastle
MIDDLESEX beat Northumberland, 13–3

1933–34 at Birkenhead
CHESHIRE beat Middlesex, 9–7

1934–35 at Birkenhead
MIDDLESEX beat Cheshire, 13–3

1935–36 at Alexandra Palace
MIDDLESEX beat Cheshire, 12–4

1936–37 at Wallasey
MIDDLESEX beat Cheshire, 11–5

1937–38 at Southend
LANCASHIRE beat Sussex, 8–8
(19 games to 18)

1938–39 at Birkenhead
MIDDLESEX beat Cheshire, 8–8
(21 games to 18)

1939 to 1946 *No Competition*

1946–47 Cheshire and Middlesex divided (unplayed)

1947–48 at Leicester
YORKSHIRE beat Surrey, 9–7

1948–49 at Wimbledon
CHESHIRE beat Surrey, 11–5

1949–50 at Birkenhead
CHESHIRE beat Surrey, 8–8
(21 games to 17)

1950–51 at Barnt Green
MIDDLESEX beat Cheshire, 9–6

1951–52 at Stamford Hill
CHESHIRE beat Middlesex, 11–4

1952–53 at Nottingham
MIDDLESEX beat Cheshire, 9–6

1953–54 at Northampton
KENT beat Cheshire, 9–6

1954–55 at Wimbledon
SURREY beat Cheshire, 12–3

1955–56 at Lytham
SURREY beat Lancashire, 10–5

1956–57 at Wimbledon
SURREY beat Lancashire, 13–2

1957–58 at Paisley
SURREY beat West of Scotland, 9–6

1958–59 at Wimbledon
SURREY beat Cheshire, 12–3

1959–60 at Paisley
KENT beat West of Scotland, 13–2

1960–61 at Wimbledon
SURREY beat Lancashire, 11–4

1961–62 at Wimbledon
SURREY beat West of Scotland, 12–3

1962–63 at Wimbledon
SURREY beat Lancashire, 12–3

1963–64 at Leyton
ESSEX beat West of Scotland, 10–5

1964–65 at Birkenhead
SURREY beat Cheshire, 11–4

1965–66 at Wimbledon
SURREY beat Lancashire, 15–0

1966–67 at Bradford
SURREY beat Yorkshire, 13–2

1967–68 at Wimbledon
SURREY beat Yorkshire, 15–0

1968–69 at Birkenhead
SURREY beat Cheshire, 10–5

1969–70 at Wimbledon
SURREY beat West of Scotland, 14–1

1970–71 at Guildford
SURREY beat West of Scotland, 14–3

1971–72 at Redbridge
SURREY beat Essex, 9–8

1972–73 at Wimbledon
SURREY beat Essex, 12–5

1973–74 at Redbridge
SURREY beat Essex, 9–8

1974–75 at Harrow
SURREY beat Kent, 9–8

1975–76 at Lytham
LANCASHIRE beat Kent, 10–7

1976–77 at Redbridge
ESSEX beat Lancashire, 10–7

1977–78 at Southampton
ESSEX beat Hampshire, 9–8

1978–79 at Sheffield
LANCASHIRE beat Yorkshire, 10–7

1979–80 at Atherton
LANCASHIRE beat Yorkshire, 11–6

1980–81 at Folkestone
LANCASHIRE beat Kent, 9–8

1981–82 at Huddersfield
SURREY beat Yorkshire 11–6

1982–83 at Wimbledon
SURREY beat Lancashire 10–7

Division Two
Results of Final Ties
(Until 1948 this was contested between county 2nd teams only.)

1937–38 at Leicester
SUSSEX 2nd beat Yorkshire 2nd, 11–5

1938–39 at Bedford
SUSSEX 2nd beat Yorkshire 2nd, 8–8
(20 games to 18)

1939 to 1946 *No Competition*

1946–47 at Barnt Green
KENT 2nd beat Cheshire 2nd, 9–5

1947–48 at Wimbledon
CHESHIRE 2nd beat Middlesex 2nd, 9–6

1948–49 at Wimbledon
CHESHIRE 2nd beat Somerset, 11–5

1949–50 at Barnt Green
ESSEX* beat Cheshire 2nd, 8–8
(21 games to 19)

1950–51 at Sydenham
HERTFORDSHIRE beat Cheshire 2nd, 9–6

1951–52 at Barnt Green
CHESHIRE 2nd beat Gloucestershire, 14–1

1952–53 at Barnt Green
BERKS, BUCKS & OXON* beat Cheshire 2nd, 9–6

1953–54 at Epsom
SOMERSET beat Derbyshire, 11–4

1954–55 at Epsom
CHESHIRE 2nd beat Kent 2nd, 11–4

1955–56 at Epsom
DERBYSHIRE* beat Hertfordshire, 12–3

1956–57 at Wimbledon
KENT 2nd beat Northamptonshire, 11–4

1957–58 at Douglas
SURREY 2nd beat Isle of Man, 9–6

1958–59 at Douglas
SURREY 2nd beat Isle of Man*, 8–7

1959–60 at Wimbledon
SURREY 2nd beat Lancashire 2nd, 13–2

1960–61 at Lytham
SURREY 2nd beat Lancashire 2nd, 9–6

1961–62 at Wimbledon
SURREY 2nd beat Lancashire 2nd, 8–7

1962–63 at Lytham
SURREY 2nd beat Lancashire 2nd, 8–7

1963–64 at Stamford Hill
MIDDLESEX* beat Lancashire 2nd, 9–6

1964–65 at Stamford Hill
HERTFORDSHIRE beat Nottinghamshire*
10–5

1965–66 at Portsmouth
HAMPSHIRE* beat Yorkshire 2nd, 10–5

1966–67 at Bradford
MIDDLESEX* beat Yorkshire 2nd, 11–4

1967–68 at Porstmouth
HAMPSHIRE beat Nottinghamshire, 13–2

1968–69 at Leeds
BERKSHIRE beat Yorkshire 2nd, 10–5

1969–70 at Abingdon
BERKSHIRE beat Derbyshire, 9–6

1970–71 at Newcastle-upon-Tyne
NORTHUMBERLAND* beat Berkshire*,
10–7

1971–72 at Derby
DERBYSHIRE beat Glamorgan, 15–2

1972–73 at Stone
HAMPSHIRE*beat Staffordshire, 12–5

1973–74 at Sydenham
KENT* beat Durham, 16–1

1974–75 at Harrow
STAFFORDSHIRE* beat Surrey 2nd, 9–8

1975–76 at Hull
    MIDDLESEX beat Yorkshire*, 9–8

1976–77 at Croydon
    SURREY 2nd beat Lancashire 2nd, 11–6

1977–78 at Birmingham
    WARWICKSHIRE beat Gloucestershire*,
    11–6

1978–79 at Finsbury
    DERBYSHIRE beat Middlesex, 10–7

1979–80 at Batley
    KENT* beat Yorkshire, 14–3

1980–81 at Redbridge
    ESSEX* beat Durham*, 10–7

1981–82 at Wimbledon
    SURREY 2nd beat Lothian*, 11–6

1982–83 at Gateshead
    DURHAM beat Middlesex, 13–4

*Also gained promotion to Division 1.

English National Championships

Previous Winners

Men's Singles

1963–64	W F Havers
1964–65	R J Mills
1965–66	R J Mills
1966–67	R J Mills
1967–68	R J Sharp
1968–69	R J Sharp
1969–70	P E Whetnall
1970–71	D Talbot
1971–72	D Talbot
1972–73	R P Stevens
1973–74	D Talbot
1974–75	P E Whetnall
1975–76	P E Whetnall
1976–77	R P Stevens
1977–78	D Talbot
1978–79	R P Stevens
1979–80	R P Stevens
1980–81	R P Stevens
1981–82	S Baddeley
1982–83	K Jolly

Ladies' Singles

1963–64	U H Smith (5)
1964–65	A M Bairstow (4)
1965–66	U H Smith (5)
1966–67	U H Smith (5)
1967–68	A M Bairstow (4)
1968–69	G M Perrin (6)
1969–70	G M Perrin (6)
1970–71	G M Gilks
1971–72	M Beck (8)
1972–73	M Beck (8)
1973–74	M Beck (8)
1974–75	M Beck (8)
1975–76	G M Gilks
1976–77	M Lockwood
1977–78	G M Gilks
1978–79	G M Gilks
1979–80	G M Gilks
1980–81	G M Gilks
1981–82	J Webster
1982–83	K Beckman

Men's Doubles

1963–64	C T Coates and A D Jordan
1964–65	J N Havers and W F Havers
1965–66	C J Beacom and A D Jordan
1966–67	R J Mills and D O Horton
1967–68	C J Beacom and A D Jordan
1968–69	J D Eddy and R A Powell
1969–70	R J Mills and A D Jordan
1970–71	E C Stuart and D Talbot
1971–72	E C Stuart and D Talbot
1972–73	R P Stevens and M G Tredgett
1973–74	E C Stuart and D Talbot
1974–75	J D Eddy and E H Sutton
1975–76	R P Stevens and M G Tredgett
1976–77	R P Stevens and M G Tredgett
1977–78	R P Stevens and M G Tredgett
1978–79	R P Stevens and M G Tredgett
1979–80	R P Stevens and M G Tredgett
1980–81	R P Stevens and M G Tredgett
1981–82	M Dew and D Bridge
1982–83	M Dew and M Tredgett

Ladies' Doubles

1963–64	U H Smith (5) and H J Pritchard (1)
1964–65	U H Smith (5) and H J Pritchard (1)
1965–66	A M Bairstow (4) and C M Barrand
1966–67	S D Pound (2) and M B Boxall (7)
1967–68	S D Pound (2) and M B Boxall (7)
1968–69	S Whetnall and M B Boxall (7)
1969–70	S Whetnall and M B Boxall (7)
1970–71	M Beck (8) and J Rickard
1971–72	J Hashman and G M Gilks
1972–73	J Hashman and G M Gilks
1973–74	N C Gardner (9) and G M Gilks
1974–75	S Whetnall and M B Boxall (7)
1975–76	S Whetnall and G M Gilks
1976–77	B Giles (10) and G M Gilks
1977–78	N Perry and A E Statt (11)
1978–79	G M Gilks and J A Webster
1979–80	N Perry and K T Puttick (12)
1980–81	K Bridge (13) and B Sutton
1981–82	J Webster and N Perry
1982–83	J Webster and N Perry

Mixed Doubles

1963–64	C J Beacom and H J Pritchard (1)
1964–65	R J Mills and C M Barrand
1965–66	A D Jordan and J E Charles (3)
1966–67	D O Horton and J Horton
1967–68	R J Mills and G M Perrin (6)
1968–69	R J Mills and G M Perrin (6)
1969–70	P E Whetnall and M B Boxall (7)
1970–71	R J Mills and G M Gilks
1971–72	D Talbot and G M Gilks
1972–73	D R Hunt and G M Gilks
1973–74	D Talbot and G M Gilks
1974–75	D Talbot and G M Gilks
1975–76	D Talbot and G M Gilks
1976–77	M G Tredgett and N C Gardner (9)
1977–78	M G Tredgett and N Perry
1978–79	M G Tredgett and N Perry
1979–80	M G Tredgett and N Perry
1980–81	M G Tredgett and N Perry
1981–82	M Dew and G M Gilks
1982–83	M Tredgett and G M Clark

(1) Later Mrs D O Horton	(5) Later Mrs L Oakley	(9) Later Mrs J P Perry
(2) Later Mrs P E Whetnall	(6) Later Mrs M A Gilks	(10) Later Mrs E H Sutton
(3) Later Mrs W R Rickard	(7) Later Mrs E J Allen	(11) Later Mrs A E Skovgaard
(4) Later Mrs H I Palmer	(8) Later Mrs R J Lockwood	(12) Later Mrs K Chapman
		(13) Later Mrs K Beckman

The All-England Championships

Once the proud preserves of the players of Great Britain; since the end of the Second World War, the Mecca for players from all over the globe. The oldest tournament in the world—the Wimbledon of badminton!

It all began on 4 April 1899. The Guildford tournament on 10 March 1898, the first ever, had been so great a success that the Badminton Association (as it was then called) felt it must join in the act. It did so first with the BA Tournament. Then, in 1902, it was known as the 'All-England', a title already used in cricket, croquet and tennis, one that gave the event paramount prestige and threw it wide open to the country as a whole.

It was played in the 'spacious and handsome' HQ of the London Scottish Rifles at Buckingham Gate. That year only doubles were played so a single day sufficed. One lady played in so vivid and elaborate a hat that 'its distraction value must have been worth several points to her'. Devon's Miss Meriel Lucas, whose 'ubiquity and return of the heaviest drives was astounding' towered above the other ladies.

In 1900, singles were added, to be won by Sidney H Smith ('as good a tennis player as the unbeatable Doherty brothers') and Ethel Thomson, who was to win it four more times. This was George Thomas's first All-England and he described it succinctly. 'With a bye, a small entry, and obliging opponents we reached the semi-final only to be well and truly dealt with by the ultimate winners', H F Mellersh and F S Collier (15–12, 15–10).

He recalls there were four courts: one at each end was overhung for half its width by a gallery which gave rise to numerous cunningly calculated 'lets'. They were marked out in chalk on the day of the tournament but needed frequent subsequent touching-up. The court had no singles lines and the doubles long-service line was also the base-line for singles! As a result Miss Ethel Thomson and Miss E Moseley put each other out fourteen times in succession without scoring! (The court was lengthened and its hour-glass shape abolished in 1901.)

Only six dozen shuttles, from which competitors had the unenviable choice of 'a rocket' or 'a slow wobbler', were used. These were uncomplainingly used by 'cracks' and 'rabbits' alike until virtually shapeless or featherless.

Players were of very varied standards. Some even used the small-headed, long-handled battledore. Miss M Hardy, in the mixed, swept impressively through 30 points in one 'hand'. Nor was there any 11-up concession to feminine frailty. In those days ladies played 15-up as did the men. Indeed, despite leg of mutton sleeves, choker collars and substantial skirts, the ladies were often comparatively better than the men. The single row of spectators was outnumbered by the players.

In 1902, a move was made to the lofty Crystal Palace Central Transept. Six courts were available for the 3-day event but not unnaturally the light was poor and, shape of things to come, there was a distinct drift, a strong air-current that altered the shuttle's true-flight. Scottish and Irish players competed for the first time. Among the few spectators not deterred by the Palace's inaccessibility was the great W G Grace of cricket fame.

In 1903, the venue changed again—to the London Rifle Brigade's City Headquarters in Bunhill Row. There conditions were cramped so that incoming players and spectators held up games as they walked behind or across the courts. Play on occasions had to be delayed to allow early morning fog to disperse. And on others, snow on the roof cast a gloom over the proceedings that gas burners could do little to dispel. In 1907 the Men's Doubles final was postponed at 7–2 because of failing light—and completed four days later.

However, it was not until 1910 that the All-England found a satisfactory and permanent home, for 25 tournaments, in the Horticultural Hall in Vincent Square behind the Army and Navy Stores.

Even so all was not initially perfect. The parquet floor was very slippery. Druggets were, as ever, likely to break from their moorings. Resin did the trick but when it was generously scattered, players were either choked by the dust, dazzled by its reflected glare, or held like flies on flypaper by its tackiness. The problem was solved only by the boarding over first of the gallery court and then of the others. Even then discussion raged as to whether the boards should have been laid at right

In 1937, Mrs V MacCrimmon saw her husband and partner win the Lincolnshire Mixed Doubles title and the Brocklesbury Cup. New to the game, she expressed a wish that one day her name might be inscribed on the same cup.

Entering for it eighteen times she was four times runner-up. In 1967, now a grandmother, and playing with her BBC commentator son, Roddy, she achieved her wish—after 30 years.

On the Horticultural Hall's Centre Court, Frank Devlin (Ireland) wins his last international by beating be-shorted R M White (England). Umpire: Sir George Thomas!

angles to or parallel with the net. The light too was unsatisfactory: championship events were therefore played by daylight though sometimes lights had to be switched on in mid-game. Sir George always found the light there difficult; like frailer mortals he too could play and miss.

Evenings were devoted to handicap events held in 1, 2 and then 3 divisions. Even the very top players entered to get all too infrequent top-class practice. Initially, there were very few 'owes' or many points that had to be knocked off before actual scoring began. International Margaret Tragett or Hazel Hogarth might be playing off 'scratch' neither 'owing' nor 'receiving' points. Sir George's pre-war partner, Frank Chesterton, was heard to remark 'These +8 fellows are such devils for hitting the wood'. Later, 'owings' were adopted but it would generally be owe 20 rather than owe a hand, (having only one serve, not two), owe 12 as in later days.

Play was also interrupted by traditional inter-national matches started on Friday afternoon. Only in 1939 was there an evening start (7.30) to encourage more spectators. Entries might well include A N Other and U N Lapin, (French for 'a rabbit'). Indeed the former, sometimes disguised Dr H N Marrett, who won the All-England title in 1908. The latter gave even less cover to Guy Sautter who 'smashing severely from all positions' won both Singles and Mixed in 1913. Some rabbit! Official records stiffly eschew such delightful oddities dreamed up by men who did not want their absence from work publicised.

The Horticultural Hall had its defects, and officials still dreamt of 'a hall of our own'. But for all that it became badminton's familiar home, the highlight of the season, where old friends could be sure of meeting off court if not on. It was the scene of the 'Best of British Badminton'.

A growing foreign entry and increasing numbers of spectators forced the BA of E to announce that in 1940 the All-England would be played at Harringay Arena: a seven-court, 12 000-seat North London stadium. Hitler decreed otherwise!

But in 1947 with British badminton and the British economy slowly creaking back into action Harringay it was. Disastrously so! The night before, a blizzard lashed London. Snow drove in horizontally through the roof ventilators and onto the spectators watching All-in Wrestling. Then, to quote Herbert Scheele, who was getting a very cold christening for his 32-year stint as All-

> *HRH the Duke of Edinburgh accepted an invitation to the 1953 All-England —but had to go to Germany instead. As Lt Mountbatten, RN, he had played regularly at Corsham (Wilts). Assessed: 'Energetic and enthusiastic—but lacking skill'.*

England referee: 'By the time the last neck had been twisted or whatever happens to conclude these extraordinary jousts, layer upon layer had frozen over the boards laid over the ice'. Next day charwomen mopped vigorously with hot water—only to see it freeze almost immediately. No more than six of 65 scheduled matches were played. And of those, one well-known lady, on the losing end, asked for a replay! As Harringay had seven courts and handicap events had at last been axed play had been scheduled for 4 not 6 days, evenings only. But on Thursday it started at 2 pm —just two hours before heating—and therefore spectators—were permitted. And a record 99 matches were cleared!

Harringay, however, was a little too spacious even for ambitious badminton. Another move was made to the five-court Empress Hall, Earls Court in 1950. And there the All-England remained until 1957 when 'structural alterations' necessitated finding another home, the seventh.

That new home of course was Wembley Pool, now Wembley Arena. There seven excellent courts are laid on the arena where Harlem Globetrotters and Russian gymnasts have thrilled and delighted; where Jungle Bunny and Bouncer have taken the double oxer in their stride, and where many a pugilist has measured his length on the canvas for the full ten seconds. Drift (inevitable in so vast a building) has played its pranks. Presentation has improved: flowers and fanfares; spotlights and champagne. A full 8000 enthusiasts from nationwide packed its high-tiered seats for the Friday evening feast of thrilling semi-final play. Now the good things are spread a little thinner with semis on the Saturday and the finals on the Sunday. But there is still that sense of occasion, of breathless excitement. And still the certainty of bumping into old friends as you walk the broad galleries or browse amongst the growing hypermarket of equipment stalls.

Seeding was not practised until 1932 and even then the seeds were not marked on the programme. Lack of it had led to early and horrid slaughter of 'top' contenders. In 1911, Champions all, A D Prebble and S M Massey had to fight it out with G A Thomas and H N Marrett in the 2nd round! Nor were qualifying rounds introduced until 1951, at Sydenham and Wimbledon. And in 1953 at Huddersfield as well.

Jack Purcell of Canada in 1931 was the first foreign entrant to put his head into the lion's mouth. The biggest Danish contingent crossed the North Sea in 1938—13 of them. Then the Danish Champion Tage Madsen spiked that famous smasher Bill White's big guns by impregnable defence; 17-year-old Jasper Bie (who played in both handicap events as well), thin and with baggy shorts down to his knees, had a bigger haul: Warrington, Field, Nichols (L), Whittaker and then, first time ever, Madsen himself! Ralph Nichols' deception, however, enabled him to overwhelm a completely over-awed and static Bie, 15–4, 15–5 in the final.

Much the same tale in the Ladies' Singles semifinal: Tonny Olsen suffering from severe toothache faded in the third game after 8–3 up against Betty Uber. A player commented: 'In 2 or 3 years these Danes will be a danger to us'. Surely the understatement of the years!

The very next season Madsen stormed back to take the Singles whilst Ruth Dalsgard and Tonny Olsen became the first non-English pair to win the Ladies' Doubles. A Canadian, Mrs W R (Dorothy) Walton, won the Singles and an Irish pair, Jim Rankin and Tommy Boyle, filched the Men's Doubles. England were left with only their usual lifebelt, the Mixed.

In 1947, English players for the first time ever, did not win one title. In contrast the Danes made a clean sweep, (Jepsen, winner of the Singles, was Swedish but Danish born) and again in 1948. And yet in 1949 no Danish man reached a final. But the pupils had surpassed their masters; England was 'to reap the whirlwind' for many seasons to come.

The writing was on the wall. From Malaysia as well as from Denmark, from Indonesia and Japan as well as from the USA, brilliant players made pilgrimage to the All-England as the unofficial World Championships. Not since 1938 has an English name appeared as a winner in the Men's Singles or Doubles. But English ladies have kept the flag flying proudly.

Space must be found to mention another All-England. One not so athletically effervescent but one warm and friendly—the All-England Veterans Men's Doubles have been played since 1905 when a compensatory bonus of a quarter of a point for each year on the downward path over 50 was given. After the War, until 1960, early rounds were played at Wimbledon—but those who reached the semifinals had a chance to renew former glories as they fought them out at the All-England proper.

1959 saw ladies at last willing to declare their age, 45. In the same year, the men lost their quarter of a point prop and the event was held at the same time as the Qualifying Rounds. The 'mix' was not welcomed; in 1960, the 'Vets' at last had it cosily to themselves at Ebbisham without 'those qualifying

Masters of mixed : Mike Tredgett and Nora Perry.

interlopers'. And with courts to spare, the sexes got together for Mixed Doubles.

1961 saw greybeards up in arms—the age limit plummeted to 45. A horrified member of the Old School commented, 'I'm aghast! Good God, man, you're going to have a lot of *boys* on the court'. In 1966, a short-lived Married Couples Competition was played at the same time as the Veterans. Did later winners as strong as England's Paul and Sue Whetnall convince the powers that be that it could well become a mere formality for years?

Records? Badminton longevity seemingly flourishes. Pat Davis won the Men's Doubles seven times, six with Cyril Denton. It was but a poor thing beside Sylvia Ripley and Margaret Bayley's breathtaking ELEVEN consecutive wins. The 1968 shoot-out winners Warwick Shute (39) and Jack McColl (31) could boast 70 English caps. Ten years later the great Iris Rogers (52) and June Timperley (44) combination (with a total of 96 caps!) took one last bow on the badminton stage. Perhaps it was just so that June could achieve her unique triple of Junior, Senior and Veteran All-England Championships! The '80s were celebrated by the arrival—and victory—of M Bopardikan and brilliant Thomas Cup star Nandu Natekar from India. And in 1982, Denmark's Erland Kops and Tonny Christensen both won titles.

The All-England has had an exciting and varied career. The very words carry a ring of promise and excitement to English ears. And still, despite official World Championships, it brings the best of the world to a tournament that has its own unique aura.

Twenty Years of All-England Highlights

52nd All-England Championships 1962
All finals were decided in two games; only one game was set; and only one other went to double figures.

There were only 16 English players in the Men's Singles out of 48 entrants.

Ursula Smith was 1–7 down in the third in her quarter-final against Heather Ward when the latter had to retire with a torn Achilles tendon.

Upset by a line decision, Ursula was on court in the final against Judy Hashman for a bare 13 minutes.

Peter Waddell and Tony Jordan beat Erland Kops and Poul Nielsen (D) in the quarters to great acclaim. On returning to court for the semi-final they received the greatest ever pre-match ovation—but it did not spur them to victory.

53rd All-England Championships 1963
Channarong Ratanasaengsuang bludgeoned Colin Beacom 15–0, 15–4; murdered H Sperre (Nor) 15–2, 15–0; and assassinated Finn Kobbero (D) 15–1, 15–2. In successive rounds at that!

In her tenth successive appearance, in the Ladies' Singles final Judy Hashman won her seventh title so beating the record of her father, Frank Devlin (Ire) and of Meriel Lucas.

In the Ladies' Doubles, sisters Judy Hashman and Sue Peard (USA) beat sisters Ulla Rasmussen and Karin Jorgensen (D).

Seventeen Danes entered for the Championships.

A play off for third place in the Men's Doubles was instituted for the first time. Peter Waddell and Tony Jordan beat Erland Kops and Poul Nielsen (D) 15–8, 15–9.

Two hundred volunteer umpires, linesmen and stewards officiated.

54th All-England Championships 1964
With 155 competitors from 16 nations, it was the largest and most widely represented hitherto held.

In winning the Ladies' Singles, Judy Hashman equalled the record five consecutive wins (1925–9) of her father, Frank Devlin, in the Men's Singles.

In the fourth round, the holder Erland Kops, was 14–9 up in the second game, having won the first, against first-time seeded Lee Kin Tat—and lost 15–6, 14–17, 13–15.

In the final of the Ladies' Doubles, sisters Sue Peard and Judy Hashman (holders) lost to sisters Ulla Rasmussen and Karin Jorgensen whom they had beaten in the previous year.

Ursula Smith reached the Ladies' Singles final after beating an Indonesian, a Canadian, a Dane, and an Irishwoman—before losing to an American.

Danish Champion Pernille Molgaard Hansen (16) was the youngest ever competitor—and won two rounds of Singles.

55th All-England Championships 1965
Ursula Smith, in winning the Ladies' Singles without dropping a game and with only one double-figure score against her, became the second English lady to win the title in 27 years.

Erland Kops regained his crown by beating Tan Aik Huang (M) (with the grace and touch of Wong Peng Soon) 15–13, 15–12 in one of the longest and most exhausting *two*-game matches—lasting 55 minutes.

If 'veteran virtuosos' Kobbero and Hammergaard Hansen (D) had won the Men's Doubles title for the seventh time, they would twice have been out-right winners of the trophies. Instead, defeated in the quarters by Malaysia's 19-year-old Tan Aik Huang and Yen Cheng Hoe, they received the greatest ever losers' ovation.

This was Hammergaard Hansen's 16th appearance in the All-England.

Ng Boon Bee, a leading Malaysian footballer was 'like a tiger sensing the kill' when he and Tan Yee Khan won the Men's Doubles without dropping a game.

After 5 years without defeat, holder and 8 times winner Judy Hashman, who had had no competitive play, lost in the 4th round to Sonia Cox (NZ) 7–11, 5–11. A defeat she accepted in exemplary fashion.

For the first time ever, many entries had had to be refused.

56th All-England Championships 1966
'English singles players were not fit enough; they had played too many minor tournaments and had not done enough practice and training' commented ex-international John Havers.

Tan Aik Huang (M) who won the Singles, beating Masao Akiyama, only Japanese man ever to reach the final, owed his footwork to 'shadow badminton —no shuttle; no opponent! Just Tan Aik Huang and the court.

Judy Hashman (with magnificent technique and temperament, and complete professionalism) gained her 9th victory despite the previous season's lay off.

Sue Peard was perhaps the dominant player when she and more famous sister Judy Hashman beat the 'Rasmussen sisters'.

Six Asians and two Danes contested the Men's Singles quarter-finals. No English player had survived!

Imre Rietveld on her second All-England appearance lost only in the Ladies' Singles finals to Judy Hashman. She returned home to a houseful of flowers and a telegram from the Dutch Minister of Sport.

57th All-England Championships 1967
Indonesian and Japanese men had not been entered—and the 'Monarchs', Kobbero and Hansen, had retired.

On her 13th appearance, Judy Hashman won her tenth title from 1–5 down in the third—on a bowl of cornflakes eaten at 5 am after a restless night.

Erland Kops, employing great strength in cross-court backhand clears and delicacy in drops and net-shots, won his seventh title in defeating a superlatively fit Tan Aik Huang. En route, in ten games, he had only one double figure score against him.

At the traditional BA of E after-Finals Dinner Dance, Judy Hashman was given an ovation lasting several minutes.

Danes won the Men's Singles and Doubles, the Mixed Doubles and a half-share in the Ladies' Doubles. On their return to Copenhagen they were given a Civic Reception.

Service judging was tougher; umpiring better.

Essex county player Janet Brennan reached the

In 1960, Heather Guntrip was drawn No 2 in each of the three All-England events, thus meeting the top seed each time. Some odds!

Ladies' Doubles final; partnered by Judy Hashman and opposed by Ulla Strand and Imre Rietveld she was not overawed in high company.

58th All-England Championships 1968

Twenty-two nations competed.

Eighteen-year-old Rudy Hartono started his great run of victories by winning the Men's Singles—at his first attempt.

Eva Twedberg became the first Swede ever to win the Ladies' Singles. (She had practised against men as there were no other comparable ladies in South Sweden). Victorious, she raced to her teammates to share her joy.

Tony Jordan, in his seventh finals appearance in twelve years won the Mixed Doubles for the fourth time—with his third partner Sue Pound. (Previously with June Timperley (2) and Jenny Pritchard).

All finals were one-sided (no game was dropped and runners-up scored only 64 points, with only one double figure score, out of a possible 132). So much so that they were completed in 3 hours 5 minutes.

The Thomas Cup was presented by IBF President, David Bloomer, to the Malaysian team who had won it by Indonesia's default in 1967. The cup had been brought from Indonesia by two IBA officials.

Finn Kobbero, winner of 15 All-England finals, despite a leg broken whilst ski-ing, took the floor at the All-England Dinner and Dance.

59th All-England Championships 1969

These, with two winners and two runners-up, were England's most successful for 30 years.

Against a succession of talented players from five different nations, Elo Hansen (D), Kojima (J), Oon Chong Hau (M), Darmadi (I), Koh Khen Siong (M), and Ray Sharp, Rudy Hartono won the title by beating Darmadi by the most crushing margin ever of 1 and 3. And with an overall loss of only 44 points in 12 games.

Only six three-game matches were played in the 63 Men's Singles matches.

Margaret Boxall, England's No 2, lost her 3rd

In 1938, the Duchess of Gloucester was the first-ever royalty to attend the All-England: she watched Tage Madsen, a youthful Dane, beat England's great Bill White.

round singles 0–11, 0–11 to Imre Nielsen (née Rietveld) but won the Ladies' Doubles with Kent partner Sue Whetnall.

60th All-England Championships 1970

Players from eighteen nations—but not Malaysia, concentrating on Thomas Cup preparations—competed before record crowds.

Margaret Boxall and Sue Whetnall beat Gillian Perrin and Julie Rickard in the Ladies' Doubles: the first time two English pairs had met in the final for over 30 years.

Only David Eddy of England's nineteen entrants, reached the last sixteen in the Men's Singles.

Etsuko Takenaka was unseeded—but won the Ladies' Singles.

Gillian Perrin got through the first round of the Ladies' Singles for the first time in 5 years.

Margaret Boxall, 11–3, 7–11, 0–10, nevertheless won (12–10) against a Danish junior—Lene Köppen!

Qualifiers David Clarke and Mike Parratt (Essex) reached the Men's quarter-finals.

61st All-England Championships 1971

Rudy Hartono in winning the Men's Singles dropped only 39 points out of 180. Apart from one 10, no one else scored more than 5 against the Master.

Danish Under-18 Junior Anni Berglund, unseeded, beat leading players of Thailand, Netherlands, Japan and Denmark before losing to Swedish Eva Twedberg in three games in the final.

The 1970 runners-up, Dave Eddy and Robert Powell, unseeded this year, were drawn against their last year's conquerors Tom Bacher and Poul Petersen (D) in the first round and lost narrowly.

'In the final the continuous calling to each other during play of Noriko Takagi and Hiroe Yuki must have been somewhat disconcerting for Judy Hashman and Gillian Gilks.'

A near capacity crowd of 8000 gave Herbert and Betty Scheele a rousing reception on the occasion of a presentation to mark the former's retirement as Secretary of the BA of E after 25 years of sterling work.

62nd All-England Championships 1972

In the throes of last-minute preparations referee Herbert Scheele had to be rushed to hospital with back trouble—shaky but invincible, he discharged himself to see his 26th Finals Day.

England had finalists in all three doubles events but failed to clinch any of them though two went to three games.

Outsiders Surrey's Colin Beacom and Keith Andrews beat top seeds Kops and Pri (15–10, 15–11); then lost to Stevens and Tredgett (unseeded) who went on to a place in the final.

Elliott Stuart and Punch Gunalan were repeatedly faulted by the service judge when the former, with Talbot, beat the latter and Ng Boon Bee, the holders.

Qualifiers C Goodman and Pauline Chitty won their first round (against another Essex pair) when Pauline served into the net! The receiver had moved before she struck the shuttle!

In the Ladies' Doubles final, the losing English pair Margaret Beck and Julie Rickard, found it was suicide to attempt to use the usually deceptive 'flick' serve against Etsuko Takenaka (J).

Dr Roger Bannister, first ever sub-four-minute miler, presented the trophies.

63rd All-England Championships 1973

English Ladies' Day? Margaret Beck won the Singles and was Ladies' Doubles runner-up. And Gillian Gilks won the Mixed Doubles and was a triple finalist.

Svend Pri took an underground train to Wembley —one travelling in the wrong direction! Arriving late, he had to hurry on court—and lost to Christian.

In the final against Hartono, Christian served 13 times with his score at 1 in the first game; in the second it took him a similar number to score 2 (15–4, 15–2).

Ed Sutton after Thursday's play drove back to Staffordshire to do a day's teaching. Time of arrival 4 am! He drove back again the same day— to lose, not surprisingly, 12 and 4 to Christian and Chandra.

In Mixed Doubles, contrary to established practice, Roland Maywald (GFR) was the first to serve— not his partner, Barbara Steden.

'Miss Nora Gardner (now Perry) carried on where she had left off the night before with some excellent low serves interspersed at intervals with flick serves all of which won points.' And that against Svend Pri—and later Derek Talbot!

64th All-England Championships 1974

Rudy Hartono won his seventh successive Men's Singles title to hold the magnificent new trophy presented anonymously in memory of former BA of E Honorary Treasurer Arthur Barron who had donated the two previous trophies—both won outright by Hartono.

Punch Gunalan (M) let slide his second game against Tjun Tjun (I) 2–15—only to slam home 15–0 in the third.

Sue Whetnall and Margaret Boxall had 9 match points when they met the Japanese Machiko Aizawa and Etsuko Takenaka in the quarter-finals. It took ten minutes of 'interminable rallies' to clinch the match from 14–9 to 15–11.

Tjun Tjun and Wahjudi (I) 'hardly lifted the shuttle at all' in defeating Christian and Sumirat (I) in an all-Indonesian final.

In the Mixed Doubles, a ricochet off Mrs M-L Zizman's (GFR) racket scored a bull's-eye on the lights—and plunged the court into darkness.

65th All-England Championships 1975

Svend Pri, the Great Dane, after eleven years constant endeavour won his first Singles title—at the same time robbing Hartono of his coveted record. First action—to rush off court to embrace his wife.

Top seeds in the Mixed were Indonesian pairs! But both went out in the quarter-finals to English pairs—one of whom Elliott Stuart and Nora Gardner gained a first ever finals win.

Karen Bridge, a 15-year-old member of the England Youth Squad, qualified for the Singles.

Heather Nielsen, 1959 winner, was still fit enough and good enough to reach the fourth round.

Margaret Beck and Gillian Gilks and Sue Whetnall and Margaret Boxall were top seeded—but both lost in the semis to Asian pairs.

66th All-England Championships 1976

Indonesia defied the Asian Badminton Confederation ban on the All-England.

So, Rudy Hartono regained his lost Singles title to 'make it eight', thus breaking Kops' record of seven wins.

Hartono's 15–7, 15–7 victory over Liem Swie King (who had decisively beaten the holder, Svend Pri) was so lack lustre that the uncharitable murmured 'Arranged'.

Gillian Gilks, supremely fit physically and psychologically, won the Singles title beating a dispirited Margaret Beck 11–0, 11–3 in a match which former champion Judy Hashman criticised as 'no credit to herself (Beck) or the game'. It was Gillian's first victory in eleven attempts!

In the semi-final, Derek Talbot 'directing his

'I've won! I've won!' After 11 years' endeavour Svend Pri beats seven times champion Rudy Hartono in 1975.

smash at Mrs Zizman's shapely figure rather than at the powerful Bochow backhand' regained control to win the third game 15–4.

But in the final it was Gillian Gilks who 'absolutely confident, dominated the net' to become Triple Champion.

The Men's Doubles final was the first all-European one for 6 years.

Defeated but admiring Danish player: 'These English girls never lift from the net; they are always pushing it down'.

After protests from the People's Republic of China, the British Foreign Office would 'neither grant nor

Wong Shoon Keat and Lee Ah Ngo trained frantically for months for the All-England—only to find that breakaway World Badminton Federation Singapore players were not eligible. No go indeed!

refuse' entry visas to the Taiwanese team who were playing in other European countries. As a result they were unable to play in the All-England.

67th All-England Championships 1977

The Wembley drift was at its worst. The shuttle was blown more than a foot—both in and out.

Yet again Mexico's Diaz Gonzales met a seed in the first round. This time no less than Flemming Delfs.

Indonesia's Chandra and Teresa Widiastuti, and Christian and Regina Masli were shown in the Mixed Doubles draw. Both however conceded walkovers stating they had never intended to enter.

Seeded 3/4, a lack lustre Svend Pri and a bubbling Ulla Strand, the former with three Mixed titles and the latter with no fewer than seven, the first won in 1962, were defeated in the first round—by Danish compatriot Elo Hansen and Holland's Joké van Beusekom, 15–0, 15–4.

Gillian Gilks dropped only six points in her first three rounds of singles against Suzanne Coates

(Surrey), Barbara Steden (GFR) and Emiko Ueno ((J).

Princess Margaret presented the trophies.

John Player started their run of financial support.

68th All-England Championships 1978

Saori Kondo (J), having lost in the Singles final to Gillian Gilks, happily spent the rest of the afternoon repairing her team-mates' rackets.

World Champion Lene Köppen (D) made her ninth unsuccessful appearance in the Singles: defeated five times in the semis, once in the final.

Sture Johnsson (S) at 4–4 (setting) in the third against Hartono had an easy 'kill' at the net after a 40-stroke rally—and hit out. So losing the chance to become the second man to beat Hartono at Wembley in ten years.

After 'drift' had played decisive tricks on Svend Pri in the Mixed, he appealed to the crowd, 'Please, shut the door'. (In vain! He lost, leaving yet another shuttle that appeared well out).

In the third round of the Men's Singles, Mike Wilks was the lone Englishman left amid three Indonesians, five Danes, one New Zealander, three Swedes, two Japanese, and one Indian.

Gillian Gilks beat Saori Kondo in the final in a bare 20 minutes; using seven rackets and a plethora of shuttles.

The 5-minute interval between the second and third games was instituted for the first time.

69th All-England Championships 1979

Lene Köppen, so long the understudy, never the star, won the Singles final to become the first Danish winner for 26 years. Saori Kondo, last year's losing finalist but again unseeded, was Lene's opponent.

In the second round of the Men's Doubles not one match went to three games. And of the 32 games, only two were set.

Uncapped Mike Wilks and Peter Bullivant defeated Denmark's Flemming Delfs and Sweden's Thomas Kihlstrom 5–15, 18–17, 18–15. A good pair beat two brilliant individuals.

Tjun Tjun and Wahjudi (I), disqualified by Umpire Arthur Jones for breach of the 5-minute interval rule, were re-instated by Referee Herbert Scheele. From 4–12 down against Japan's Iino and Tsuchida they fought back to win their semi-final 18–16.

As little Imelda Wigoeno (I), all flowers, smiles, trophy and champagne bottle, turned from the

Gillian Gilks (England) : the epitome of elegance.

presentation by the Minister of Sport, Dennis Howell, she was preceded by a small dark-skinned boy who danced ecstatically before her waving the Indonesian flag.

Europe's 'Strictly Private' Mixed game preserves were cunningly despoiled by Indonesian poachers, Christian and Imelda Wigoeno, first ever Asian winners.

Doping controls were instituted for the first time.

Four titles out of five: Indonesia's biggest haul ever.

70th All-England Championships 1980

The *first* 'Open' All-England: £1000 prize money for the Men's Singles winner.

The Indonesian aura of invincibility waned: Prakash Padukone's (Ind) half smashes to the sideline and held, attacking clears shattered Liem Swie King's (I) hopes of permanently annexing the Singles trophy.

Lene Köppen imperiously dismissed Verawaty.

Stevens (blue-shorted) and Tredgett outgunned Christian and Chandra in the semi-final; shellshocked Tjun Tjun and Wahjudi in the final by winning the first game but could not quite destroy them in the next two.

Mike Tredgett and a scintillating Nora Perry dethroned Christian and Imelda Wigoeno.

With the Championships lengthened by an extra day, was it a question of 'Never on a Sunday' for the other Indonesians?

To give added point to the upheld Danish protest at Lius Pongoh (I) being seeded higher than Delfs, the latter crushed the former in the quarters 8 and 4.

Liem Swie King was Indonesia's thirteenth successive finalist—and had an unbeaten run of seventeen matches to his credit.

Having cut herself adrift from the BA of E, Gillian Gilks foundered 1–11, 1–11 against the 18-year-old Danish 6-foot bean-pole Kirsten Larsen. And, with Svend Pri, was torpedoed 5–15, 4–15 by David Eddy and Barbara Sutton. But, paired with Nora Perry, she won the Ladies' Doubles against Atsuko Tokuda and Yoshiko Yonekura (J) (all voluble excitement)—and then declared herself 'unavailable' to the BA of E for the Uber Cup.

Bengt Froman on the 'Sidek Serve': 'It's hopeless. The shuttle moves this way and that. It could destroy the game.'

Trophies presented by the Duke of Beaufort.

71st All-England Championships 1981
Nora Perry and Jane Webster showed remarkable consistency in reaching the final (after 8 games) at a cost of a mere 15 points—an incredible under 2 a game. No wonder they won the all-English final!

Prize money: £10 525.

A stunned crowd watched their favourite, holder Lene Köppen, at her wit's end against South Korea's surprise weapon, the strongly built 19-year-old, Sun Ai Hwang, on her first Wembley appearance. Rumour ran riot: Sun had trained in a convent; was chastised by her coach when she made errors.

Unseeded, and drawn against Hartono in the first round, a defeated and disappointed Delfs quipped, 'I only came to see the England–Spain soccer match!'

Birds on court are commonplace: birds on camera, a novelty. An errant pigeon perched on a TV camera, held up play, and made his début on the 'box'.

Prakash Padukone (Ind) beat the wizard Hartono but lost to the sorcerer's apprentice Liem Swie King (I) in the final.

Tjun Tjun and Wahjudi were robbed of a record-breaking seventh win by yet another brilliant Indonesian pair, Kartono and Heryanto.

> 'If you want to know the score ask a player': umpire on a Lilleshall course.

Unhappy birthday! A 21st at that! Karen Bridge trounced 11–1, 11–2 by Lene Köppen.

72nd All-England Championships 1982
Players from a record 26 nations competed—including a biggest ever squad of 27 from first time entrants People's Republic of China.

All seven 1981 champions failed to reach the final.

In the quarter-finals of the Ladies' Singles Lene Köppen was the only European left; the remaining seven were all Chinese. And in the Men's Singles, China had five out of eight semi-finalists.

Both finalists in the Men's Doubles, winners Razif and Jalaini Sidek (M) and losers Gilliland and Travers (Sco) were unseeded.

In the final of the Ladies' Doubles, China's Wu Dixi, holding the shuttle base up, nearly made the game a farce with virtually unplayable backhand spin-serves. The shuttle swerved late—and fully 2 feet!

Comparatively unknown Martin Dew, having started the season by a fine surprise win in the Friends' Provident Men's Doubles, concluded it brilliantly by winning the Mixed Doubles (with Gillian Gilks).

73rd All-England Championships 1983
Of the 356 entries from 25 countries (including 114 for the Men's Singles) only 223 could be accepted direct into the Wembley Championships.

Phil Sutton created a Welsh record by reaching the 4th round of the Singles before succumbing to 'Frost'-bite.

Lene Köppen crashed 3–11, 0–11 to Xu Rong, one of China's six quarter-finalists. Sadly, Lene later came 'on court' to make a farewell curtsey to a great roar of applause.

Mike Tredgett and Martin Dew reached the Men's Doubles final after beating the holders, the Sidek brothers, but could not contain the Swedes, Kihlstrom and Karlsson.

Unseeded youngsters Niel Tier (Hants) and Gillian Gowers (Sussex) reached the semi-final of the Mixed, an event won by the Anglo-Swedish combination of Nora Perry and Thomas Kihlstrom.

Seeded Danes, Steen Fladberg and Jesper Helledie were knocked out in the 1st round by Indian unknowns. A month later they won the World Championships!

In the Ladies' Singles, all 6 Chinese seeds reached the quarters; none of them conceded more than 7 points!

For the All-England semi-finals, Wembley Arena's seven Hova courts, ringed by red sweatered linespersons, are reduced to th

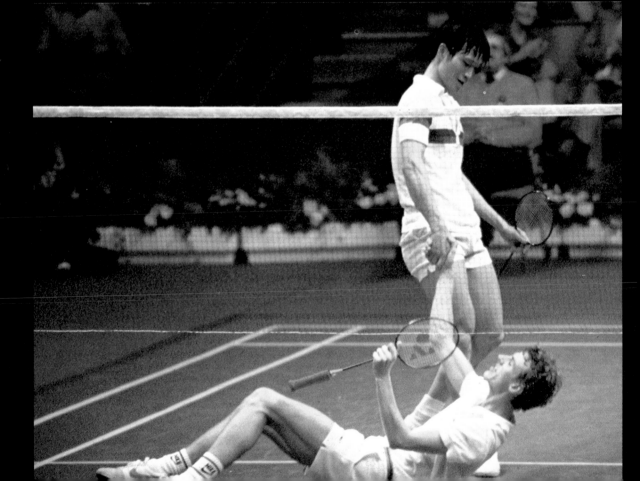

oing-up!" A perfectly controlled net-shot by China's
ng Ailing.

Scotland's Billy Gilliland and England's Karen Puttick,
runners-up in the All-England Mixed Doubles 1982.

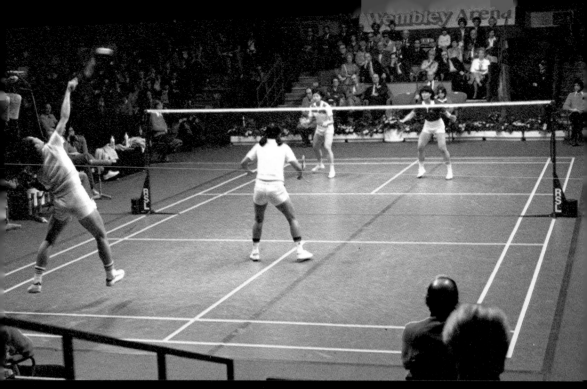

All action and athleticism! A badminton ballet. Indonesia's Damayanti and Verawaty overcome China's Great Wall, Zhang Ailing and Liu Xia.

Top A memorable final. Wu Dixi (left-hander), with Liu Ying, massacred Verawaty (smashing) and Damayanti, with her viciously swerving cut-serve.

Above England's Kevin Jolly shows dash and determination as he chases a deceptive lob deep to his forehand corner.

Right Denmark's No 1, Morten Frost, in full flow as he smashes to victory in the All-England Singles final.

Gillian Gilks, the world's finest all-rounder ever, collects rackets, tracksuit, bouquet . . . and All-England Singles trophy.

Denmark's Lene Köppen salutes the crowd after winning the All-England Singles.

Morten Frost, "Mr Perpetual Motion", only the third European All-England Singles winner in fifteen years.

Gold for Helen Troke—England's winner of the European Junior Championships Singles title!

The Queen and Prince Philip at the Thomas Cup Final at the Albert Hall.

Millions world-wide have thrilled and laughed at "Badminton on Ice": Shirley Marie, Reg and Hugh Forgie.

Striking both in looks and action, Indonesia's Queen of the Courts, Wiharjo Verawaty-Fajrin.

Above *Ladies' Doubles demands super fitness: Ann Statt* (left) *and Gillian Gilks train with . . . why, soccer star Kevin Keegan!*
Right *'Champions All' foregather at Wembley : Finn Kobbero (Denmark), Ian Maconachie (Ireland), Svend Pri (Denmark), Rudy Hartono (Indonesia), Judy Hashman (USA), Sue Peard (USA), Tony Jordan (England), Eva Twedberg (Sweden), June White (England).*

All-England Championships

Previous Winners

Men's Singles

1899	*No Competition*	
1900	S H Smith	
1901	Capt H W Davis	
1902	Ralph Watling	
1903	Ralph Watling	
1904	H N Marrett	
1905	H N Marrett	
1906	N Wood	
1907	N Wood	
1908	H N Marrett	
1909	F Chesterton	
1910	F Chesterton	
1911	G A Sautter	
1912	F Chesterton	
1913	G A Sautter	
1914	G A Sautter	
1915 to 1919	*No Competition*	
1920	Sir G A Thomas, Bart.	
1921	Sir G A Thomas, Bart.	
1922	Sir G A Thomas, Bart.*	
1923	Sir G A Thomas, Bart.	
1924	G S B Mack (Ire)	
1925	J F Devlin (Ire)	
1926	J F Devlin (Ire)	
1927	J F Devlin (Ire)*	
1928	J F Devlin (Ire)	
1929	J F Devlin (Ire)	
1930	D C Hume	
1931	J F Devlin (Ire)	
1932	R C F Nichols	
1933	R M White	
1934	R C F Nichols	
1935	R M White	
1936	R C F Nichols	
1937	R C F Nichols*	
1938	R C F Nichols	
1939	Tage Madsen (D)	
1940 to 1946	*No Competition*	
1947	Conny Jepsen (S)	
1948	Jorn Skaarup (D)	
1949	D G Freeman (USA)	
1950	Wong Peng Soon (M)	
1951	Wong Peng Soon (M)	
1952	Wong Peng Soon (M)*	
1953	E B Choong (M)	
1954	E B Choong (M)	
1955	Wong Peng Soon (M)	
1956	E B Choong (M)	
1957	E B Choong (M)*	
1958	Erland Kops (D)	
1959	Tan Joe Hok (I)	
1960	Erland Kops (D)	
1961	Erland Kops (D)	
1962	Erland Kops (D)*	
1963	Erland Kops (D)	
1964	K A Nielsen (D)	
1965	Erland Kops (D)	
1966	Tan Aik Huang (M)	
1967	Erland Kops (D)	
1968	R Hartono (I)	
1969	R Hartono (I)	
1970	R Hartono (I)*	
1971	R Hartono (I)	
1972	R Hartono (I)	
1973	R Hartono (I)*	
1974	R Hartono (I)	
1975	S Pri (37) (D)	
1976	R Hartono (I)	
1977	F Delfs (D)	
1978	Liem Swie King (I)	
1979	Liem Swie King (I)	
1980	P Padukone (Ind)	
1981	Liem Swie King (I)	
1982	M Frost (D)	
1983	L Jin (Ch)	

Ladies' Singles

1899	*No Competition*	
1900	E Thomson (1)	
1901	E Thomson (1)	
1902	M Lucas (21)	
1903	E Thomson (1)	
1904	E Thomson (1)*	
1905	M Lucas (21)	
1906	E Thomson (1)	
1907	M Lucas (21)	
1908	M Lucas (21)	
1909	M Lucas (21)*	
1910	M Lucas (21)	
1911	M Larminie (2)	
1912	M Tragett	
1913	L C Radeglia	
1914	L C Radeglia	
1915 to 1919	*No Competition*	
1920	K McKane (3)	
1921	K McKane (3)	
1922	K McKane (3)*	
1923	L C Radeglia	
1924	K McKane (3)	
1925	M Stocks	
1926	M Barrett	
1927	M Barrett	
1928	M Tragett	
1929	M Barrett	
1930	M Barrett	
1931	M Barrett	
1932	L M Kingsbury (4)	
1933	A Woodroffe (5)	
1934	L M Kingsbury (4)	
1935	E. Uber	
1936	T Kingsbury (16)	
1937	T Kingsbury (16)	
1938	D M C Young (17)	
1939	D Walton (C)	
1940 to 1946	*No Competition*	
1947	Marie Ussing (25) (D)	
1948	Kirsten Thorndahl (24) (D)	
1949	A Schiott Jacobsen (D)	
1950	Tonny Ahm (D)	
1951	A Schiott Jacobsen (D)	
1952	Tonny Ahm (D)	
1953	Marie Ussing (25) (D)	
1954	J Devlin (27) (USA)	
1955	M Varner (33) (USA)	
1956	M Varner (33) (USA)	
1957	J Devlin (27) (USA)	
1958	J Devlin (27) (USA)	
1959	H M Ward (28)	
1960	J Devlin (27) (USA)*	
1961	J Hashman (USA)*	
1962	J Hashman (USA)	
1963	J Hashman (USA)*	
1964	J Hashman (USA)	
1965	U H Smith (34)	
1966	J Hashman (USA)	
1967	J Hashman (USA)	
1968	E Twedberg (39) (S)	
1969	H Yuki (J)	
1970	E Takenaka (43) (J)	
1971	E Twedberg (39) (S)	
1972	N Nakayama (J)	
1973	M Beck (42)	
1974	H Yuki (J)	
1975	H Yuki (J)	
1976	G Gilks	
1977	H Yuki (J)*	
1978	G Gilks	
1979	L Köppen (D)	
1980	L Köppen (D)	
1981	S A Hwang (K)	
1982	Z Ailing (Ch)	
1983	Z Ailing (Ch)	

*Trophy won outright.

Men's Doubles

1899	D Oakes and S M Massey
1900	H L Mellersh and F S Collier
1901	H L Mellersh and F S Collier
1902	H L Mellersh and F S Collier*
1903	S M Massey and E L Huson
1904	A D Prebble and H N Marrett
1905	C T J Barnes and S M Massey
1906	H N Marrett and G A Thomas
1907	A D Prebble and N Wood
1908	H N Marrett and G A Thomas
1909	F Chesterton and A D Prebble
1910	P D Fitton and E Hawthorn
1911	H N Marrett and G A Thomas
1912	Dr H N Marrett and G A Thomas*
1913	F Chesterton and G A Thomas
1914	F Chesterton and G A Thomas
1915 to 1919	No Competition
1920	A F Engelbach and R du Roveray
1921	Sir G A Thomas, Bt., and F Hodge
1922	J F Devlin (Ire) and G A Sautter
1923	J F Devlin and G S B Mack (Ire)
1924	Sir G A Thomas, Bt., and F Hodge
1925	H S Uber and A K Jones
1926	J F Devlin and G S B Mack (Ire)
1927	J F Devlin and G S B Mack (Ire)
1928	Sir G A Thomas, Bt., and F Hodge
1929	J F Devlin and G S B Mack (Ire)*
1930	J F Devlin and G S B Mack (Ire)
1931	J F Devlin and G S B Mack (Ire)
1932	D C Hume and R M White
1933	D C Hume and R M White
1934	D C Hume and R M White*
1935	D C Hume and R M White
1936	L Nichols and R C F Nichols
1937	L Nichols and R C F Nichols
1938	L Nichols and R C F Nichols*
1939	T H Boyle and J L Rankin (Ire)
1940 to 1946	No Competition
1947	Tage Madsen and Poul Holm (D)
1948	Preben Dabelsteen and Borge Frederiksen (D)
1949	Ooi Teik Hock and Teoh Seng Khoon (M)
1950	Preben Dabelsteen and Jorn Skaarup (D)
1951	E L Choong and E B Choong (M)
1952	E L Choong and E B Choong (M)
1953	E L Choong and E B Choong (M)*
1954	Ooi Teik Hock and Ong Poh Lim (M)
1955	Finn Kobbero and J Hammergaard Hansen (D)
1956	Finn Kobbero and J Hammergaard Hansen (D)
1957	J C Alston (USA) and H A Heah (M)
1958	E Kops and P E Nielsen (D)
1959	Lim Say Hup and Teh Kew San (M)
1960	Finn Kobbero and P E Nielsen (D)
1961	Finn Kobbero and J Hammergaard Hansen (D)
1962	Finn Kobbero and J Hammergaard Hansen (D)*
1963	Finn Kobbero and J Hammergaard Hansen (D)
1964	Finn Kobbero and J Hammergaard Hansen (D)
1965	Ng Boon Bee and Tan Yee Khan (M)
1966	Ng Boon Bee and Tan Yee Khan (M)
1967	E Kops and H Borch (D)
1968	E Kops and H Borch (D)
1969	E Kops and H Borch (D)*
1970	T Bacher and P Petersen (D)
1971	Ng Boon Bee and P Gunalan (M)
1972	Christian and Ade Chandra (I)
1973	Christian and Ade Chandra (I)
1974	Tjun Tjun and J Wahjudi (I)
1975	Tjun Tjun and J Wahjudi (I)
1976	B Froman and T Kihlstrom (S)
1977	Tjun Tjun and J Wahjudi (I)
1978	TjunTjun and J Wahjudi (I)*
1979	Tjun Tjun and J Wahjudi (I)
1980	Tjun Tjun and J Wahjudi (I)
1981	Kartono and R Heryanto (I)
1982	R Sidek and J Sidek (M)
1983	T Kihlstrom and S Karlsson (S)

Ladies' Doubles

1899	M Lucas (21) and Miss Graeme
1900	M Lucas (21) and Miss Graeme
1901	St John and E M Moseley (6)
1902	M Lucas (21) and E Thomson (1)
1903	M C Hardy (7) and D K Douglas (8)
1904	M Lucas (21) and E Thomson (1)
1905	M Lucas (21) and E Thomson
1906	M Lucas (21) and E Thomson (1)*
1907	M Lucas (21) and G L Murray
1908	M Lucas (21) and G L Murray
1909	M Lucas (21) and G L Murray*
1910	M Lucas (21) and M K Bateman (14)
1911	A Gowenlock and D Cundall (9)
1912	A Gowenlock and D Cundall (9)
1913	H Hogarth and M K Bateman (14)
1914	M Tragett and E G Peterson
1915 to 1919	No Competition
1920	L C Radeglia and V Elton
1921	K McKane (3) and M McKane (10)
1922	M Tragett and H Hogarth
1923	M Tragett and H Hogarth
1924	M Stocks and K McKane (3)
1925	M Tragett and H Hogarth
1926	A M Head and V Elton
1927	M Tragett and H Hogarth*
1928	M Barrett and V Elton
1929	M Barrett and V Elton
1930	M Barrett and V Elton*
1931	E Uber and M Horsley
1932	M Barrett and L M Kingsbury (4)
1933	T Kingsbury (16) and M Bell (11)
1934	T Kingsbury (16) and M Henderson
1935	T Kingsbury (16) and M Henderson*
1936	T Kingsbury (16) and M Henderson
1937	E Uber and D Doveton
1938	E Uber and D Doveton
1939	R Dalsgard and T Olsen (19) (D)
1940 to 1946	No Competition
1947	K Thorndahl (24) and T Olsen (19) (D)
1948	K Thorndahl (24) and G Ahm (D)
1949	E Uber and Q M Allen (20)
1950	K Thorndahl (24) and G Ahm (D)
1951	K Thorndahl (24) and G Ahm (D)*
1952	A Jacobsen and G Ahm (D)
1953	I L Cooley (23) and J R White (22)

1954	S Devlin (26) and J Devlin (27) (USA)
1955	I L Cooley (23) and J R White (22)
1956	S Devlin (26) and J Devlin (27) (USA)
1957	A Hammergaard Hansen and K Granlund (D)
1958	M Varner (33) (USA) and H M Ward (28)
1959	I Rogers and J Timperley
1960	S Devlin (26) and J Devlin (27) (USA)
1961	S Peard (Ire) and J Hashman (USA)*
1962	T Holst-Christensen (D) and J Hashman (USA)
1963	S Peard (Ire) and J Hashman (USA)
1964	K Jorgensen and U Rasmussen (29) (D)
1965	K Jorgensen and U Strand (D)
1966	S Peard (Ire) and J Hashman (USA)
1967	I Rietveld (30) (N) and U Strand (D)
1968	Minarni (40) and R Koestijah (I)
1969	M B Boxall (41) and S Whetnall
1970	M B Boxall (41) and S Whetnall
1971	N Takagi (38) and H Yuki (J)
1972	M Aizawa and E Takenaka (43) (J)
1973	M Aizawa and E Takenaka (43) (J)
1974	M Beck (42) and G Gilks
1975	M Aizawa and E Takenaka (43) (J)
1976	G Gilks and S Whetnall
1977	E Ueno and E Toganoo (J)
1978	A Tokuda and M Takada (J)
1979	Verawaty and I Wigoeno (I)
1980	G Gilks and N Perry
1981	N Perry and J A Webster
1982	Liu Ying and Wu Dixi (Ch)
1983	Xu Rong and Wu Jianqiu (Ch)

Mixed Doubles

1899	D Oakes and Miss St John
1900	D Oakes and Miss St John
1901	F S Collier and E M Stawell-Brown (12)
1902	L U Ransford and E M Moseley (6)
1903	G A Thomas and E Thomson (1)
1904	H N Marrett and D K Douglass (8)
1905	H N Marrett and H Hogarth
1906	G A Thomas and E Thomson (1)
1907	G A Thomas and G L Murray
1908	Norman Wood and M Lucas (21)
1909	A D Prebble and D Boothby (13)
1910	G A Sautter and D Cundall (9)
1911	G A Thomas and M Larminie (2)
1912	E Hawthorn and H Hogarth
1913	G A Sautter and M E Mayston (15)
1914	G A Thomas and H Hogarth
1915 to 1919	No Competition
1920	Sir G A Thomas, Bt., and H Hogarth
1921	Sir G A Thomas, Bt., and H Hogarth*
1922	Sir G A Thomas, Bt., and H Hogarth
1923	G S B Mack (Ire) and M Tragett
1924	J F Devlin (Ire) and K McKane (3)
1925	J F Devlin (Ire) and K McKane (3)
1926	J F Devlin (Ire) and E G Peterson
1927	J F Devlin (Ire) and E G Peterson
1928	A E Harbot and M Tragett
1929	J F Devlin (Ire) and M Horsley
1930	H S Uber and E Uber
1931	H S Uber and E Uber
1932	H S Uber and E Uber*
1933	D C Hume and E Uber
1934	D C Hume and E Uber

1935	D C Hume and E Uber*
1936	D C Hume and E Uber
1937	I Maconachie (Ire) and T Kingsbury (16)
1938	R M White and E Uber
1939	R C F Nichols and B M Staples (18)
1940 to 1946	No Competition
1947	P Holm and T Olsen (19) (D)
1948	J Skaarup and K Thorndahl (24) (D)
1949	Clinton Stephens and P Stephens (USA)
1950	P Holm and T Ahm (D)
1951	P Holm and T Ahm (D)
1952	P Holm and T Ahm (D)*
1953	E L Choong (M) and J R White (22)
1954	J R Best and I L Cooley (23)
1955	F Kobbero and K Thorndahl (24) (D)
1956	A D Jordan and J Timperley
1957	F Kobbero and K Granlund (D)
1958	A D Jordan and J Timperley
1959	P E Nielsen and I B Hansen (D)
1960	F Kobbero and K Thorndahl (D)
1961	F Kobbero and K Thorndahl (D)*
1962	F Kobbero and U Rasmussen (29) (D)
1963	F Kobbero and U Rasmussen (29) (D)
1964	A D Jordan and H J Pritchard (31)
1965	F Kobbero and U Strand (D)
1966	F Kobbero and U Strand (D)*
1967	S Andersen and U Strand (D)
1968	A D Jordan and S D Pound (32)
1969	R J Mills and G M Perrin (36)
1970	P Walsoe and P Molgaard Hansen (35) (D)
1971	S Prie (37) and U Strand (D)
1972	S Prie (37) and U Strand (D)
1973	D Talbot and G Gilks
1974	J D Eddy and S Whetnall
1975	E C Stuart and N C Gardner (44)
1976	D Talbot and G Gilks
1977	D Talbot and G Gilks
1978	M G Tredgett and N Perry
1979	Christian and I Wigoeno (I)
1980	M G Tredgett and N Perry
1981	M G Tredgett and N Perry
1982	M Dew and G Gilks
1983	T Kihlstrom (S) and N Perry

*Trophies won outright.

(1)	Mrs D R Larcombe	(23)	Mrs W C E Rogers
(2)	Mrs R C Tragett	(24)	Mrs P Granlund
(3)	Mrs L A Godfree	(25)	Mrs A Nylen
(4)	Mrs H Middlemost	(26)	Mrs F W Peard
(5)	Mrs R J Teague	(27)	Mrs G C K Hashman
(6)	Mrs Allen	(28)	Mrs E B Nielsen
(7)	Mrs Lionel Smith	(29)	Mrs U Strand
(8)	Mrs Lambert Chambers	(30)	Mrs K A Nielsen
(9)	Mrs B L Bisgood	(31)	Mrs H J Horton
(10)	Mrs A D Stocks	(32)	Mrs P E Whetnall
(11)	Mrs M Henderson	(33)	Mrs W G Bloss
(12)	Mrs Hemsted	(34)	Mrs L Oakley
(13)	Mrs A C Geen	(35)	Mrs K Kaagaard
(14)	Mrs Flaxman	(36)	Mrs M A Gilks
(15)	Mrs Walker	(37)	Formerly S Andersen
(16)	Mrs C W Welcome	(38)	Mrs N Nakayama
(17)	Mrs J Warrington	(39)	Mrs E C Stuart
(18)	Mrs J B Shearlaw	(40)	Mrs Soedaryanti
(19)	Mrs G Ahm	(41)	Mrs E J Allen
(20)	Mrs F G Webber	(42)	Mrs R J Lockwood
(21)	Mrs King Adams	(43)	Mrs E Toganoo
(22)	Mrs E J Timperley	(44)	Mrs J P Perry

Seven/**International Events**

World Championships

First World Championships 1977
Malmo, Sweden, 3–8 May

Flemming Delfs returned to the court 3 minutes late after the 5-minute interval. Only sporting Ray Stevens' appeals persuaded referee Ole Mertz (D) to change his 'Delfs is scratched' edict.

Standing ovation for 'local boy' Thomas Kihlstrom when he beat Indonesia's hope, Liem Swie King in the third round (15–11, 9–15, 15–12).

Mixed semi-finals: two English pairs (Talbot and Gilks and Tredgett and Perry); one Scottish (Gilliland and Flockhart), and one Danish (Skovgaard and Köppen).

Lene Köppen 'played the best mixed doubles of her life' to outclass Gillian Gilks.

Margaret Lockwood, with strained knee ligaments strapped up, lost 3–11, 0–11 in the semi-final to Lene Köppen's 'relentless pressure and retrieving activity'. Tragically, it was to be Margaret's last competitive appearance on court.

Gillian Gilks had to race from the Championships to fly back in time for a BBC women's 'Superstars' programme. En route the heating failed in the chartered British Caledonian eight-seater aircraft. Gillian huddled beneath every blanket on board. She arrived home at 1 am and was up again at 6 am to undergo canoe-capsize tests.

And it was 'Gold' for Gillian!

The Zambian team withdrew for political reasons.

> *Lynn Braden, playing a single at the Cardiff National Sports Centre, struck simultaneously a clear played by her opponent and a mishit from the adjoining court. A million to one chance!*

Results

Men's Singles F Delfs (D) beat S Pri (D) 15–6, 15–5.

Ladies' Singles L Köppen (D) beat G Gilks 12–9, 12–11.

Men's Doubles Tjun Tjun and J Wahjudi (I) beat H Christian and A Chandra (I) 15–3, 15–4.

Ladies' Doubles E Toganoo and E Ueno (J) beat J van Beusekom and M Ridder-Luesken (N) 15–10, 15–11.

Mixed Doubles S Skovgaard and L Köppen (D) beat D Talbot and G Gilks 15–12, 18–17.

Second World Championships 1980
Jakarta 26–31 May

14 000 spectators crammed into space for 10 000 —and the temperature hit the high humidity, upper 90sF. Perspiration streamed from players' arms as from a tap.

Spectators chaired Hadiyanto (I) off court after he had defeated All-England Champion Prakash Padukone.

Rudy Hartono came out of retirement and to the familiar chant of 'Ru-dy! Ru-dy!' beat seven years younger Liem Swie King by pinpoint placement and impenetrable defence.

Tears from petite Lie Ivana as she was swept off court by the Amazon Wiharjo Verawaty, to the boos and jeers of the crowd (11–1, 11–3).

Fifteen English enthusiasts outcheered 14 985 Indonesians when Nora Perry and Jane Webster captured a solitary title from the all-conquering Indonesians.

Denmark lost all its three titles but perhaps found consolation in the appointment of Copenhagen as venue for the World Championships in 1983.

Tjun Tjun held his wedding party at the Inter-Continental Hotel on the night after the finals. Everyone attended: racket manufacturers *Kawasaki* paid!

'Wonderful, wonderful Copenhagen!' Jubilant 1983 World Championships medallists on the rostrum.

Results

Men's Singles   R Hartono (I) beat Liem Swie King (I) 15–9, 15–9.

Ladies' Singles   W Verawaty (I) beat L Ivana (I) 11–1, 11–3.

Men's Doubles   Chandra and Christian (I) beat Kartono and Heryanto (I) 5–15, 15–5, 15–7.

Ladies' Doubles   N Perry and J Webster beat I Wigoeno and W Verawaty (I) 15–12, 15–3.

Mixed Doubles   Christian and I Wigoeno (I) beat M Tredgett and N Perry 15–12, 15–4.

Third World Championships 1983

Copenhagen 2–8 May

4000-seater Bronby Hallen was a complete sell-out for all finals long before 2 May.

The finals were patronised by Queen Margaret II of Denmark, and Juan Samaranch, I.O.C. President.

Lene Köppen was the player featured on a specially issued Dkr. 2.70 blue stamp.

World famous Tivoli Gardens gave a spectacular firework display to mark the close of the Championships.

'Times' correspondent Richard Eaton said there was 'frenzied tension' in hall—but it didn't deter England's joker Sally Podger from putting on a purple, white and grey make-up to kid Team Manager Ciro Ciniglio that she was unfit!   ·

Danish police rushed Joké van Buesekom to the hall when she 'missed the bus'.

South Korea's Yun Ya Kim and Bronby Hallen drift beat Denmark's idol, Lene Köppen, although she was 7–1 up in the third.

Nora Perry chose to play with Thomas Kihlstrom (S), oldest player in the Championships, and beat her former Mixed partner Mike Tredgett (and Karen Chapman) in the semi-final.

4000 cheering Danes were sadly silenced as Icuk Sugiarto (I) unbelievably massacred Morten Frost 15–3, 15–5.

'Placidly athletic' 18-year-old Helen Troke, neither England's No 1 nor National Champion, was first ever English girl to reach the Singles semis, losing 10–12, 6–11 to ultimate winner.

Results

Men's Singles   Icuk Sugiarto (I) beat Liem Swie King (I) 15–8, 12–15, 17–16.

Ladies' Singles   Li Lingwei (Ch) beat Han Aiping (Ch) 8–11, 11–6, 11–7.

Men's Doubles   S Fladberg and J Helledie (D) beat M Dew and M Tredgett 15–10, 15–10.

Ladies' Doubles Wu Dixi and Liu Ying (Ch) beat N Perry and J Webster 15–4, 15–12.

Mixed Doubles T Kihlstrom (S) and N Perry beat S Fladberg and P Nielsen (D) 15–1, 15–11.

World Games 1981

Minor sports, unable to oust established major Olympic ones, banded together in common cause to show their qualities. The World Games were held at Santa Clara, California, on 22–28 July, 1981. Unfortunately, largely through maladroit organisation they were something of a damp squib; there was no blaze of publicity.

At least it served to warn the badminton world of a new force: the Chinese. Taking full advantage of their recently acquired IBF membership, they took four of the five titles!

Results

Men's Singles Chen Changjie (Ch) beat M Frost Hansen (D) 9–15, 15–7, 15–12.

Ladies' Singles Zhang Ailing (Ch) beat Sun Ai Hwang (K) 9–11, 11–9, 12–9.

Men's Doubles Sun Zhian and Yao Ximing (Ch) beat T Kihlstrom and S Karlsson (S) 12–15, 15–4, 15–6.

Ladies' Doubles Zhang Ailing and Liu Xia (Ch) beat N Perry and J Webster 11–15, 15–4, 15–8.

Mixed Doubles T Kihlstrom (S) and G Gilks beat M Tredgett and N Perry 15–6, 18–14.

Friends' Provident Masters Open Championship

First Championship 1979

The Royal Albert Hall, London, 19–22 September

Gillian Gilks, wearing a logo on her sweater twice the size allowed (20 cm²), was asked to take the latter off—only to reveal still bigger lettering on her shirt. As Gillian had no alternative kit, back on went the sweater.

Though programmed as Lene Ropke, Lene Köppen asked to be announced by her maiden name. (Danish wits christened Hans Ropke, Mr Köppen).

7–11, 11–1: Gilks v Kondo (J). Third game was even shorter than the interval, 11–1 again to Gillian.

Lene Köppen's 12–10, 11–4 final's victory over

Gillian Gilks earned her £3000—as an unlicensed player she had to hand it over to the Danish BA. Other players too weren't licensed so out of £20 700 prize money only £5400 went direct into players' pockets.

Mixed doubles were not included.

With the shuttle deceptively lobbed over his head, Svend Pri walked forward to congratulate opponent Thomas Kihlstrom—only to hear linesman's call, 'Out'.

7500 spectators paid £24 000 gate money.

Results

Men's Singles P Padukone (Ind) beat M Frost (D) 15–4, 15–11.

Ladies' Singles L Köppen (D) beat G Gilks 12–10, 11–4.

Men's Doubles T Kihlstrom and B Froman (S) beat R Stevens and M Tredgett 18–16, 15–9.

Ladies' Doubles N Perry and J Webster beat Y Yonekura and A Tokuda (J) 15–2, 8–15, 15–10.

Prize money Winners: Singles: £3000
Doubles: £750 each
Runners up: Singles: £1500
Doubles: £375 each

Second Championship 1980

The Royal Albert Hall, London, 23–27 September

A very sharp Ray Stevens attributed his speed revival to training under new manager Gordon Richards. From 4–14, he fought back against Rudi Hartono to win the first game 17–14! But the Maestro took the next two.

'Man of the Doubles Match'? Undoubtedly crew-cut 'Big Ade' Chandra. No longer with the speed of a whippet tank, he nevertheless still mounted the fire-power and had the armour-plating of a 'Chieftain'.

Mike Tredgett and Nora Perry, who lost in the World Championships final to Christian and Imelda Wigoeno (I), had sweet revenge: 10–15— and then in just 7 minutes, an unbelievable 15–0, followed by 9–0 (finally 15–2 in just 6 minutes).

But it was still Christian and Wigoeno and Anglo-Scottish outsiders Gilliland and Karen Puttick who contested the final—by a slender games advantage!

A new-look Gillian Gilks, fitter and more confident, took the court: nose reshaped by cosmetic surgery and hair in a newly styled bubble-cut.

40 per cent of the prize money went to Indonesians —or, as they are amateurs, to their Association.

Friends' Provident Life Office

20·00·00 T

BARCLAYS BANK LIMITED 072522
54, LOMBARD STREET, E.C.3.

DATE 4.1.78 PAY TO THE ORDER OF THE BADMINTON ASSOCIATION OF ENGLAND £15000-00

The Sum of £15000=00

FOR AND ON BEHALF OF **Friends' Provident Life Office**

R.A.Uth

PAYMENTS ACCOUNT

⑆072522⑆ 20⑈0000⑉ 204158 20⑈

For badminton, a generous cheque for all *winners; for tennis, not enough for* one *singles winner.*

Results

Men's Singles	Liem Swie King (I) beat R Hartono (I) 15–11, 15–3.
Ladies' Singles	L Köppen (D) beat Y Yonekura (J) 9–12, 11–5, 11–8.
Men's Doubles	Christian and A Chandra (I) beat T Kihlstrom and S Karlsson (S) 15–12, 17–16.
Ladies' Doubles	Y Yonekura and A Tokuda (J) beat N Perry and J Webster 18–14, 6–15, 15–12.
Mixed Doubles	Christian and I Wigoeno (I) beat W Gilliland (Sco) and K Puttick 15–6, 15–6.

Third Championship 1981

The Royal Albert Hall, London, 22–26 September

No fewer than eight foreign players withdrew, for both acceptable and unacceptable reasons: they included Korea's enigmatic Sun Ai Hwang, All-England destroyer of Lene Köppen; and Indonesia's Liem Swie King, Rudy Hartono's successor.

Martin Dew, dramatically called from his PhD computer technology studies at Hatfield Polytech-

In the Kent Open Championships only one lady entered the singles—so winning a two guinea £2.10 voucher, a cup and the title without hitting a single shuttle.

nic, substituted for Ray Stevens who had trapped his thumb in a drawer—and won the Men's Doubles title! To say nothing of £750.

The BBC disappointed millions—by last-minute withdrawal of television coverage. 'Viewing rating not even a million' was the terse reason given. Salt was rubbed into the wound by showing darts hot-shots no fewer than eight times; and filming the last day's play—for export only!

Superlatively agile Chinese players, on their first strictly competitive appearance in Europe, cornered three titles and £9000 with some ease.

Ticket sales up—but first day's seats still empty. Later BA of E advertised for FP Masters Promoter.

Ray Stevens had several hundred pounds' worth of equipment—including 12 rackets—stolen from virtually under his nose in the changing rooms.

Hire charges for the Albert Hall galloped along at £400 for half an hour.

Recently married to her coach, Indonesian star Verawaty left the Albert Hall—bound for a pilgrimage to Mecca.

Presentations made to Kevin Jolly (22) and Jane Webster (25) for their 50 caps for England: Sir George Thomas in 28 years' play bagged only 29! Times change!

Uninvited? Disgusted Flemming Delfs—who had beaten Luan Jin only a week before?

Dispute! Referee Frank Wilson conscripted Mike Tredgett to test shuttles after a Jolly–Kihlstrom argument.

Results

Men's Singles Luan Jin (Ch) beat P Padukone (Ind) 15–9, 15–8.

Ladies' Singles Zhang Ailing (Ch) beat L Köppen (D) 11–6, 11–12, 11–6.

Men's Doubles M Tredgett and M Dew beat T Kihlstrom and S Karlsson (S) 15–9, 2–15, 15–10.

Ladies' Doubles Liu Xia and Zhang Ailing (Ch) beat Y Yonekura (J) and G Gilks 15–10, 3–15, 15–6.

Mixed Doubles M Tredgett and N Perry beat M Frost Hansen and L Köppen (D) 15–5, 15–5.

Commonwealth Games

Commonwealth Games 1966
Kingston, Jamaica

The Kingston Arena was specially built at a cost of £500 000.

Temperatures soared above 100°F *38°C.*

Jamaican players had been trained for weeks before the Games as linesmen and umpires.

Colin Beacom was the only English player to come home without a medal.

Results

Men's Singles Tan Aik Huang (M) beat Yew Cheng Hoe (M) 15–8, 15–8.

Ladies' Singles A Bairstow beat S Whittaker (C) 11–5, 11–3.

Men's Doubles Tan Aik Huang (M) and Yew Cheng Hoe (M) beat Ng Boon Bee (M) and Tan Yee Khan (M) 15–8, 15–5.

Ladies' Doubles J Horton and U Smith beat A Bairstow and I Rogers 15–7, 15–7.

Mixed Doubles R Mills and A Bairstow beat A Jordan and J Horton 7–15, 15–9, 15–12.

Commonwealth Games 1970
Edinburgh, Scotland

England won ten out of the fifteen medals.

Canadian Jamie Paulson sank to his knees in emotion on winning the Singles; his coach Thailander Ratanasaengsuang permitted himself a gentle smile.

Ladies' semi-finalists: Miss Tan and Miss Ng; Men's finalists: Tan and Ng. Not related!

J J McCarry (Referee) 'of the lugubrious voice'

earned umpires' gratitude by announcing their names as well as those of the players.

Results

Men's Singles J Paulson (C) beat P E Whetnall 10–15, 15–13, 15–10.

Ladies' Singles M Beck beat G Perrin 3–11, 11–3, 11–8.

Men's Doubles Ng Boon Bee and Gunalan (M) beat Tan Soon Hooi and Ng Tat Wei (M) 15–3, 15–3.

Ladies' Doubles M Boxall and S Whetnall beat G Perrin and J Rickard 15–9, 15–2.

Mixed Doubles D Talbot and M Boxall beat R Mills and G Perrin 8–15, 15–12, 15–12.

Commonwealth Games 1974
Christchurch, New Zealand

English players won four of the five 'Golds' and four of the five 'Silvers'. All ten members of the team won either 'Gold' or 'Silver'.

Paul Whetnall damaged the Achilles tendon sheath whilst beating Tan Aik Mong (M) and could offer only token resistance to Jamie Paulson (C) in the next round. And had to scratch in the Mixed.

The Prince of Wales attended the Men's Doubles final and found it 'a real education'.

Gillian Gilks won 'Triple Gold'.

Ray Stevens contracted chicken-pox but recovered in time to play.

Results

Men's Singles P Gunalan (M) beat J Paulson (C) 15–1, 15–6.

Ladies' Singles G Gilks beat M Beck 11–8, 11–8.

Men's Doubles D Talbot and E Stuart beat R Stevens and M Tredgett 15–6, 6–15, 15–11.

Ladies' Doubles M Beck and G Gilks beat S Whetnall and M Boxall 15–7, 15–5.

Mixed Doubles D Talbot and G Gilks w.o. P Whetnall and N Gardner scratched.

> *The English team's plane en route to South Africa in 1948 was grounded on the Equator at Entebbe for a 4-day repair. Hitching a lift in a freighter, they found the only other passenger was a corpse.*

Commonwealth Games 1978

Edmonton, Canada

Herbert Scheele escorted the Queen to her car at the end of the Opening Day.

David Eddy was forced to withdraw because of mumps—caught from his own children. He was awarded not a Gold Medal but a digestive biscuit on the Terry Wogan Show.

'Come on, Canada!' greeted England's Ann Statt every time she served to a Canadian player. Shades of Jakarta jingoism!

Nora Perry, service faulted several times, was refused explanation by the service judge. Team Captain John Havers asked for a replacement—and got it.

In the key match, Talbot v Czich (C), the latter, despite the umpire's appeal for quiet, asked the crowd for support—and got it thunderously. Ice-cool, Talbot won despite shedding a shoe in the final rally.

Play was held in the Ice Arena but heat and humidity turned it into a sauna.

Results

Men's Singles	Prakash Padukone (Ind) beat D Talbot 15–9, 15–8.
Ladies' Singles	Sylvia Ng (M) beat Katherine Teh (M) 11–5, 11–3.
Men's Doubles	R Stevens and M Tredgett beat F L Moo and T B Ong (M) 15–10, 15–5.
Ladies' Doubles	N Perry and A Statt beat C Backhouse and J Youngberg (C) 10–15, 15–5, 15–12.
Mixed Doubles	M Tredgett and N Perry beat W Gilliland and J Flockhart (Sco) 15–7, 15–7.

Commonwealth Games 1982

Brisbane, Australia

Frank Shannon, Scotland team captain, found the Aussie crowd 'very partisan'.

The team event was divided into two groups:
1 Scotland, India, Australia, Northern Ireland, Kenya and England.
2 Canada, New Zealand, Hong Kong, Isle of Man, Zimbabwe and Malaysia.

In winning the team event England set up a new record by winning all seven ties, 5–0.

England's No 1, Steve Baddeley, notched up a temperature of 103°F *39°C* on the opening day. Staggered through one game and then had to retire to hospital with a temperature of 105°F *41°C*.

Gillian Clark and Karen Beckman must have been dazzled by 'Gold'. In the final against Johanne Falardeau and Claire Backhouse, having won the first game, they were 13–8 up in the second. Only to lose the match—and title!

Karen Beckman and Duncan Bridge were first ever sister and brother partnership to reach the Mixed final.

Results

Men's Singles	S Modi (Ind) beat N Yates 7–15, 15–6, 15–5.
Ladies' Singles	H Troke beat S Podger 4–11, 11–3, 11–5.
Men's Doubles	R Sidek and B Ong (M) beat M Dew and N Yates 15–10, 17–15.
Ladies' Doubles	C Backhouse and J Falardeau (C) beat G Clark and K Beckman 12–15, 15–7.
Mixed Doubles	M Dew and K Chapman beat D Bridge and K Beckman 18–16, 15–3.

European Championships

The European Badminton Union was founded on 24 September 1967 at Frankfurt. Credit for it must be given to Herr Hubert Brohl in particular and to his association, the Deutscher Badminton Verband (West Germany) in general.

Founder members were Austria, Belgium, Czechoslovakia, Denmark, England, Finland, West Germany, Netherlands, Norway, Sweden and Switzerland. (Wales and Scotland merely 'indicated their approval').

Plans were immediately laid for the holding of European Championships, starting in April 1968 in West Germany and being held thereafter every second year at a different venue. Initially it was solely an individual championship. A Junior championship however was swiftly added the following year and team events in 1972 (Senior) and 1975 (Junior).

H P Kunz, Switzerland, was elected President of the Union whilst Stellan Mohlin and Hubert Brohl were added to the small committee of three to be responsible for the overall management of the Union.

One of the team leant against the emergency exit to put on his flannels. And suddenly found himself out in the street—distinctly underclothed.

European Individual Championships

Men's Singles

1968	S Johnsson (S)
1970	S Johnsson (S)
1972	W Bochow (GFR)
1974	S Johnsson (S)
1976	F Delfs (D)
1978	F Delfs (D)
1980	F Delfs (D)
1982	J P Nierhoff (D)

Ladies' Singles

1968	I Latz (GFR)
1970	E Twedberg (S)
1972	M Beck
1974	G Gilks
1976	G Gilks
1978	L Köppen (D)
1980	L Blumer (Swi)
1982	L Köppen (D)

Men's Doubles

1968	J D Eddy and R A Powell
1970	E Hansen and P Walsoe (D)
1972	W Braun and R Maywald (GFR)
1974	W Braun and R Maywald (GFR)
1976	R P Stevens and M Tredgett
1978	R P Stevens and M Tredgett
1980	C Nordin and S Karlsson (S)
1982	S Karlsson and T Kihlstrom (S)

Ladies' Doubles

1968	M B Boxall and S Whetnall
1970	M B Boxall and S Whetnall
1972	G Gilks and J Hashman
1974	G Gilks and M Beck
1976	G Gilks and S Whetnall
1978	N Perry and A Statt
1980	N Perry and J Webster
1982	G Gilks and G Clark

Mixed Doubles

1968	A D Jordan and S Whetnall
1970	J D Eddy and S Whetnall
1972	D Talbot and G Gilks
1974	D Talbot and G Gilks
1976	D Talbot and G Gilks
1978	M Tredgett and N Perry
1980	M Tredgett and N Perry
1982	M Dew and G Gilks

Supremo Judy Hashman (just sacked by the BA of E!) in the midst of her victorious England team, 1978 European Team Championships winners. Standing: Ray Stevens, Mike Tredgett, Maurice Robinson (coach), Judy Hashman, Derek Talbot. Kneeling: Karen Bridge, Jane Webster, Nora Perry. Sitting: Barbara Sutton, Ann Statt.

European Team Championships

Seniors

1968 Bochum—*No Competition*
1970 Port Talbot—*No Competition*
1972 Karlskrona—1 England, 2 Denmark
1974 Vienna—1 England, 2 Denmark
1976 Dublin—1 Denmark, 2 England
1978 Preston—1 England, 2 Denmark
1980 Groningen—1 Denmark, 2 England
1982 Boblingen—1 England, 2 Sweden

Juniors

1969 Voorburg (Holland)
1971 Gottwaldov (Czechoslovakia) } No team event held
1973 Edinburgh
1975 Copenhagen—1 Denmark, 2 England
1977 Ta Qali (Malta)—1 England, 2 Denmark
1979 Mulheim (GFR)—1 Denmark, 2 England
1981 Edinburgh—1 Denmark, 2 England, 3 Sweden
1983 Helsinki—1 England, 2 Denmark

European Junior Individual Championships

Boys' Singles

1969 F Delfs (D)
1971 R Ridder (N)
1973 J Helledie (D)
1975 B Wackfeldt (S)
1977 A Goode
1979 J P Nierhoff (D)
1981 M Kjeldsen (D)
1983 K Thomsen (D)

Girls' Singles

1969 A Berglund (D)
1971 A Berglund (D)
1973 M Nyhre (D)
1975 P Nielsen (D)
1977 K Bridge
1979 K Larsen (D)
1981 H Troke
1983 H Troke

Boys' Doubles

1969 K P Arthur and R P Stevens
1971 P J Gardner and J C Stretch
1973 S Karlsson and W Nilsson (S)
1975 B Wackfeldt and G Sterner (S)
1977 U Johansson and S Carlsson (S)
1979 Antonsson and P Isaaksson (S)
1981 M Kjeldsen and M Christiansen (D)
1983 C Rees and L Williams (W)

Girls' Doubles

1969 J van Beusekom and M Luesken (N)
1971 A Berglund and L Köppen (D)
1973 A Forrest and K Whiting
1975 L Gottsche and L B Pedersen (D)
1977 K Bridge and K Puttick
1979 S Leadbeater and G Clark
1981 D Kjaer and N Nielsen (D)
1983 J Shipman and L Chapman

Mixed Doubles

1969 G Perneklo and K Lindquist (S)
1971 P J Gardner and B Giles
1973 J Helledie and S Johansen (D)
1975 T Stokes and K Puttick
1977 N Tier and K Puttick
1979 J P Nierhoff and C Pilgaard (D)
1981 D Tailor and M Leeves
1983 A Nielsen and G Paulsen (D)

Olympic Games Demonstration

Badminton, ever since it cast off the swaddling clothes of battledore and shuttlecock and became recognised as an energetic and skilful racket game in its own right, has gazed enviously at the slopes of Mount Olympus.

In 1972 it came nearest to fulfilling its ambition when it was staged in ill-fated Munich as a demonstration sport. Twenty-five players from 11 major badminton nations, under the auspices of the Deutscher Badminton Verband and the IBF played before large and appreciative audiences.

But it was not enough. With the advent of Open Badminton, the IBF, ever hopeful, left the door ajar in its regulations so that those who preferred amateur glory to professional profit could walk proudly through it should the invitation ever come. It never did. Nor with the huge growth of the Games and their cost does it seem likely to do so. The IBF/WBF split certainly did not help badminton's cause.

Results

Men's Singles R Hartono (I) beat S Pri (D) 15–6, 15–1.

Ladies' Singles N Nakayama (J) beat U Dewi (I) 11–5, 11–3.

Men's Doubles Chandra and Christian (I) beat Ng Boon Bee and P Gunalan (M) 15–4, 2–15, 15–11.

Mixed Doubles D Talbot and G Gilks beat S Pri and U Strand (D) 15–6, 18–16.

FIRST OLYMPIC BADMINTON DEMONSTRATION
Munich 1972 IBF

Nordic Games

Men's Singles

1962 K A Nielsen (D)
1963 K A Nielsen (D)
1964 E Kops (D)
1965 E Kops (D)
1966 E Kops (D)
1967 E Kops (D)
1968 E Kops (D)
1969 S Johnsson (S)
1970 J Mortensen (D)
1971 S Pri (D)
1972 S Johnsson (S)
1973 S Pri (D)
1974 S Pri (D)
1975 S Johnsson (S)
1976 F Delfs (D)
1977 S Pri (D)
1978 M Frost (D)
1979 M Frost (D)
1980 M Frost (D)
1981 M Frost (D)
1982 M Frost (D)

Ladies' Singles

1962 K Jorgensen (D)
1963 U Rasmussen (D)
1964 U Rasmussen (D)
1965 U Rasmussen (D)
1966 U Strand (D)
1967 E Twedberg (S)
1968 J Föge (D)
1969 I R Nielsen (D)
1970 L von Barnekow (D)
1971 E Twedberg (S)
1972 E Twedberg (S)
1973 L Köppen (D)
1974 L Köppen (D)
1975 L Köppen (D)
1976 L Köppen (D)
1977 L Köppen (D)
1978 L Köppen (D)
1979 L Köppen (D)
1980 L Köppen (D)
1981 L Köppen (D)
1982 N Nielsen (D)

Men's Doubles

1962 B Glans and G Wahlquist (S)
1963 K A Nielsen and H Borch (D)
1964 O Mertz and J Sandvad (D)
1965 E Kops and K Kaagaard (D)
1966 E Kops and H Borch (D)
1967 E Kops and H Borch (D)
1968 S Pri and P Walsoe (D)
1969 S Pri and P Walsoe (D)
1970 S Pri and P Walsoe (D)
1971 S Pri and P Walsoe (D)
1972 S Pri and P Petersen (D)
1973 E Hansen and F Delfs (D)
1974 S Pri and P Petersen (D)
1975 T Kihlstrom and B Fröman (S)
1976 T Kihlstrom and B Fröman (S)
1977 T Kihlstrom and B Fröman (S)
1978 F Delfs and S Skovgaard (D)
1979 T Kihlstrom and B Fröman (S)
1980 M Frost and S Fladberg (D)
1981 M Frost and S Fladberg (D)
1982 M Frost and S Fladberg (D)

Ladies' Doubles

1962 U Rasmussen and K Jorgensen (D)
1963 U Rasmussen and K Jorgensen (D)
1964 L von Barnekow and P Molgaard Hansen (D)
1965 U Rasmussen and K Jorgensen (D)
1966 U Strand and K Jorgensen (D)
1967 U Strand and L von Barnekow (D)
1968 A Flindt and P Molgaard Hansen (D)
1969 A Flindt and P Molgaard Hansen (D)
1970 A Flindt and P Molgaard Hansen (D)
1971 A Flindt and P Molgaard Hansen (D)
1972 L Köppen and A Berglund (D)
1973 U Strand and P Kaagaard (D)
1974 L Köppen and I R Nielsen (D)
1975 L Köppen and I Borgstrom (D)
1976 L Köppen and P Nielsen (D)
1977 L Köppen and I Borgstrom (D)
1978 L Köppen and S Berg (D)
1979 L Köppen and I Bergstrom (D)
1980 L Köppen and P Nielsen (D)
1981 L Köppen and P Nielsen (D)
1982 N Nielsen and D Kjaer (D)

Mixed Doubles

1962 P E Nielsen and U Rasmussen (D)
1963 H Borch and U Rasmussen (D)
1964 F Kobbero and U Rasmussen (D)
1965 E Kops and U Rasmussen (D)
1966 P Walsoe and U Strand (D)
1967 E Kops and U Strand (D)
1968 P E Nielsen and P Molgaard Hansen (D)
1969 P Walsoe and P Molgaard Hansen (D)
1970 S Pri and U Strand (D)
1971 P Walsoe and P Kaagaard (D)
1972 E Hansen and U Strand (D)
1973 E Hansen and U Strand (D)
1974 E Hansen and P Kaagaard (D)
1975 S Skovgaard and L Köppen (D)
1976 S Skovgaard and L Köppen (D)
1977 S Skovgaard and L Köppen (D)
1978 S Skovgaard and L Köppen (D)
1979 S Skovgaard and L Köppen (D)
1980 S Skovgaard and L Köppen (D)
1981 S Skovgaard and L Köppen (D)
1982 S Skovgaard and H Adsbol (D)

Lene Köppen won the Nordic Triple Crown seven times in succession, making 25 titles in all.

Thomas Kihlstrom overcame Flemming Delfs in the 1980 Nordic Championships after 75 minutes—and 45 shuttles.

*Eight/*The Team Events

Thomas Cup

	Year	Competing Nations	Result	Venue
1st	1948–49	10	Malaya 8 Denmark 1	Preston, England
2nd	1951–52	12	Malaya 7 USA 2	Singapore
3rd	1954–55	21	Malaya 8 Denmark 1	Singapore
4th	1957–58	19	Indonesia 6 Malaya 3	Singapore
5th	1960–61	19	Indonesia 6 Thailand 3	Jakarta
6th	1963–64	26	Indonesia 5 Denmark 4	Tokyo
7th	1966–67	23	Malaysia 6 Indonesia 3	Jakarta
8th	1969–70	25	Indonesia 7 Malaysia 2	Kuala Lumpur
9th	1972–73	23	Indonesia 8 Denmark 1	Jakarta
10th	1975–76	26	Indonesia 9 Malaysia 0	Bangkok
11th	1978–79	21	Indonesia 9 Denmark 0	Jakarta
12th	1981–82	24	China 5 Indonesia 4	London

In 1939, just 5 years after the formation of the IBF which by now had 15 members, Sir George Thomas, Bart, its President, felt the time was ripe to moot an international men's championship. More, he offered to give a trophy.

The idea and the offer were eagerly accepted but before detailed plans could be made, the eruption of War shattered all such hopes. Nevertheless, the trophy was made and presented by Sir George to Vice-President A D Prebble, on 3 July 1940.

The famous Thomas Cup and its even more famous donor, Sir George Thomas, Bart.

The cup, by Atkin Bros of London, is of hammered silver-gilt. It stands 28 in *71 cm* high with a span including the handles of 16 in *40 cm*. It is made in three pieces, plinth, cup and lid; a figure of a player, static, surmounts the latter. On the back and on the plinth there is space for winners' names.

In 1946, at the first AGM since 1940, plans were laid for the first competition to be held in 1948–9. In deference to the donor the venue decided upon was England. Sir George himself made the draw of the ten entrants and presented the trophy at Preston's Queen's Hall to an elated Malayan team.

The competition's format of five men's singles and four men's doubles, played over two evenings, has not changed. Nor has it altered from being a triennial event though proposals to make it biennial have been rejected, largely on grounds of cost. Ireland's A G Trapnell did suggest that both Thomas and Uber Cups be replaced by a mixed team event: 'It would be more economical and more interesting' he maintained. His idea was rejected but the IBF are perhaps resurrecting it in the currently proposed World Team event.

Two major changes, however, have taken place. The finals may no longer be played twice successively in the winner's country. Had this proviso not been made the Cup might well have taken permanent root in Jakarta so heavily does its steamy climate favour the Indonesians. And the challenge round, in which the holders played their sole match against the winner of the inter-zone finals, was abolished after the 1966–7 series. Now, the holders and the host nation are exempt until the inter-zone ties.

Nations are divided into four zones: Pan American, Asian (two sections, East and West); Australasian, and European. Where there are 6–12 entrants, the finalists in the previous competition are exempt until the semi-final; if more than 12, then all four semi-finalists are exempt until the quarter-finals. To the four winners are added the host nation and the holders who participate in the inter-zone ties.

Play on the whole has been in the sporting spirit generally inherent in badminton and doubtless wished for by Sir George. Unfortunate incidents, however, have occurred three times; in each case, Asian countries, where fanatical partisanship and national prestige spark off an indescribable bedlam in a jam-packed stadium, were involved.

In 1964, the Danes were barracked and distracted by a claque of Indonesian students in Tokyo who helped their country through to a 5–4 victory. In 1967, spectator disturbance at Jakarta was so great when Indonesia were on the brink of defeat by Malaysia that the match was abandoned and Indonesia conceded the re-arranged tie. In 1970, the boot was on the other foot: Indonesia's protest as to unfair conditions when playing Thailand in the Western Section final of the Asian Zone was upheld—and it was Thailand, under protest, who conceded.

England's record makes sad reading. Never yet has she won even the European Zone with its right to participate in the inter-zone ties. On five occasions she has lost in the final to the might of little Denmark. And on six occasions she has perished earlier to Denmark (2), Sweden (2), West Germany and even South Africa. None of the other Home Countries has ever reached the final.

Stop Press. The IBF have proposed that the Thomas and Uber Cup competitions be held jointly in 1984 and every 2 years thereafter. The nine-match format will be changed to 5, i.e. 3 singles and 2 doubles. Zones will be abolished but 3 qualifying events will be held in different parts of the world. From these 8 countries will fight out the final ties.

First Thomas Cup 1948–9

In the European Zone, Denmark showed complete mastery with 9–0 victories over Ireland, Sweden, and, in the final, England. In the Pan-American Zone, USA beat Canada 8–1 whilst Malaya, in the Pacific Zone, passed through unopposed.

The inter-zone ties were played on the courts of the country which had first envisaged the competition—England. USA met Malaya at the Kelvin Hall, Glasgow, neither side ever having played or even met any of the other's team. Dave Freeman beat both Wong Peng Soon and Ooi Teik Hock but the fast-hitting, aggressive Malayan pairs took all four doubles—and so the match 6–3. In his game against Wong, Freeman incredibly moved from 4–4 to 15–4, 14–0 (15–1) thus dropping only one point in 26.

In the final tie, played at Queen's Hall, Preston, Malaya were even more convincing. When the draw had been made from Wynn Rogers' Stetson hat, Wong Peng Soon had been omitted because of an arm injury suffered before the USA match. Later, when his injury was found to be less severe, Denmark sportingly agreed to his inclusion—but regulations did not permit it. Law Teik Hock's deception and a slightly slippery floor led to Skaarup's downfall from 3–0 to 5–15, 0–15 in just 21 minutes, and to a 4–0 Malayan lead. This they capitalised to 8–1, only the 19-year-old Jutlander Mogens Felsby winning a game.

Sir George Thomas presented the cup to the Malayan Team Captain Lim Chuan Geok and personal gifts of medals to all players and officials. Immediately these two were besieged by autograph hunters, the latter on all fours in the centre of the court.

Inter-Zone Final Tie

Malaya 8—Denmark 1
At the Queen's Hall, Preston, on 25 and 26 February. Scores (Malayan names first):
Singles: Law Teik Hock beat J Skaarup, 15–5, 15–0; lost to M Felsby, 11–15, 1–15. Ooi Teik Hock beat Felsby, 15–9, 15–2; beat Skaarup, 14–18, 15–13, 15–9. Ong Poh Lim beat P Holm, 17–14, 15–8.
Doubles: Yeoh Teck Chye and Chan Kon Leong beat P Holm and I Olesen, 15–4, 15–6; beat J Skaarup and P Dabelsteen, 15–2, 15–4. Teoh Seng Khoon and Ooi Teik Hock beat Skaarup and Dabelsteen, 15–11, 15–10; beat Holm and Olesen, 15–6, 15–7.

Second Thomas Cup 1951–2

In the first inter-zone tie, India v Denmark, the latter started at a great disadvantage. A cancelled flight from Bangkok caused a three-day delay so they arrived only 8 hours before their match, to be played in stifling heat and with shuttles faster than the slow ones to which they were accustomed. As a result Poul Holm and Jorn Skaarup, both All-England Champions, each lost two singles, for India to gain a surprise 6–3 victory.

In the second inter-zone tie, the Final, played in the Happy World Stadium (105°F *41°C*) before 8500 delirious fans, it was India's turn to be on the receiving end. 1–4 down to the USA, they fought back magnificently to 4–4. And in the final match Seth and Guha were 15–6, 8–2 up before FBI man Joe Alston, exhausted by a gruelling singles, and Wynn Rogers bravely rallied to give America the edge.

In the Challenge Round between holders Malaya and USA, the ventilating system broke down. Not only were tickets at a premium on the black market but also hand-fans. America, already bereft of Dave Freeman who had retired, suffered a severe blow when Joe Alston was refused an extension of leave. Again in stifling conditions they fought gallantly but were beaten by a better team.

Martin Mendez extended Wong Peng Soon in the second game and defeated Ooi Teik Hock who retired with cramp at one game each. Wynn Rogers and Alston's replacement, Robert Williams, gained a meritorious win over Malayan champions Chan Kon Leong and Abdullah Piruz, and, 12–10 up in the third, took Ismail Bin Marjan and Ong Poh Lim to the limit.

Tremendous Press coverage ensured packed houses that recouped all travelling expenses. Organisation by Mr Loke Wan Tho, a millionaire ex-Oxford honours graduate was superb; it even included US Team Manager Ken Davidson's famous comedy act.

Challenge Round

Malaya 7—USA 2

At Singapore on 31 May and 1 June. Scores (Malayan names first):

Singles: Wong Peng Soon beat A M Mendez, 15–1, 15–10; beat R Mitchell, 15–8, 15–5. Ooi Teik Hock beat Mitchell, 15–9, 15–11; lost to Mendez, 15–11, 10–15, retired. Ong Poh Lim beat R Williams, 15–1, 15–6.

Doubles: Chan Kon Leong and Abdullah Piruz lost to W Rogers and R Williams, 15–9, 16–18, 9–15; beat C Loveday and R Mitchell, 15–2, 15–2. Ong Poh Lim and Ismail bin Marjan beat Loveday and Mitchell, 15–5, 15–4; beat Rogers and Williams, 15–12, 13–15, 15–12.

Third Thomas Cup 1954–5

All inter-zone ties were played in Singapore's new Badminton Hall before 8000 spectators who produced record gate receipts.

After 2–2 on the first evening, America's Joe Alston, 15–7, 9–7 up against India's Nandu Natekar, uncharacteristically went to pieces to lose the key match. T N Seth (Ind) clinched the issue (6–3) by defeating R B Mitchell who twice fought back unavailingly from 1–7.

Against Denmark, Australia won only one game when Don Murray beat Finn Kobbero 15–9 only to be smartly rapped 2–15 in the third.

Denmark were 4–1 up in the singles in the Final tie against India. Eilersten and Mertz (D) lost both doubles but Kobbero and Hammergaard Hansen

(D) compensated handsomely dropping only 28 points in 4 games (6–3).

In the opening game of the Challenge Round, Eddy Choong set the pace by beating Kobbero (D) 6 and 4. Wong Peng Soon although 1–4 down took the first game 15–5 from Jorn Skaarup (D) and was 3–12 down in the second before rallying to 13 all only to lose 16–18. In the third an exhausted Skaarup lost 4–15.

Kobbero raised Danish hopes by taking his first game against Wong from 8–12 to 15–12 only to reap the whirlwind 0–15, 7–15.

Denmark's only success was a men's doubles victory in which Hammergaard Hansen weakly supported by a weary Kobbero smashed his way to victory.

The trophy was presented to Malayan captain Wong Peng Soon by Sir George Thomas who travelled to and from Malaya by sea. He in turn was presented with a tea-set on a tray engraved with the names of all players and officials.

Challenge Round

Malaya 8—Denmark 1

At Singapore on 4 and 5 June. Scores (Malayan names first):

Singles: E B Choong beat F Kobbero, 15–6, 15–4; beat J Skaarup, 15–10, 15–9. Wong Peng Soon beat Skaarup, 15–5, 16–18, 15–4; beat Kobbero, 12–15, 15–0, 15–7. Ong Poh Lim beat O Jensen, 15–10, 15–8.

Doubles: Lim Kee Fong and Tan Jin Eong beat O Eilertsen and O Mertz, 15–9, 15–3; lost to F Kobbero and J Hammergaard Hansen, 13–18, 15–4, 6–15. Ooi Teik Hock and Ong Poh Lim beat Kobbero and Hammergaard Hansen, 15–4, 15–8; beat Eilertsen and Mertz, 15–8, 15–1.

Fourth Thomas Cup 1957–8

Denmark having brushed England aside in the European Zone for the loss of just two doubles had to face new entrants Indonesia in the inter-zone tie in Singapore. But the cream of Europe, with Kobbero's brilliance unhappily discounted by a lack lustre display by Erland Kops after a too long sea voyage, could not match them. To the known genius of Ferry Sonneville was added that of unknown 19-years-old Tan Joe Hok whilst Tan King Gwan and Njoo Kiem Bie started a doubles

George Thomas reached the semi-final of the 1900 All-England Men's Doubles within three months of taking up the game.

run of success unbroken throughout the ties save for a single defeat—and that caused by injury.

In the other inter-zone tie, Thailand, with few players and fewer clubs, beat USA 7–2. The latter were without Dave Freeman; Joe Alston had retired from singles, and Wynn Rogers was now in the veteran class. But in Jim Poole they had a class player who had beaten Kobbero, and in Ron Palmer, a superbly fit and stylish newcomer.

In the Final, Indonesia won all the singles without dropping a game and cantered home 8–1 against near neighbour Thailand.

And, incredibly, in the Challenge Round, the Malayan holders could not win even one single! Sadly, Eddy Choong, hero of so many All-Englands, who had given the game so much and asked so little, on this, his farewell appearance, was shamefully barracked. Indonesia's Tan Joe Hok and Ferry Sonneville played superlative singles but together lost both doubles (the last 1–15, 1–15) whilst Malaya's veterans Choong and Ooi Teik Hock renewed past glories with two wins. But it was not enough to prevent the first of Indonesia's many victories, 6–3, on their first appearance in the competition.

Challenge Round

Indonesia 6—Malaya 3

At Singapore on 14 and 15 June. Scores (Indonesian names first):

Singles: F A Sonneville beat E B Choong, 15–12, 15–4; beat Teh Kew San, 13–15, 15–13, 18–16. Tan Joe Hok beat Teh Kew San, 18–14, 15–4; beat Choong, 15–11, 15–6. E Yusuf beat A Piruz, 6–15, 15–10, 15–8.

Doubles: Tan King Gwan and Njoo Kiem Bie beat H A Heah and Lim Say Hup, 7–15, 15–5, 18–15; lost to E B Choong and Ooi Teik Hock, 15–13, 9–15, retired. Tan Joe Hok and F A Sonneville lost to Choong and Ooi Teik Hock, 15–18, 5–15; lost to Heah and Lim Say Hup, 1–15, 1–15.

Fifth Thomas Cup 1960–1

In the European Zone Final, Denmark did a 9–0 demolition job on England. In the Asian Zone—sensation! Thailand, without masters Charoen Wattanasin and Thanoo Khajadbhye, fielded a completely new team—average age 19. Against three-time winners Malaya they lost the first match—but took the next six (7–2). The scoring for this tie was done in Thai, not the customary English.

All inter-zone ties were played in the magnificent Senayan Hall in Jakarta, specially designed and built for badminton.

Thailand continued victoriously (9–0) against the Australians who garnered only 37 points from 10 singles games. Denmark beat USA (7–2) with rather more trouble than the score suggests but wilted by the reverse score against Thailand in the final tie.

Indonesian umpires and linesmen were accepted by the Thais for the Challenge Round as, due to late notification, Malayan officials had not arrived. Indonesia (2–1 up) seemed certainties when Tan King Gwan and Njook Kiem Bie were leading 15–12, 14–4 up. At this point, the latter became so ill that he could only stagger round the court unable even to hit the shuttle. The Thais snatched the game out of the fire 17–14—and the match, for Njook then retired. So 2–2!

Then Yusuf (I) beat Bhornchima in a gamesmanship 'circus', Tan Joe Hok (I) executed Boonyasukhanonda 2 and 5 whilst Sonneville, as ever, rose to the Thomas Cup occasion. So at 5–2, proceedings came to an abrupt if temporary halt as Acting President Dr Djuanda presented the trophy, hitherto under armed guard, to Indonesian non-playing captain, Lt Col Muljoeno in front of a swarming mass of cheering spectators amid scenes of unprecedented enthusiasm. Not surprisingly, the remaining doubles were of purely academic interest.

Challenge Round

Indonesia 6—Thailand 3

At Jakarta on 10 and 11 June. Scores (Indonesian names first):

Singles: Tan Joe Hok beat Channarong Ratanasaengsuang, 15–9, 15–5; beat Somsook Boonyasukhanonda, 15–2, 15–5. F A Sonneville beat Boonyasukhanonda, 15–3, 15–11; beat Ratanasaengsuang, 15–9, 15–4. E Yusuf beat Narong Bhornchima, 18–14, 15–7.

Doubles: Tan Joe Hok and Lie Po Djian lost to Narong Bhornchima and Raphi Kanchanaraphi, 7–15, 13–15; beat Chavalert Chumkum and Chucart Vatanatham, 15–5, 13–15, 18–17. Tan King Gwan and Njoo Kiem Bie lost to Chumkum and Vatantham, 15–12, 14–17, retired. Tan King Gwan and F A Sonneville (sub) lost to Bhornchima and Kanchananaraphi, 13–15, 15–13, 5–15.

Sixth Thomas Cup 1963–4

A record 26 entries saw several nations entering in zones distant from their own to help further their hopes of reaching the inter-zone ties. Pakistan in European, Malaya in Australasian, Japan in Pan-American. In the latter group, Mexico, playing Japan, suspended their own No 1 singles player, S A Fraustro, and replaced him in his two remaining matches.

England, now almost as by habit, succumbed weakly (1–8) to Denmark. And so the latter, with Japan, Thailand and Malaya (coached by Eddy Choong) travelled to Tokyo and its echoing (often sparsely filled) 9000 seater Municipal Gymnasium. Denmark decisively beat Malaya (7–2) and, in the final, Thailand (6–3) to make them firm favourites for the Challenge Round against the Indonesian holders for whom Sonneville was ageing and Tan Joe Hok playing only sporadically.

Denmark for their part could boast All-England Singles Champions Knud Nielsen and Erland Kops as well as Hammergaard Hansen and Finn Kobbero who had been monarchs in the world of men's doubles for a decade. And the Tokyo climate was no tropical hothouse.

But Kops lost both singles; while the veteran Sonneville yet again rose to the occasion to win both his: that against Kops from 13–18, 6–14! Indonesia gained a completely unexpected 4–1 advantage in singles. One which even two doubles wins, one by the 'Great Danes' and one by Kops and Borch, could not wipe out.

Throughout, a claque of orchestrated Indonesian fanatics had perfervidly indulged in singing, flag-waving, feet-stamping—and flashlight photo-graphy—*only when facing the Danes*. Official appeals and even the arrival of siren-wailing police cars were ineffective.

This mob rule had risen to a crescendo in the vital men's doubles (4–3 to Indonesia) when the Danes, Kops and Borch won the first game. Play had to be abandoned for 20 minutes. On resumption, the Danes, concentration broken, lost 12–15, 6–15. The Cup was Indonesia's.

As David Bloomer in a superbly written im-partial *Gazette* account said, 'International bad-minton is not what it was. And, unless something is done by the IBF to stop organised hooliganism and a caterwauling atmosphere of anti-sportsman-ship, never again will be.'

(Mr Bloomer had flown at 24 hours' notice to Tokyo as IBF representative after Herbert Scheele, who should have officiated, had been suddenly taken ill at Jakarta.)

Challenge Round
Indonesia 5—Denmark 4
At Tokyo on 21 and 22 May. Scores (Indonesian names first):
Singles: Tan Joe Hok beat E Kops 5–15, 15–1, 15–9; lost to K A Nielsen 15–11, 14–17, 9–15. F A Sonneville beat Nielsen 12–15, 15–6, 15–6;

beat Kops 13–18, 17–14, 17–14. Ang Tjin Siang beat H Borch 15–10, 15–5.
Doubles: Tan King Gwan and A P Unang lost to F Kobbero and J Hammergaard Hansen 5–15, 6–15; beat E Kops and H Borch 12–15, 15–12, 15–6. F A Sonneville and Tutang Djamaludin lost to Kops and Borch 12–15, 2–15; lost to Kobbero and Hammergaard Hansen 14–17, 5–15.

Seventh Thomas Cup 1966–7
England and Denmark, by virtue of being the previous year's European zone finalists, received byes into the semi-final. There similarity ended. England perished ingloriously 3–6 to South Africa who had had a walkover when East Germany refused to play them on political grounds. Den-mark, 3–4 down, scraped home against Sweden 5–4, the narrowest margin ever between these two countries. Finally, Denmark beat South Africa (8–1).

Japan, Malaysia and USA coasted through meagre entries in the other Zones.

With tickets at a premium on the black market, 12 000 spectators jammed the Senayan Stadium for the first inter-zone clash.

Denmark arrived only 48 hours before the match but they had practised *en route* in Thailand. On the first night, they held Malaya 2–2 when Kops beat second string Yew Cheng Hoe, and Andersen (Pri) and Walsöe beat second string Tan Aik Huang and Teh Kew San. But on the second night the Danes failed to win a single match (7–2) in a 96°F oven.

In the other semi-final, Japan beat USA by a similar margin. The fitness of the Japanese (reported to have trained by playing singles for two hours without a break—or a drink) was exemplified by rubber-ball Ippei Kojima, a shuttle-chaser who bounced from net to base-line and made incredible defensive returns.

For the Americans, burly 35-year-old Jim Poole was accorded tremendous vocal support because of his indomitable determination and infectious enjoyment.

Malaysia had little difficulty overcoming Japan in the Final (6–3) to challenge holders Indonesia.

With 36-year-old Sonneville losing both his singles (and, sadly, being jeered off-court), Malay-sia ran up a seemingly indestructible lead 4–1.

Ooi Teik Hock and Teoh Seng Khoon never lost a Thomas Cup match—and also won the star-studded 1949 All-England.

On the second evening 17-year-old Rudy Hartono (formerly Nio) won his second single as comfortably as his first, and Muljadi beat a strangely hesitant Teh Kew San (4–3).

The trophy's fate now hinged on the Ng Boon Bee/Tan Yee Khan v Muljadi/Susanto match. The former were hot favourites and underlined the fact by racing to 15–2 in 11 minutes and then smashing on to 10–2. At this point, the crowd erupted as it had done in Tokyo. Worse, it deliberately jeered the Malaysians every time they were about to serve. Despite appeals by the Danish umpire Tom Bacher and the English referee Herbert Scheele the struggle sputtered on spasmodically amid pandemonium for the Indonesians to snatch the game 18–13 from the palpably distressed Malaysians.

At this stage Herbert Scheele, receiving no support from Indonesian officials, bravely called a halt to this travesty of badminton. And with the Indonesians refusing to restart the game behind closed doors or to go to neutral courts, the IBF later awarded the match 6–3 to Malaysia.

Challenge Round
Malaysia 6—Indonesia 3
At Jakarta on 9 and 10 June. Scores (Malaysian names first):
Singles: Yew Cheng Hoe beat F Sonneville 15–9, 15–7; lost to R Hartono 5–15, 9–15. Tan Aik Huang lost to Hartono 6–15, 8–15; beat Sonneville 15–4, 15–2. Teh Kew San lost to Muljadi (formerly Ang Tjin Siang) 15–18, 4–15.
Doubles: Tan Yee Khan and Ng Boon Bee beat A P Unang and Darmawan Supatera (formerly Tan King Gwan) 15–6, 15–7; V Muljadi and A Susanto 15–2, 13–18 abandoned. Tan Aik Huang and Teh Kew San beat Muljadi and Susanto 16–17, 15–6, 15–12.

Play abandoned in the eighth match. Subsequent decision of the IBF awarded the tie to Malaysia 6–3.

Eighth Thomas Cup 1969–70
Despite high hopes that England might reach the inter-zone ties for the first time ever, she succumbed, after beating Norway 9–0 and West Germany 7–2, for the sixth time to Denmark (3–6). Paul Whetnall defeated Erland Kops (England's only singles victory) and David Eddy and Derek Talbot won both their men's doubles but it was not enough against a sound Danish side that included a rampant Svend Pri. Nor could Sweden, who had beaten South Africa on neutral territory in Haarlem in a morning game behind locked doors

Tjun Tjun and Wahjudi (Indonesia): one of the greatest ever men's doubles pairs.

for fear of anti-apartheid demonstrations, make any impression on the Danes (1–8) in the final.

Meantime, sensation in the Asian zone. In Bangkok, Indonesia were 3–2 up against Thailand. At 12–12 in the sixth match, Muljadi (I) refused to carry on and the Indonesian team as a whole also declined to play as 'neither the conduct of the tie nor the spirit of the competition was as it should be'. Thailand thus took the tie 6–3. But a hastily convened IBF meeting in London upheld the Indonesian protest, set the score at 3–3, and ordered continuation in Japan (venue of the next round). Thailand declined—and Indonesia passed on narrowly to defeat Japan 5–4, largely thanks to Rudy Hartono winning all his four matches.

Prior to the inter-zone ties in the Negara Stadium at Kuala Lumpur it was agreed that, after the first game only, players could change clothing at the courtside. So great was the interest that even the Indonesian 9–0 massacres of New Zealand and Canada attracted gates of 10 000.

Meantime, after an 8 months' training camp

stint, Malaysia had had its share of drama against Denmark. Leading 3–1, Malaysia saw Abdul Rahman Mohamed winning 15–3, 9–3 against Henning Borch. The latter levelled at 13 all, when Rahman's stamina and nerve ran out simultaneously, and won 18–13. At 12–12 in the third, an exhausted Rahman scrambled to 14–12 only to be violently sick by the umpire's chair. Forced to continue, he did not score another point. So 3–2, 3–3, then 4–4. All hinged on the last match. But bounding Boon Bee and black panther Punch Gunalan were altogether too good for All-England winners Tom Bacher and Poul Petersen (5 and 2).

The final was played before the Sultans and Sultanahs of Kedah and Selangor, the Malaysian Prime Minister, and a packed house of badminton enthusiasts. But the issue was never in doubt. Hartono yet again won all four. And Malaysia's heralded 'Bold Gamble' of a singles reshuffle and the splitting of the brothers Tan by replacing Aik Mong by newcomer Ng Tat Wei failed. Muljadi, beating Rahman to bring the Cup back to Indonesia (5–1), was chaired round the arena by wildly enthusiastic supporters. The final score: 7–2.

Gate receipts amounted to M$271 832 (£36 734).

Final Round

Indonesia 7—Malaysia 2
At Kuala Lumpur on 5 and 6 June. Scores (Indonesian names first):
Singles: Muljadi beat P Gunalan 15–9, 15–5; beat Abdul Rahman Mohamed 15–5, 15–5. R Hartono beat Abdul Rahman 15–12, 15–2; beat Gunalan 17–16, 12–15, 15–3. Darmadi lost to Tan Aik Huang 12–15, 12–15.
Doubles: R Hartono and Indra Gunawan beat Tan Aik Huang and Ng Tat Wai 15–9, 15–11; beat Ng Boon Bee and P Gunalan 9–15, 17–16, 15–6. Indratno and Minjarti lost to Ng Boon Bee and Gunalan 7–15, 15–13, 10–15; beat Tan Aik Huang and Ng Tat Wei 10–15, 18–16, 15–10.

Ninth Thomas Cup 1972–3

England having beaten the Netherlands without the loss of a game unexpectedly succumbed to West Germany (4–5) in the last match of the tie after 1–4 down.

In the Australasian zone India had an equally exciting encounter with New Zealand. The brothers Ghoosh beat the brothers Purser to make it 4–4. And in a 13–18, 15–10, 15–12 game of 75 hectic minutes that finished just after midnight, Asif Parpia and Prakash Padukone finally carried the day for India.

In the Asian zone Malaysia beat Japan 5–4 when

their second string doubles pair beat Japan's first—to complete a tie that had lasted a record breaking 11 hours. In the American zone, Mexico achieved their first ever success in beating a USA team that included 40+ Jim Poole playing in his sixth Thomas Cup series.

The inter-zone first round match was another cliff-hanger for India. Prakash creeping up from 6–14 in the third wrested 10 match points from Canada's Jamie Paulson to set the pattern of India's four singles victories. But Canada's Jamie Paulson and Yves Pare (whose lively personality captured Indonesian hearts) and their two Thailanders, Channarong Ratanasaengsuang and Raphi Kanchanauraphi, took all four doubles—and the tie.

By contrast the semi-finals were one-sided. Thailand's only success was achieved by Bandid Jaiyen's granite defence exhausting Indonesia's veteran Muljadi (8–1). Denmark, thanks to Pri's consistency, Hansen's defence, Borch's accuracy and Delfs' stroke artistry gave Canada even shorter shrift (9–0).

12 000 eager fans packed the hall to see first blood for Indonesia in the Final. An apparently exhausted Muljadi found new reserves of strength to stave off Elo Hansen, the only Dane seemingly unaffected by the heat. But Pri, having thrown the second game, saved four match points after Hartono had stormed from 8–11 to 14–11 in one hand—and with calmness and pin-point smashing took a fine match, 17–15, after 73 minutes. But with Hansen ill and unable to play and Denmark's doubles pairs able to average only 6 points a game, it was their only victory.

So Indonesia won the Thomas Cup for the fifth time in six attempts—before a well-behaved audience.

Final Round

Indonesia 8—Denmark 1
At Jakarta on 2 and 3 June. Scores (Indonesian names first):
Singles: Muljadi beat E Hansen 15–6, 10–15, 15–10; beat S Pri 15–11, 15–1. R Hartono lost to Pri 12–15, 15–5, 15–17; w.o. Hansen retired. A Nurman beat F Delfs 11–15, 15–4, 15–4.
Doubles: Christian and Ade Chandra beat P Petersen and T Bacher 15–3, 15–6; beat S Pri and H

It was reported that after 'spinning' none of the four veterans could clearly see or feel 'rough' or 'smooth'. The racket had to be handed to a spectator!

Borch 15–2, 15–8. R Hartono and Tjun Tjun beat Pri and Borch 15–7, 15–6; beat Petersen and Bacher 15–11, 15–5.

Tenth Thomas Cup 1975–6

England in with a chance against bogeymen Danes? 2–2 at the end of the first evening thanks to a death or glory effort by Ray Stevens against Svend Pri, 15–11, 12–15, 15–11, only his second ever European zone defeat, and David Eddy (with Ed Sutton) maintaining his unbeaten Thomas Cup record. And that in defiance of a resurrected Per Walsoe's 'I wish to pronounce publicly that Eddie Sutton is serving overhand!' in reverberating, faultless English. But England could not stay the pace (3–6). And it was Denmark who, after a last game 5–4 defeat of Sweden, took the plane for Bangkok.

In the first round Thailand whitewashed a hesitant Canada (9–0). New Zealand on the other hand fought bravely if unavailingly against a young Malaysian team captained by Punch Gunalan (3–6).

In the second round, Pri set Denmark on a favourite's course. But Delfs was overcome by the heat and Denmark's doubles heavyweights Poul Petersen and Per Walsoe were out-punched by Malaysia's dancing lightweights, Soong and Chong. Again it was left to Pri, rising above heat and humidity, thriving on banter and barracking, to shepherd young Steen Skovgaard to victory—and 2–2.

The next evening Hansen lost his singles but the indomitable Pri won his (3–3). But in the stifling heat Delfs wilted again—and even Pri could not rise to a fourth victory. Delirious Malaysian supporters revelled in a 5–4 victory against the book.

In the other semi-final Hartono set the pace with a 15–1, 15–1 victory over a luckless Suharitadamrong. In a superb veteran's battle, Thailand's Bandid Jaiyen chastened extrovert Ie Sumirat but Tjun Tjun and Wahjudi breached Thailand's defences in a 16-minute blitzkrieg 15–0, 15–6 victory. And, unstoppable now, Indonesia smashed through 8–1.

So too in the Final. The Indonesian juggernaut

The Oxfordshire county team in 1968 consisted of J P Lord, D Barrett, C Ciniglio, J Warwick—and their wives. Also P Wills and C Saunders (brother of Mrs Barrett). And Mrs Wills was reserve!

brushed aside unavailing Malaysian resistance: 9–0, only a single game dropped—and that by carelessness.

Final Round

Indonesia 9—Malaysia 0

At Bangkok on 4 and 5 June. Scores (Indonesian names first):

Singles: Liem Swie King beat Phua Ah Hua 15–12, 15–1; beat Saw Swee Leong 18–13, 15–3. R Hartono beat Saw Swee Leong 15–7, 15–5; beat Phua Ah Hua 15–6, 15–1. Tjun Tjun beat J Selvaraj 15–1, 15–7.

Doubles: Ade Chandra and Christian Hadinata beat J Selvaraj and Moo Foot Lian 15–4, 15–1; beat Phua Ah Hua (sub) and Cheah Hong Chong 15–6, 15–11. Tjun Tjun and J Wahjudi beat D Soong and Cheah Hong Chong 13–15, 15–7, 15–6; beat Selvaraj and Moo Foot Lian 15–6, 15–2.

Eleventh Thomas Cup 1978–9

With Ray Stevens setting a cracking pace, 15–0, 10–0 (15–2) against Tony Dawson, England beat Scotland 9–0. A fine start for David Eddy entering his fifth series. Belgium suffered similar ignominy.

Stevens again set the scene against Sweden when after 70 minutes he overcame Kihlstrom 18–15, 3–15, 15–9. With the score 3–3, Kevin Jolly had no fewer than 13 hands at 13–8 against Stefan Karlsson—and lost 13–18. Other English pairs were similarly unable to clinch games that seemed well in hand. And so Sweden won 6–3— only to lose 2–7 to Denmark, winners of the European zone for the 11th time.

Politics wreaked havoc elsewhere. In the American zone, Mexico refused to play Taiwan so the latter withdrew to prevent exacerbation. And Mexico then gave Canada a walkover! In the Asian zone, Sri Lanka and Singapore, as members of the newly founded World Badminton Federation withdrew. Pakistan and Thailand vacillated interminably—and were scratched. India, defeating Malaysia, emerged from the chaos (5–4).

In the Jakarta inter-zone finals, the usual early massacres occurred. Japan dropped only one match to Canada (reputed to have had five sports psychologists in their squad to learn how to assess world class potential). Denmark, inspired by Pri's fantastic recovery in debilitating heat from 6–13 to 17–14, and 15–3 against Prakash, romped home against India, 7–2.

Against Japan's Zeniya, Liem Swie King from 9–14 pulled back 10 game points to win 17–16 and then rampant took the next 15–1. This in a sauna heat so intense that the Japanese invariably

Maestro Rudy Hartono (Indonesia) : the 'greatest'?

shuddered to a virtual standstill in the second game —completely out of steam (9–0).

In the Final, Ie Sumirat having won the vital battle of the veterans against Pri (11–15, 15–7, 15–10) indulged in frenetic star jumps before being joyously engulfed by the whole Indonesian entourage. In the next three matches, the rest of the Danes collected a bare 24 points! And whilst they did better the next day, the Danish giants Steen Skovgaard and Flemming Delfs were reduced to pygmy proportions by the heat. And fittingly it was Hartono who clinched the issue 5–0.

Vice-President Malik presented the Cup to the Indonesian Titans. And her vain challengers departed to the strains, incongruously clashed out by brisk majorettes on drums and cymbals, saxophones and xylophones, of 'Auld Lang Syne'.

Final Round

Indonesia 9—Denmark 0

At Jakarta, on 1 and 2 June. Scores (Indonesian names first):

Singles: I Sumirat beat S Pri 11–15, 15–7, 15–10; beat M Frost Hansen 11–15, 15–9, 15–9. Liem Swie King beat Frost Hansen 15–3, 15–6; beat Pri 15–8, 15–1. R Hartono beat F Delfs 15–10, 15–2.

Doubles: Tjun Tjun and Wahjudi beat S Skovgaard and F Delfs 15–2, 15–3; beat Frost Hansen and S Fladberg 15–9, 15–5. Christian and King beat Hansen and Fladberg 15–8, 15–2; beat Skovgaard and Delfs 17–16, 15–4.

Twelfth Thomas Cup 1981–2

The first time the Thomas Cup had been concluded outside Asia since the 1949 inaugural meeting.

In the European Zone, Scotland trounced both Austria and the Netherlands 9–0 before suffering the same fate against Denmark who went on to eclipse Sweden in the final 8–1.

Malaysia and Japan coasted through the Australasian and Pan-American zones. In the Asian zone West, China and India both gained 9–0 wins before clashing in another 9–0 fiasco—for China. In the East zone, Thailand beat Korea 7–2 but

> *Singapore, for its Thomas Cup match v Thailand, issued a programme in the shape of an outsize shuttle. Its stiff pages spread out to form a much-needed fan.*

went down by the same margin against China in the Zone Final.

In the inter-zone ties held in England, the latter, hitherto exempt as host nation, squeezed home 5–4 in the last match against three-time-holders Malaysia. Denmark beat Japan by a similarly narrow margin.

The semi-final clearly showed the shape of things to come. China acupunctured Danish pride 8–1 with Han Jian setting the pace with a 15–2, 15–1 annihilation of Steen Fladberg. Delfs and Skovgaard gained Denmark's only victory.

England suffered much the same fate. Swie King beat England's new No 1 Steve Baddeley by the odd score 11–15, 15–0, 15–9. Equally erratic was Kartono and Heryanto's 15–2, 2–15, 15–5 victory over the new pairing of Andy Goode and Ray Stevens. It was left to the last match for England's Mike Tredgett and Martin Dew to gain revenge and score their country's only victory 15–10, 15–1.

The final, graced by Her Majesty the Queen and Prince Philip, was perhaps the most exciting ever played. Indonesia on the first night had Swie King's singles and two closely fought three-game doubles under their belts to more than off-set the expected defeat of Pongoh (3–1).

On the second, Hartono fought bravely but predictably could not match Luan Jin's speed, stamina and power (3–2). Everything hinged on Swie King v Han Jian—Prince Philip, a one-time player himself, was deaf to his aide's whispers of another engagement. In a match of incredible defence and net play Han Jian—and China—inched home (3–3). Lius Pongoh played till he dropped—vainly (3–4).

In the key game (for a pair as powerful as Christian and Swie King were unlikely to yield to anything less than a barrage of thunderbolts) Sun Yian and Yao Ximing crept home 17–14 against Kartono and Heryanto, then somersaulted 3–15. Could the Chinese come back from a near knock-out? They did! In an incredible 5 minutes the Indonesians were whirlwinded to the canvas 15–1 (3–5).

The legend of Chinese impassivity was shattered! Magnificent play and sportsmanship in a perfect setting!

Final Round

China 5—Indonesia 4

At the Albert Hall, London, on 20 and 21 May. Scores (Chinese names first):

Chen Changjie lost to Liem Swie King 8–15, 13–15. Han Jian beat Lius Pongoh 15–5, 15–7. Luan Jin and Lin Jiangli lost to Kartono and Rudy

Top *At their first attempt, the Chinese narrowly wrested the Cup from holders and seven-time winners Indonesia.*

Above *1983 Thomas Cup final: the Queen is introduced to EBU's Emil ter Metz by IBF President Craig Reedie. Referee Frank Wilson looks on.*

Heryanto 8–15, 15–13, 9–15. Sun Zhian and Yao Ximing lost to Christian and Liem Swie King 10–15, 15–12, 8–15. Luan Jin beat Rudy Hartono 15–9, 1–15, 15–9. Han Jian beat Liem Swie King 15–12, 11–15, 17–14. Chen Changjie beat Lius Pongoh 18–17, 15–12. Sun Zhian and Yao Ximing beat Kartono and Rudy Heryanto 17–14, 3–15, 15–1. Luan Jin and Lin Jiangli lost to Christian and Liem Swie King 4–15, 11–15.

Badminton's Day of Shame

Badminton has long had a reputation for good sportsmanship. Many tournaments were played without linesmen—players could be relied upon to give their own scrupulously fair decisions. Even in county matches—with success and prestige hanging on the result—there were no umpires. Players faulted themselves if a shuttle grazed racket or hair, or if they touched the net; they even, often unnecessarily, penalised themselves by calling 'clean woods' as 'slings'. Crowds applauded brilliant play impartially; defeat was taken with good grace.

Badminton's saddest day was 10 June 1967. The scene: the Senayan Stadium in Djakarta. The occasion: the Challenge Round of the seventh Thomas Cup competition between Malaysia and Indonesia. The offenders: the 12 000 spectators watching it.

In some extenuation it should be stressed that Indonesians are volatile, without English phlegm or reserve. That they do not have a centuries old tradition of 'fair play', 'let the best man win', behind them. That, as a young emergent nation, victory in sport is essential national prestige, a symbol of their new-found freedom.

The inter-zone ties had been played before fervent but fair audiences. In Indonesia, visiting players have to learn to live with a bedlam of fiercely partisan applause not merely between rallies but often during them. Even the Indonesians' own idols once found to have feet of clay will be callously jeered off court.

On the last day of the Challenge Round the score was 3–3. With Ng Boon Bee and Tan Yee Khan 15–2, 10–2 up on Muljadi and Susanto, the Malaysians were poised for a break-through. Then things went sadly awry. Cheering reached storm intensity not on good play but on Malaysian errors. Rattled, the latter saw the score slide to 10–6. Now the crowd were on their feet, gesticulating, screaming, letting off flash-bulbs, but only when the *Malaysians* served. 13–11.

At this juncture, the Danish umpire, Tom Bacher, whose appeals for silence had met with no success, summoned the referee Herbert Scheele. He too was howled down.

Mr Scheele desperately tried to persuade a stalling Padmo Soemasto, President of the Indonesian BA, to leave his box and, in the crowd's own tongue, ask for fair play. But in vain. Meantime, the Indonesian pair had snatched the second 'stop-go' game 18–13 from the now thoroughly frightened Malaysians.

During the customary 5-minute interval, Mr Scheele asked for the hall to be cleared and play resumed behind locked doors. Mr Soemasto refused. And eventually smilingly announced the abandonment of play 'with the agreement of both teams and the Referee'. A statement patently untrue. Meantime, the court had been surrounded by military police.

Mr Scheele was hurriedly led to an ante-room —in which was a huge (6 ft × 4 ft *1.8 m × 1.2 m*) floral emblem bearing the words 'Indonesia Must Win'. Before leaving the hall, he again, unsuccessfully, urged resumption of play behind locked doors. Indeed the Indonesian team had left the hall, and the court was being swiftly dismantled. Indonesia had no intention of continuing play!

Then back to his hotel, with an escort of outriders. There, accompanied by two military policemen, he discussed the situation with court officials and the Malaysian captain. All, despite great inconvenience, were prepared to cancel flights to continue play behind locked doors the next day. Mr Soemasto visited the hotel at 1.30 am —but he refused to meet Mr Scheele.

At 5.30 am Mr Scheele was escorted by Ferry Sonneville to the airport. There he was handed an official letter of protest (*sic*) by the Indonesian non-playing captain Col Moljoeno.

10th June, 1967

Mr H A E Scheele
Honorary Referee Thomas Cup 1967
Djakarta.

Dear Sir,

1 We'd like to kindly advice you herewith that the Indonesian team strongly protest against the decision taken by the Honorary Referee, to stop the Challenge Round matches, on June 10th which was being played between the Malaysian and Indonesian team at Djakarta.

2 As the decision to stop all matches was officially taken by the Referee, while there was not any protest from the participating teams, the whole matter should entirely be the responsibility of the Honorary Referee himself.

3 We'd also like to draw the attention, that the decision was taken at a moment when the Indonesia team was at a crescendo line and beginning in gaining advantage.

4 Thanking you in advance for your attenties we are,

Yours sincerely,

(Signed) Moljoeno

Moeljoeno Col M P
Manager Indonesia
Thomas Cup Team 1967

In all his decisions, Mr Scheele was backed by his officially appointed Danish advisers A Bruun and K A Nielsen. He stressed that the situation had been brought about solely by the spectators; players of both sides and court officials had behaved impeccably throughout.

At the official enquiry, the IBF decided the tie should be concluded in New Zealand. Malaysia agreed; Indonesia refused. The Challenge Round was awarded to Malaysia 6–3.

A sad conclusion indeed to a memorable event. The more so perhaps as after the vote of censure promulgated by the Danish BA (in connection with similar unsporting Indonesian crowd behaviour in the previous 1964 finals in Tokyo) Ferry Sonneville had, doubtless sincerely, voiced his opinion that 'no such disturbances would occur in Indonesia'.

How mistaken can one be?

In all fairness to Indonesia it must be pointed out that Indonesian *players* have always shown the highest standards of sportsmanship. And that, although Indonesian crowds are as vociferously enthusiastic as ever, there has been no such repetition.

Uber Cup

Although no war intervened, it took the Ladies' International Badminton Championship for the Uber Cup (to honour it with its full title) some 7 years to reach fruition.

It was New Zealand, far from badminton's main traffic routes, who in 1950 mooted the idea shortly

	Year	Competing Nations	Result		Venue
1st	1956–57	11	USA 6	Denmark 1	Lytham St Anne's
2nd	1959–60	14	USA 5	Denmark 2	Philadelphia
3rd	1962–63	11	USA 4	England 3	Wilmington
4th	1965–66	17	Japan 5	USA 2	Wellington
5th	1968–69	19	Japan 6	Indonesia 1	Tokyo
6th	1971–72	17	Japan 6	Indonesia 1	Tokyo
7th	1974–75	14	Indonesia 5	Japan 2	Jakarta
8th	1977–78	16	Japan 5	Indonesia 2	Auckland
9th	1980–81	15	Japan 6	Indonesia 3	Tokyo

Betty Uber presents her fine trophy, for the first time, to USA's Margaret Varner, the 'Texan Bronze'.

after the first successful Thomas Cup Championship. It was Betty Uber, England's greatest and most gracious pre-War player, Sir George Thomas's female counterpart, who offered a trophy. The time was not considered ripe financially but in 1953 the plan was agreed in principle. And in 1956 Betty Uber formally presented the trophy and made the draw from it.

This was a distinguished piece of craftsmanship made to Mrs Uber's own design by London's famous silversmiths, Mappin and Webb. The trophy, suitably inscribed, stands 18 in high and consists of a swivel-globe surmounted by a shuttle on which is poised an active lady player.

Unhappily, the New Zealanders were unable to make the journey from the other side of the world to participate in England. The US team however crossed the Atlantic to gain the first of three successive victories. And it was they who then sportingly suggested that they should not again receive the advantage of home courts.

Fittingly the venue then chosen was New Zealand. There Japan defeated USA and began a run of five successes broken by Indonesia only in 1974–5. The format was virtually the same as for the Thomas Cup except that each tie consisted of seven matches (three singles; four doubles) completed in one day, until 1981 when it was increased to nine, played over 2 days, as in the Thomas Cup.

England has a far better record for the Uber Cup than for the Thomas Cup. Indeed she might well have won it on three occasions but for a shock result when Ursula Smith lost to unknown Miss H MacGregor Stewart in 1963; when Sue Whetnall had tonsillitis in 1969; and when Gillian Gilks was 'unavailable' in 1981. England has reached the inter-zone ties on five occasions and the Challenge Round or final once.

And let it be said no scenes have ever occurred in Uber Cup inter-zone ties whether they were held at Lytham or Jakarta, Philadelphia or Tokyo.

First Uber Cup 1956–7

In the European zone, Ireland beat Sweden and Scotland to reach the final but England (her team composed of four Surrey players) fell to Denmark. With England's hopes, Iris Rogers and June Timperley, both beaten (the latter lost a game in $2\frac{1}{2}$ minutes!) it was left to All-England Junior Champion Heather Ward to gain England's first win. In a preview of the All-England final, A Hammergaard Hansen and Karen Granlund beat Iris Rogers and June Timperley to pave the way to a 5–2 victory. To such a powerful Danish side Ireland could offer no real opposition (1–6).

In the Asian zone, India narrowly beat Malaya 4–3. The match was, only momentarily, held up by the predominantly Indian crowd vociferously dissenting against the umpire's ruling in favour of one of the all-Chinese Malayan team.

In the inter-zone tie USA, having previously dispatched Canada 7–0 losing only one game, were equally ruthless in defeating India by the same margin—dropping the one game by a single point.

In the final, played at Lytham St Annes before a paltry 250 crowd, USA swamped Denmark. Their powerful singles line up of Margaret Varner, Judy Devlin and Lois Alston gave them a 3–0 lead. Veterans Ethel Marshall ('here, there and everywhere') and Bea Massman ('serving atrocious') took the next doubles to clinch the match. Denmark's only win came in the last match when Marshall and Massman's strict back and front formation found its defence easily pierced (6–1).

Betty Uber herself presented the trophy to Margaret Varner.

Final Round

United States of America 6—Denmark 1
At Lytham St Anne's, 18 March. Scores (USA names first):

Singles: Miss J Devlin beat Mrs T Ahm 11–2, 11–8; Miss M Varner beat Miss A Schiott Jacobsen 11–7, 11–1; Mrs J C Alston beat Miss T Petersen 8–11, 11–8, 11–6.

Doubles: Miss E Marshall and Miss B Massman beat Miss Schiott Jacobsen and Mrs B Kristiansen 15–11, 15–11; lost to Mrs K Granlund and Mrs A Hammergaard Hansen 4–15, 9–15. Miss S Devlin

Betty Uber, playing with R M White, was the only player to serve when they beat two Danish players 15–0, 15–0.

and Miss J Devlin beat Mrs Granlund and Mrs Hammergaard Hansen 15–8, 15–4; beat Miss Jacobsen and Mrs Kristiansen 15–4, 15–12.

Second Uber Cup 1959–60

The draw was made by the Maharani of Jaipur. In the Australian Zone, New Zealand, largely through whose efforts the Uber Cup Competition finally came into being, emerged as winners on their first appearance. They beat cold-benumbed Thailanders 4–3 at southerly Dunedin and then dispatched Australia (6–1) who had beaten Indonesia (5–2), also appearing for the first time. The latter included hints of later greatness in the persons of 15-year-old Minarni (she had no first name!) and Retno Koestijah, and also the sisters Megah, of whom Liem Swie King is the brother.

In the European Section, Denmark proved altogether too strong. She defeated England, Scotland and Ireland in turn with the loss of only three matches. Indeed, England, losing 0–7, scored double figures in only two games. But they had lost Heather Ward and Barbara Carpenter (living in South Africa) and Iris Rogers.

In the inter-zone ties, New Zealand continued her good work with a 4–3 win over Canada but was whitewashed in the final by a strong Danish side who had previously beaten India 6–1.

In the Challenge Round, USA retained the Cup by defeating Denmark 5–2. The latter's only two victories were at the expense of Margaret Varner and newcomer Dorothy O'Neil. But things might easily have swung the other way for Judy Devlin had to set in both games in her singles and she and her sister Sue only scraped home 18–16 in the third when their combination became so ragged under pressure from Kirsten Thorndahl and Hanne Jensen that they had to resort to back (Judy) and front (Sue).

Challenge Round

United States of America 5—Denmark 2
At Philadelphia on 9 April. Scores (USA names first):
Singles: Miss J M Devlin beat Mrs T Holst Christensen, 12–9, 12–9. Miss M Varner beat Miss H Jensen, 11–8, 11–6. Miss D O'Neill beat Miss Hasselsteen, 11–8, 7–11, 11–7.
Doubles: Miss M Varner and Miss D O'Neill lost to Mrs K Thorndahl and Miss H Jensen, 14–17, 5–15; lost to Mrs B Kristiansen and Mrs A Winther, 8–15, 17–16, 14–17. Miss J M Devlin and Miss S F Devlin beat Mrs Kristiansen and Mrs Winther, 15–5, 15–3; beat Mrs Thorndahl and Miss Jensen, 5–15, 15–6, 18–16.

Third Uber Cup 1962–3

With Denmark, challengers in 1960, not competing, England had only to defeat Ireland 6–1 to have qualified for the inter-zone finals on the courts of the American holders. An appeal by Sir George Thomas to clubs and players to meet the £1500 travelling costs met with an excellent response.

England, boasting three such top-class players as Iris Rogers, Angela Bairstow and Ursula Smith seemed to have an excellent chance of bringing the Cup home at last. Especially as Judy Hashman was the only powerful survivor from the great 1957 team. And the American second doubles pair were 16 years old!

The odds shortened still more. After a 22-hour flight, England crushed Canada (coached by the great Wong Peng Soon) who only once reached double figures. And at Bronxville, New York, with the temperature in the near nineties, they beat the Indonesian dark horses 5–2. Notification of the arrival of their team, which averaged 18–19 years, had been received only a fortnight before the match.

The Challenge Round was played at Brandywine High, Wilmington. Judy Hashman as expected, beat Angela Bairstow but the anticipated decisive swing of the pendulum did not materialise when Miss MacGregor Stewart in her first international match defeated Ursula Smith (runner-up in the All-England singles in the two preceding years) who veered disastrously between hitting out and hitting short. Nevertheless the score was 3–3 when Iris Rogers and Jenny Pritchard faced Judy Hashman and Carlene Starkey—a player of no outstanding merit and one whom she had never partnered before. But so brilliantly did Judy play and so astutely general their tactics that England's 4–0 lead in the third slumped sadly to 6–8, and, after a deadly war of attrition, the Americans garnered a point at a time to win the game, match and trophy 15–9.

Never again was England to have so handsome a chance of victory and surrender it so ingloriously.

Challenge Round

United States of America 4—England 3
At Wilmington on 6 April. Scores (USA names first):
Singles: Mrs G C K Hashman beat Miss A M Bairstow, 11–2, 11–1. Miss H M Stewart beat Miss U H Smith, 11–4, 11–7. Miss D O'Neill lost to Mrs W C E Rogers, 6–11, 7–11.
Doubles: Mrs G C K Hashman and Mrs C Starkey beat Miss U H Smith and Mrs G W Barrand, 15–8,

18–15; beat Miss H J Pritchard and Mrs W C E Rogers, 15–8, 8–15, 15–9. Miss T Barinaga and Miss C Jensen lost to Miss Pritchard and Mrs Rogers, 8–15, 1–15; lost to Miss Smith and Mrs Barrand, 10–15, 14–18.

Fourth Uber Cup 1965–6

The European Zone, with Denmark not having entered for financial reasons, saw England in a class of their own with victories over Netherlands (6–1), Ireland (7–0) and Federal Republic of Germany (7–0).

Other inter-zone finalists had equally easy passages. Indonesia (Australasian) dropped one match in 14; Japan (Asian) had a walkover from Hong Kong and a whitewash against Thailand; Canada (Pan-American) were unopposed.

In the inter-zone ties, at Dunedin, England beat Canada 6–1, although Ursula Smith, 1965 All-England Champion, lost surprisingly to Sharon Whittaker.

Wisely England had dispatched coach Ian Palmer to Napier in North Island to weigh up the unknown Indonesians in their match against Japan. Despite interminable rallies, the latter put the cat among the pigeons with a comfortable 5–2 victory – at 2.30 am. (And the local paper headlined 'England Send Spy to Napier').

For the final round, the Auckland hall with transverse strip lighting and TV spotlights presented problems. England lost all three singles, winning only 24 points, pulled back the next two doubles, but lost the third and the match in a tense finish.

In the Challenge Round, it was much the same tale with even USA's Judy Hashman unable to overcome the little-known Japanese captain Noriko Takagi. Judy gained revenge in the following doubles but it was a victory that USA's second pair could not sustain.

A fine win for first-time entrants Japan – and probably the latest ever trophy presentation, 1.15 am.

Challenge Round

Japan 5—United States of America 2
At Wellington on 21 May. Scores (Japanese names first):
Singles : Miss N Takagi beat Mrs G C K Hashman 12–9, 11–7. Miss F Yokoi beat Miss C Jensen, 12–11, 11–3. Miss M Yokoyama beat Miss T Barinaga 11–3, 11–8.
Doubles : Miss Takagi and Miss K Goto lost to Mrs Hashman and Mrs R. Jones, 14–18, 9–15; beat Miss Jensen and Miss Barinaga 15–2, 17–16. Miss

H Amano and Miss T Takahashi beat Miss Jensen and Miss Barinaga 9–15, 15–9, 15–7; lost to Mrs Hashman and Mrs Jones 8–15, 4–15.

Fifth Uber Cup 1968–9

Politics reared its head in the European Zone. In view of the invasion of Czechoslovakia, the Netherlands refused to play East Germany (subsequently defeated 6–1 by Scotland). In the Denmark v South Africa match in Copenhagen smoke-bombs were ignited by anti-apartheid students – who spent the night in custody.

In beating Denmark 5–2 (weakened by the absence of Ulla Strand: strengthened by the inclusion of Holland's Imre Rietveld who had recently married Danish Knud Nielsen) inexperienced England chalked up their first victory against that country for 35 years by winning all four doubles!

Inter-zone ties, excellently organised, were played in the huge central Tokyo Municipal Gymnasium. Electric score-boards were plentiful, duplicated result sheets handed out, and linesmen wore white gloves with which they indicated 'in' or 'out' for every shot.

England and Indonesia both had convincing 7–0 wins against Thailand and USA respectively. The latter lost their first five matches all in under 20 minutes. In the final, Indonesia (conceding the last game) beat England (4–3). After a fine start by Margaret Boxall they disappointed as a whole and Sue Whetnall, suffering from tonsillitis, was practically out on her feet and had to be substituted in the second match.

In the Challenge Round, Indonesia's tactics were distinctly dubious. They placed Minarni, the finest singles player in the ties, No 2, where she massacred Hiroe Yuki 6 and 2. As No 1 they publicly sacrificed Poppy Tumengkol who had not even played a single in previous rounds. Routed by Noriko Takagi 0 and 0 in just 9 minutes, she left the arena weeping. The remaining five matches all went to Japan. Indonesia's only consolation was a spirited fight by Minarni and Retno Koestijah against the rocklike Jap combination of Noriko Takagi and Hiroe Yuki in a brilliant, see-sawing match deservedly re-shown in its entirety on television the next day.

Challenge Round

Japan 6—Indonesia 1
At Tokyo on 4 June. Scores (Japanese names first):
Singles : Miss N Takagi beat Miss P Tumengkol 11–0, 11–0. Miss H Yuki lost to Miss Minarni 6–11, 2–11. Miss T Takahashi beat Miss Utami Dewi Kurniawan 11–3, 11–8.

Doubles : Miss N Takagi and Miss H Yuki beat Miss Minarni and Miss Retno Koestijah 8–15, 15–5, 15–12; beat Miss Nurhaena and Miss Hesty Lianawati 15–3, 15–3. Miss H Amano and Miss T Takahasi beat Miss Nurhaena and Miss Lianawati 15–4, 15–5; beat Miss Minarni and Miss Koestijah 15–8, 15–8.

Sixth Uber Cup 1971–2

The only match lost by England against the Netherlands was that of Judy Hashman, making her first Uber Cup appearance for England, against Agnes van de Meulen-Geene who 'ran her legs down to her knees'. In the European Zone final, Denmark avenged their previous defeat by a 5–2 win—Gillian Gilks had a racket in both English victories. But the fastest shuttles available at Gentofte were 78's!

In the inter-zone finals, the Japanese organisation was again excellent though eight huge arc lights erected for colour TV transmission had to be re-aligned before play could begin in front of badminton enthusiast Princess Chichibu. In her box stood the Uber Cup flanked – not by brawny military police but two petite and pretty Japanese girls.

As expected, Indonesia crushed both Canada and New Zealand 7–0. On paper Japan had a much tougher contest but nevertheless beat Denmark equally easily—7–0. (Owing to exams, the latter however could field neither of their brilliant youngsters, Anni Berglund and Lene Köppen, and Ulla Strand bravely played one doubles before, unable to continue, she was rushed to hospital).

So, on the hottest day of the year, Japan faced Indonesia in the final before an enthusiastic 10 000 crowd. (The huge racket and shuttle – carefully set at an angle of 45°!—made of ice, which graced the after-match buffet might have been still more acceptable at this juncture.) Indonesia took the first single played—and that was all. Japan won the other six games by convincing margins for Ferry Sonneville to present the Cup to a tearfully happy Noriko Nakayama.

Final Round

Japan 6—Indonesia 1
At Tokyo on 11 June. Scores (Japanese names first):
Singles : Mrs N Nakayama beat Miss Utami Dewi, 11–2, 11–0. Miss H Yuki beat Miss Taty Sumirah, 11–4, 11–3. Miss K Takasaka lost to Miss Intan Nurtjahja, 9–11, 11–7, 3–11.
Doubles : Miss M Aizawa and Miss E Takenaka beat Miss Intan Nurtjahja and Miss Regina Masli, 15–5, 11–15, 15–7; beat Miss Retno Koestijah and Miss P Tumengkol, 15–8, 15–9. Mrs N Nakayama and Miss H Yuki beat Miss Koestijah and Miss Tumengkol, 15–9, 15–11; beat Miss Nurtjahja and Miss Masli, 15–8, 15–8.

Seventh Uber Cup 1974–5

In the European Zone Final, England, with 40 practices and a 5–2 away victory over Holland under their belts, faced Denmark confidently at Plymouth, in the presence of Betty Uber herself. A powerful England team (Beck, Gilks, Nielsen, Whetnall, Boxall—all former All-England winners) lost two singles: Gillian Gilks going down to Lene Köppen ('in a stunning pair of the briefest of blue shorts').

But they won all four doubles for a 5–2 win.

England flew to Malaysia for a first ever match (and a 5–0 victory) as part of the acclimatisation process. Although Jake Downey accompanied them as a coach, they had no doctor—but in Djakarta they received generous help from Canada's medico and Manchester United's (!) trainer to overcome inevitable stomach upsets, and strains.

In the first round, in a Commonwealth clash, Canada narrowly beat Australia 4–3, and Indonesia, showing the flag, obliterated Malaysia 7–0. In the second round, Japan too showed its might with a clear-cut 6–1 victory over Canada (Hiroe Yuki won her singles without dropping a point).

Indonesia met England in a Senayan Stadium as packed and seething with excitement as for a Thomas Cup match. And it was this clamorous support in a key game that boosted Tati Sumirah from 1–6 down in the third to 11–6—at the same time shattering Margaret Beck's confidence. Gillian Gilks won her singles against Teresa Widiastuti and her doubles (with Margaret Beck) against the still redoubtable Minarni and Regina Masli. Despite two spirited three-gamers, it was Indonesia 4, England 2 before, well after midnight, the latter threw in the sponge 2–15, 1–15 in the last doubles.

So to the final. Holders Japan were 2–1 with convincing wins by Yuki and the ace-up-the-sleeve, retired, former All-England champion, Noriko Nakayama. But that was the end of Japan's hopes of a fourth successive victory for Indonesia surprisingly took all four doubles with the Japanese showing little cohesion and less of their characteristic determination.

Mrs M Soedaryanto, the former Miss Minarni, was the Indonesian captain—the first time this position had been given to a woman.

Happy Japs: 1978 Uber Cup winners. Y Yonekura, E Ueno, M Takada, A Tokudo, S Kondo, H Yuki (with cup), H Amanoe (Coach) and T Itagak (Manager).

Final Round

Indonesia 5—Japan 2

At Jakarta on 6 June. Scores (Indonesian names first):

Singles: Miss T Widiastuti lost to Miss H Yuki 7–11, 1–11. Miss T Sumirah beat Miss A Tokuda 11–5, 11–2. Miss Utami Dewi lost to Mrs N Nakayama 5–11, 3–11.

Doubles: Mrs M Soedaryanto and Miss R Masli beat Miss M Aizawa and Miss E Takenaka 15–6, 6–15, 15–9; beat Miss H Yuki and Miss M Ikeda 15–8, 15–11. Miss I Wigoeno and Miss T Widiastuti beat Miss Yuki and Miss Ikeda 15–4, 15–9; beat Miss Aizawa and Miss Takenaka 17–14, 15–0.

Eighth Uber Cup 1977–8

No surprises in the European zone up to the final. In the semi-finals England defeated the Netherlands, bereft of Marjan Ridder, by a surprisingly comfortable 6–1 in view of the fact that their opponents had beaten Sweden 4–3 and Canada 5–2. Scotland beat Norway 5–2 in the tiny Shetland village of Brae, three hours' flight from Glasgow. They enjoyed a narrow victory over Germany 4–3 before being mercilessly crushed 7–0 by Denmark.

In the final, on their players' own Gentofte courts, Denmark took the first two singles which included a right-against-the-book 11–0, 6–0 (later 8–10, 12–10) by Pia Nielsen against Margaret Lockwood. And our ladies' doubles pairs (Nora Perry and Ann Statt, and Jane Webster and Barbara Sutton) who had done so well in the preceding Swedish and German Championships managed to win only one doubles, though two others were set in the third game (5–2).

The inter-zone finals in Auckland were redrawn. In the first round 'dark horses' USA discourteously but methodically murdered the host nation New Zealand 7–0. And Japan who had, unexpectedly, been forced to fight for their lives in Malaysia (4–3) to reach this stage were equally severe with New Zealand's antipodean neighbour Australia (7–0) who, with the minimum team of four, put up a brave but futile resistance, scoring a total of only six points in the Singles!

In a Uber Cup match in 1969 Japan's Noriko Nakayama took just 3½ minutes to win the first game against Indonesia's Poppy Tumengkol, and 5½ for the second.

In the second round, Indonesia's 7–0 victory against a never-say-die USA gave no hint of the suddenly increased tempo to come. Sadly Team Manager Suharso had to fly back to Indonesia to a very sick father, leaving the team in the hands of Christian.

Denmark protested against Japan's replacing Hiroe Yuki as their No 1 by Saori Kondo; a protest upheld by the IBF. And the former perished against Lene Köppen.

Now Japan's turn: Atsuko Tokuda 11–1, 5–0 up with only two service changes against Pia Nielsen. The Danish girl fought back magnificently to 10–6 up but an even more determined Tokuda finally squeezed home 12–10. Saori Kondo proved her proposed No 1 ranking had been fully justified with fleet footedness and aerial smashes. Japan's two All-England final pairs (Atsuko Tokuda and Mikiko Takada; Emiko Ueno and Yoshiko Yonekura) never looked like dropping a match (6–1).

In a truly great final, the Japanese, spearheaded by an airborne Kondo uttering martial cries, and master-minded by the impassive 'Little General' Tokuda, were just too good even for a powerful Indonesian side. Only the Amazonian Wiharjo Verawaty, playing above herself, could, with two fine wins, delay the inevitable recapture of the Uber Cup (5–2) and its presentation to a tearful Hiroe Yuki.

Final Round
Japan 5—Indonesia 2
At Auckland on 20 May. Scores (Japanese names first):
Singles: S Kondo beat L I Hoa 11–3, 11–3. H Yuki lost to W Verawaty 3–11, 6–11. A Tokuda beat Tjan So Gwan 11–5, 11–4.
Doubles: E Ueno and Y Yonekura lost to I Wigoeno and W Verawaty 15–10, 8–15, 12–15; beat R Masli and T Widiastuti 15–11, 15–12. M Takada and A Tokuda beat Masli and Widiastuti 15–10, 15–8; beat Wigoeno and Verawaty 15–5, 15–7.

Ninth Uber Cup 1980–1
Fittingly, in the ninth series the format was changed to that of the Thomas Cup—nine matches.

In the European zone semi-final, England decisively beat Taiwan, 7–2 conquerors of Scotland, on court 9–0, never losing a game and only once the lead. Off court, it was the cheongsam clad Taiwanese who won handsomely in harmonising song.

The final against Denmark resulted in the latter's defeat 5–4 before crowds only 250 strong. Lene Köppen won three of her four games and exacted stinging revenge (11–0, 11–1) for her recent first

round Copenhagen Cup defeat by Sally Leadbeater. But teenagers Nette Nielsen, Dotte Kjaer, Kirsten Larsen and Rikki Sorensen lacked big match experience.

In the Asian zone, Indonesia showed awesome power in brushing aside New Zealand, without the loss of a game, and India, vanquisher of Australia who averaged no more than two points a game in eight of the matches. Wiharjo Verawaty's results read astoundingly 11–3, 11–2, 11–0, 11–1, 15–0, 15–1, 15–1, 15–3.

This one-sidedness unhappily continued in the inter-zone finals in Tokyo. Canada, having crossed the Pacific, scored just 58 points in 18 games against Japan; Indonesia conceded only 3 more (6 love games) against Malaysia in sessions that lasted—just 90 minutes!

The slide seemed likely to continue when Indonesia raced to a 3–0 lead against England which included the surprise defeat of World Champions Nora Perry and Jane Webster by Wiharjo Verawaty and Ruth Damayanti. England fought back gamely to 4–4: youngsters Sally Leadbeater and Karen Chapman won a doubles, Karen Bridge, despite recent mumps, beat Taty Sumirah, and Jane Webster, Ivana Lie. But a majestic Verawaty scored her fourth victory to clinch the match 5–4.

The final was given a swinging start by a regiment of baton-twirling majorettes in sequined bathing costumes before a full house who had paid up to £16 for a ticket. Verawaty, with two victories, again dominated to put the score 2–2 (all three-setters) at the end of the first evening. But it was Japan's little bouncing Saori Kondo who started the slide next day with a decisive win over Verawaty (her only defeat of the series). Inspired, the Japanese slammed home the next two matches to win the Uber Cup yet again (6–3).

Final Round
Japan 6—Indonesia 3
At Tokyo, on 22 and 23 May. Scores (Japanese names first):
Singles: S Kondo beat I L I Hoa 11–7, 10–12, 11–3; beat V Wiharjo 11–6, 11–8. Y Yonekura lost to V Wiharjo 11–2, 2–11, 6–11; beat I L I Hoa 3–11, 11–7, 12–9. A Tokuda beat T Sumirah 11–4, 11–9.
Doubles: S Kondo and M Takada lost to V Wiharjo and R Damayanti 15–11, 12–15, 3–15; beat I Wigoeno and T Widiastuti 15–8, 15–11. A Tokuda and Y Yonekura beat I Wigoeno and T Widiastuti 17–18, 15–11, 15–7; lost to V Wiharjo and R Damayanti 15–9, 9–15, 12–15.

Nine/**Famous Names and Games**

Memorable Matches

These could well fill a book on their own—and their choice be hotly debated. The following all-too-short selection has been made on grounds of high drama and lively style in addition to brilliance of play. All were originally printed in the *Badminton Gazette*.

Dave Freeman (USA) v Wong Peng Soon (M)
Thomas Cup 1949

The second evening commenced with the Freeman v Wong match, the principal feature of which was the really superb play of the American captain. He showed form of a standard considerably higher than had been seen in the British Isles in singles play for a great number of years.

His length was a good deal more consistent and accurate than on the previous day, and throughout the whole of the match he was calling the tune in practically every rally.

Wong was on terms at 4–all, but thereafter, he was successful in obtaining only one more point, and that only after Freeman had advanced to 14–0 in the second game largely by the aid of his deceptive cross-court drops, made equally well on the forehand as on the backhand. The Californian ran from 6–4 to 11–4 in one hand, and he similarly annexed the final four points in the first game also in one hand.

In the second game, Wong attempted to play more aggressively, but Freeman's defence was equal, not only to returning all the Malayan's smashes, but to returning them most accurately indeed, and exactly where he wanted. He ran from 4–0 to 11–0 in one hand, and thereafter the Malayan got in only three times before the American ran out 15–4, 15–1, after only 21 minutes' play.

'*Invicta*'

A N Other was once top-seeded.

David and Eddy Choong (M) v J Skaarup and Paul Holm (D) and v Ong Poh Lim and I bin Marjan
All-England Championships 1951

E L Choong and E B Choong reached the doubles final over the bodies of Skaarup and Holm. Holm's genius was at its best, and it required the superb generalship of David (E L) Choong to rescue the match out of the fire (17–14, 8–15, 18–13).

The Choongs are known as aggressive stroke-makers. But they were outmatched in this direction in the final by both Ong and Marjan, both of whom have splendid smashes and are very quick indeed on their feet. The Choongs were put on the defensive continually, and little Eddy fairly brought the house down on many occasions with his amazing retrieves.

There was one rally in which he returned smashes from Ong's racket five times in a row when actually sitting on the floor! Eventually David was able to rescue his brother and the Choongs actually won the point. So it went on to the great enjoyment of the large gallery.

To the applauding public Eddy was the complete hero; to the cognoscenti, the palm of success was granted to the quieter and less dramatic David (9–15, 15–7, 15–10). And it was Eddy who was singled out for the thunder of the Singapore rackets.

'*Invicta*'

D Smythe (C) v J Heah (M)
All-England Championships 1953

It was a battle between meticulous accuracy and unflagging energy, and after the most exciting and exhausting rallies, Heah just won the first game after setting. With the change of ends there was a change also in the tide of battle. Smythe got his smash working better, and won many points down the side-lines, whilst in the long rallies Heah seemed to be tiring. When Smythe won the game quite easily I thought that Heah had 'had it', and I think most people thought the same.

Top *Malaya's Eddy Choong and Wong Peng Soon can still joke about their gruelling three-game singles epic (1955).*

Above *J Hammergaard Hansen and Finn Kobbero (Denmark), men's doubles masters, look with anticipatory appraisal at their All-England tankards.*

However, again there was a change. Heah regained the accuracy he seemed temporarily to have lost in the second game and, again taking the centre of the court, made Smythe do all the running. But it was a grim struggle, the Canadian was giving nothing away, and point by point they crept up towards game, until Heah led 14–12.

Still the service went in and out, and then with Heah serving and leading 14–12 there was a tremendous rally during which Smythe in order to reach a beautiful drop shot of his opponent's, threw himself full length on the floor and played the shot while on the ground. Heah cleared the shuttle again to the back of the court, and Smythe, picking himself up, chased it, and returned the

shuttle into court again. The rally went on, but at last Heah stroked one near the corner of the net, and again in his efforts to reach it Smythe measured his length on the floor.

But this time, Smythe, racket and shuttle seemed to touch the floor at the same moment, and the match was Heah's. The crowd roared their approbation, the applause being for the winner, who so well deserved it, and also for the loser who had helped to make such a lovely match possible.

Betty Uber

Finn Kobbero and Hammergaard Hansen (D) v Ng Boon Bee and Tan Yee Khan (M)
All-England Championships 1966

Kobbero and Hammergaard Hansen played very well and were a trifle unlucky not to win it. They have played worse and won the title. At one stage Kobbero's play about the net and forecourt completely bewildered Ng Boon Bee and Tan Yee Khan. Hammergaard hit as hard as he has ever done, and that is harder than anyone in my memory. His smash is produced so fluently that the pace and penetration of it confound his opponents. The Malaysian pair both hit very hard themselves, but Hammergaard's extra power was most evident. One shot that most of us will be practising hard before next season is the delayed forehand cross-court flick that he plays when receiving the short service. A piece of very powerful spring steel inserted in the wrist will be essential for most normal players!

John Havers

Robert McCoig (Sco) v Roger Mills
Scotland v England 1968

On court came the pride in Scottish Pride, Robert McCoig, intent on avenging all the wrongs inflicted on us by the English. It just so happened that Roger Mills was in the way. The match started at a spanking pace, and it seemed only a question of who would drop first. The hall was like an oven and before long even the fit, ebullient Mills was breathing a bit more often and bouncing a bit less, and McCoig's shoe laces seemed to be giving him endless trouble. The Scot, however, acclimatised first, and, after a long, hard struggle, reached game point. A subtle shuttle change, two quick smashes and Scotland was a game up.

At this point, Mills decided that a low service, long rallies and a refusal to smash would win the day, so he slowly and effectively ground his opponent into the floorboards. But McCoig has never let Scotland down, and no one can say he lacks guts.

In fact, although horribly tired, he staged a late revival and came to 10–12 in the third game, but here his steam ran out.

The crowd, although missing the delicacy of the tactics, was voluble and appreciative in its applause. A match that will be long remembered in Perth.

'Scotia'

Rudy Hartono (I) v Elo Hansen (D)
Kelvin Hall 1972
Then, sometimes to a stunned silence, Hartono took Hansen to the proverbial cleaners. The Dane eventually resorted to his famous trick shots, but even this gambit found the Indonesian machine totally unimpressed. Hartono's subsequent steamrollering of Kojima left no one in doubt as to the result of the men's singles.

Cock o' the North

Svend Pri (D) v Rudy Hartono (I)
All-England Championships 1975
Denmark's Svend Pri after 11 years' endeavour to win the All-England title is 15–11, 12–8 in the lead against Rudy Hartono, who has won the title seven times in succession and needs only one more victory to beat Erland Kops' record.
Hartono, unruffled as ever, immediately won six points to lead 14–12 and one thought of poor Gunalan last year. Could Pri remain staunch of heart and win a third game. Pri had other ideas and in three rallies, Hartono was electing to set to 3. A tentative hand apiece at love all and then Pri had match point. Hartono fought this off, but at the next time of asking Pri was not to be denied and it was game and match 15–11, 17–14.

The waves of applause that greeted the end were compounded of many emotions. Acknowledgement of a fine match between two great players; one achieving the pinnacle of a life-time after so many 'heart-aches' in the past and the other reflecting on his first defeat at Wembley in eight years' competition against the world's best. All done with great grace and the crowd wondering whether they were witnessing the passing of an era or whether this fabulous young man would return to conquer new heights. We all hope so.

Pri—arms raised to the crowd in salute—then raced off court to where his wife waited to greet him. The great truth had dawned—he was the champion! A worthy champion, indeed, for though he dropped a couple of games during the tournament, he never appeared to be in the slightest trouble. Any player would do well to ponder Svend Pri's persistence in striving for this

title. He had been so near before, but he had the courage to train, concentrate and not be diverted from the final goal. Such a victory was more than good for Pri and good for Denmark—it was good for Badminton!

Arthur Jones

Rudy Hartono (I) v Liem Swie King (I)
All-England Championships 1976
Rudy Hartono duly achieved the fantastic record of eight All-England titles, the sole purpose of his trip to Europe and the main reason for his country's decision to defy the Asian ban. In so doing, he beat the record of Erland Kops of Denmark who collected the title seven times between 1958 and 1967 and was an interested spectator of the final between Hartono and his fellow countryman, Liem Swie King, conqueror of last year's champion, Svend Pri, at the quarter-final stage.

Having recorded these facts and paid tribute to the incredible and well deserved achievement of Hartono, it must be reported that the final which should have been the climax of 9 years' endeavour did not exactly provide the most exciting of spectacles for the large crowd and the millions of television viewers. Those who feel charitable may accept the Indonesian explanation that the players involved play each other every day in life, thus the predictability of the match. Those feeling less charitable may have other ideas but suffice to say there was little to keep even the most ardent spectator on the edge of his seat or, for that matter, away from the bar.

The crowd rose generously to applaud Rudy as he collected his record breaking trophy and title but one felt it was this overall achievement they were recognising rather than the match they had just witnessed.

Tommy Marrs

Flemming Delfs (D) v Liem Swie King (I)
All-England Championships 1977
John Vincent catches the atmosphere of a great final won by Delfs 15–17, 15–11, 15–8.
The extremity of the game soon became apparent in the vulnerability of the shuttles. Such was the pace, so extreme the angling, that shuttles even hit

In a Kelvin Hall final in Glasgow, Finn Kobbero handed the shuttle to his partner, Marjorie Russell, at 10–5. Without any further error they won 15–5, 15–0.

cleanly often survived only one or two rallies and the surrounding scene soon resembled a Yorkshire moor on the 12th August. Surely there has never been such cheering and lively chatter, such spontaneous appreciation of ploys which ranged from the subtle to the esoteric. The clamour of one rally carried over to the next, rising and falling like storm-waves on the seashore. Had King Canute been able to say 'Quiet, please' in every European and Oriental language he would have had no more success than did the Wembley umpire.

John Vincent

Lene Köppen (D) v Hiroe Yuki (J)
All-England Championships 1977
Lene Köppen with 'the tactical precision of a chess player' wins the first game 11–7 but in the second is out-rallied 3–11.

The third game followed the pattern of the other two: control changing from point to point and often from shot to shot. Köppen got ahead to 5–1 and 6–3 at the change. Yuki eventually pulled level at 7–7 and after many more rallies she got to 9–7. Then, after 45 minutes of absorbing badminton, Köppen's fine resolve gave way at last and two tired rallies let Yuki run out at 11–7. Perhaps the older girl's stamina was that bit greater; perhaps after three previous championships her self-confidence was that bit more certain but anyway one of them had to come out on top and Yuki it was.

The most emotional moment came at the end. Then, after the trophies had been presented by Princess Margaret, Miss Köppen raised Miss Yuki's arm to acknowledge the applause. They both deserved it.

John Woolhouse

Mike Tredgett and Nora Perry v S Skovgaard and Lene Köppen (D)
All-England Championships 1978
So the two top seeds met in the final; a repeat of the final of the Danish Championship the week before, won by the Danes. The problem facing the English pair was to prevent the towering Skovgaard from annihilating the service and from using his devastating smash on the rallies, and this demanded extremely accurate services. To begin with, honours were about even, but gradually Tredgett and Mrs Perry started to pull away, and began to play very well indeed, giving an object lesson in how to tame an aggressor by thoughtful and controlled shuttle manipulation, so much so that they came to 9–0 in the second game. The Danish cause then flickered to life, but at 4–9 a

fine winning return by Mrs Perry of one of Skovgaard's fiercest smashes extinguished their hopes and the home pair ran out at 15–4 to give Tredgett his first, and Mrs Perry her second, All-England title.

Arthur Salway

Rudy Hartono (I) v Sture Johnsson (S)
All-England Championships 1978
But, surely, the greatest match of the week, and one worthy to be ranked among the best ever played, was that between Hartono and Sture Johnsson of Sweden. The third game was an experience to be remembered as blow for blow and point for point the score crept up to 13–all with an exhibition of badminton which would have been worth recording. The popular Swede took hold of himself at this point and went into a 4–1 lead with match point to come.

Could he do it? Was he to be the second man to beat Hartono at Wembley? Service changed hands several times in long rallies and perhaps Johnsson scenting victory tried too hard to make winners too soon and the Indonesian caught up to 4–all. Then followed one of the longest rallies seen all week; something approaching 40 shots were exchanged before Johnsson forced a weak return from his opponent. Only to see his golden chance vanish when he hit a 'sitter' at the net out of court. Thus he let Hartono off the hook and gave him the match 15–9, 10–15, 18–17.

And so to the final – an All-Indonesian affair. Here the greater experience of Hartono took him to an early lead at 10–7 from which score he did not collect another point until his opponent was 6-love up in the second game!

Hartono's game fell right away and a stunned audience rubbed their eyes in disbelief as error after error came from the 'Master's' racket. Liem Swie King took full advantage of the situation and went on to win the second game and the title 15–10, 15–3.

This was not a final to remember. What a pity that the memory of one of the greatest champions of all time should be dimmed by such a performance!

Mike Harvey

Tjun Tjun and Wahjudi (I) v Iino and Tsuchida (J)
All-England Championships 1979
Indeed it might well have been a final with no Indonesians at all. In the semi-final holders Tjun Tjun and Wahjudi, having won the first game against the fast and aggressive Japanese, Yoshitaka

Japan's Iino and Tsuchida who uncomplainingly lost an All-England semi-final after their opponents had been disqualified by the umpire but reinstated by referee Herbert Scheele.

Iino and Masao Tsuchida, 15–6, had their ears pinned back unceremoniously 14–17 in the second. With the Japanese pair on court and ready to play, the Indonesians returned late after the 5 minute interval to hear umpire Alan Jones announcing their disqualification. To a storm of booing from a packed auditorium, he brushed aside their protests and left the arena. Almost immediately, Herbert Scheele limped on court, overruled the decision and beckoned Michael Gilks to the vacant umpire's chair to equally thunderous applause. The Japanese made no word or gesture of protest.

The Indonesians played like men in a dream still seeing the shadow of the noose. With Tsuchida making powerful jump smashes and intercepting equally agilely at the net, the Japanese swept to 12–4. Virtue was surely going to have its own reward!

Tjun Tjun, however, had other ideas. Counter attacking, the Indonesians levelled at 13–all. Soon 0–3 down in the setting, it was the Japanese turn to fight back to 4–3 only to reap the Tjun Tjun

whirlwind and lose the match which had been awarded them.

Pat Davis

Liem Swie King (I) v Han Jian (Ch)

Indonesia v China 1980

With two-victory King to play China's second string, 23-year-old Han Jian, Indonesian confidence grew. To their consternation Jian took the first game 15–11 only to be unceremoniously brought to heel in the second, 4–15. Undeterred, Jian stormed back, but King led 13–11, and again 4–2. Almost in sight of victory, King found he could neither out-run nor out-play his opponent.

He lost his head. A half-court smash was netted and—uncharacteristically—King's racket followed it. 'I was so frustrated—it was beyond my consciousness'. And it was Jian who took the game 18–17 when King smashed again—and smashed out. Said Jian: 'To lose his cool was King's greatest mistake'.

After 75 minutes of ever-increasing tension, Jian was hoisted shoulder-high by the fans who swarmed over the court in Cup-Tie style. Only then did the inscrutable Hou (Chinese coach) allow himself a quiet smile.

Our Far Eastern Correspondent

Dhany Sartika (I) v Luan Jin (Ch)

Indonesia v China 1980

Came the second night's play and Indonesia again broke the deadlock when an ecstatic Sumirat smothered Yan Yujiang, who played like a shepherd who had lost his flock, 15–7, 15–7 in 22 minutes.

But one of the biggest and most costly mistakes the Indonesians made was to pit Dhany Sartika against Luan Jin in the third singles slot. Sartika was a let-down, preferring to stop play to wipe sweat puddles on his half of the court, and even wring his socks dry, when he should have been capitalising on Luan's pulled muscle in the second game.

There was Indonesia's Ferry Sonneville and several others on the sidelines, yelling out to him to keep pushing Luan beyond the limits of human endurance, but the young Indonesian turned a deaf

A statue of Liem Swie King was erected in his home town; it was pulled down when he lost to China's Han Jian!

141

IBF Presidents all! Left to right, *Ferry Sonneville (Indonesia), Humphrey Chilton (England), David Bloomer (Scotland), Stuart Wyatt (England), Stellan Mohlin (Sweden), and, standing, Craig Reedie (Scotland).*

ear to them, taking his sweet time to test shuttle after shuttle, as Luan rubbed some ointment on his thigh and took a breather. In the final analysis, Luan prevailed 15–12, 15–13 after 65 minutes of interrupted play that dragged into a bore for the 8000 fans in the stuffy hall.

Our Far Eastern Correspondent

Kartono and Heryanto (I) v Tjun Tjun and Wahjudi (I)

All-England Championships 1981

In the final Kartono and Heryanto impishly snatched a quick 5–1 lead and looked as though they would be overhauled at 10–9. Then, with Kartono returning a point-blank Tjun Tjun smash and pressurising the hitherto steady Wahjudi into error, the anxious holders, seeking a record-breaking seventh win, were down 9–15.

In the second game (surely a cross between the speed of greyhound racing and the punch of light-weight boxing) much the same, until 7–6. Then Kartono and Heryanto romped away to 12–6. Wahjudi's defence halted the slide but for once Tjun Tjun seemed to have little heart for the fight, to hammer through Kartono's buffer defence or withstand Heryanto's lethal poison-tipped attack into the body. Perhaps the marriage idyll had

Fifty-four strokes were counted in a rally between Wong Peng Soon and Eddy Choong in an All-England final, 1955.

blunted Tjun Tjun's normally razor-sharp aggression.

A well-deserved victory for the younger Indonesians. There seems no light at the end of the tunnel for English men. The two pocket blitzkriegs, Kartono and Heryanto, will undoubtedly be about for some years to come. And mighty fast about at that!

Pat Davis

Famous Officials

WILFRED BADDELEY

At 19 the youngest ever player to win the Wimbledon Singles—three times. With his brother Herbert, he also won the Men's Doubles (four times) before, at the age of 25, ill health forced him to give up tennis. He took up badminton, restarted the famous Bee Club, and was President of the Badminton Association (1913–19).

PETER BIRTWISTLE

Though 'Bertie' to all, he deservedly ranks high in the badminton hierarchy. A man of pushing enthusiasm and limitless drive, he played for Lancashire II until the War pitched him as a 2nd Lieutenant with the BEF into France—and five years' captivity. There he zealously organised badminton leagues and tournaments with the same fanatical devotion and eye to detail with which he later voluntarily umpired, and organised major BA of E tours and international matches for which he received first the Queen's Jubilee Medal, then the Rothman's Service to Sport Trophy. Capped five times for England in the lean years 1948–52 despite a 40 per cent shoulder disability acquired when strafed by American Mustangs whilst he was marching to a Nuremburg Oflag—and a starvation diet.

In the summer, he is often seen on television screens, as experienced a tennis umpire as a badminton one.

Living at Mynton Court, Chorley, this ex-textile-tycoon is the man who took some of the 'bad' out of badminton.

BRIAN BISSEKER

Winning hockey and tennis 'blues' at Cambridge, and seven years as England hockey trialist, left Bisseker no time to handle badminton rackets. Articled as a Law Clerk, he volunteered to face the rigours of war rather than those of Final Exams. Emerging as a Captain of Marines he went into advertising before becoming BA of E Secretary (1970–8) to shoulder the Herculean task of following 'Mr Badminton'—Herbert Scheele.

Quiet, pipe-smoking, he is a man of infinite patience who consolidated his distinguished predecessor's work and set his own mark on the germination of badminton's beanstalk growth in the '70s.

DAVID L BLOOMER

It was Glasgow's good fortune that he was born there in 1913. In its 3000-seater Kelvin Hall, he and 'Honest John' McCarry acted as conscripted impresarios when they staged the famous Malaya v USA semi-final in the first ever Thomas Cup (1949). Staged it so successfully that there followed some 15 Kelvin Hall World Invitation Tournaments that brought the world's finest players to Scotland (and, in 1951, included Ken Davidson's 'Gladminton' act).

A rotund figure invited bodyline attack but pertinacity and a superb backhand defence helped him gain eight Scottish caps (1947–51). From being the USA's representative on the IBF he became the latter's Chairman (1962–9) and its President (1965–9).

An insurance broker, he was addicted, 'with lurid asides, to a game loosely called golf'; was a born raconteur; and brought wit and wisdom blended in felicitous style to the *Gazette*'s columns.

Still going strong!

HUMPHREY FARWELL CHILTON

Though born in Somerset (1911), Chilton, of puckish face and good humour, lives not inappropriately at Gnomes Cottage, Penn, Bucks.

Played much at the Eton In and Out BC (so called because of its members' between-games incursions to neighbouring pubs). He lost the sight of one eye when hit on the head by a full-toss whilst playing cricket for the Old Boys at King's School, Canterbury. Nevertheless became a County player whose deception 'could make the best players look silly, though he was inclined to overdo things'. As a result was regarded with some awe in America where he was posted as a member of the British Army Staff Supplies; and had already caught the Queen's eye with his agility when she opened Slough Community Centre.

With a reputation for putting more back into the game than he took out, he occupied virtually all administrative posts for Berks, Bucks and Oxon. BA of E Vice-President (1959–), Chairman of the Council (1970–5), and President of the IBF (1969–71).

A man of charm and vision.

J PLUNKETT-DILLON

An enthusiastic but never brilliant player, this Dublin solicitor kept a firm hand on the reins of the Badminton Union of Ireland as its Hon Secretary (1924–42). Plunkett-Dillon was amongst the founders of the IBF and its President from 1955–7 and fathered all the Irish 'greats' from Devlin to Rankin.

COLONEL S S C DOLBY

Not only the founder of the Badminton Association in 1893 and its President until 1898, but also its Hon Secretary and Treasurer from 1893–9

David Bloomer, Scottish international, IBF President, and masterly raconteur.

143

when he was ordered to the Boer War. On his return he played at the Services Club in Southsea and later at Ealing BC of which he was Hon Secretary until 1920. In the meantime he had won the All-England Veterans' Men's Doubles in 1912.

RENÉ GATHIER

Remembered today for 'Gathier Strings' he was Managing Director of RSL as well as of Wimbledon Squash and Badminton Club. As the French delegate to the IBF, he never missed a meeting in 35 years. And he was a driving force of the French Championships after which he invariably held memorable Montmartre parties. He even insisted on one being held in 1940 as 'a morale booster'— and himself won the Men's Doubles with Henri Pelizza.

F W HICKSON

Table tennis's gift to badminton! As founder of the Alexandra Palace Ping Pong Club in 1900 he flirted with that game but within a year found his true love as an official of Alexandra Palace BC. He played a large part in forming the London League (1908)—battleground of leading internationals— and the Middlesex BA (1927), repeated ICC winners. Such organisational skill and love of detail made him a natural choice to become the BA's first paid Secretary (1927–37) and the IBF's Hon Secretary (1934–7). His name is perpetuated in the Hickson Permanent Memorial Trophy, given by his wife, and awarded, together with the Championship Cup, to the All-England Men's Singles winner.

COLONEL ARTHUR HILL

A name to be linked with those pillars of badminton, Sir George Thomas and Herbert Scheele. As a player his contribution was meagre for he took up the game only in his later years. But for many years he travelled twice weekly 30 miles each way to the famous Southsea Club, and put down his racket only in his 80th year.

As an untiring, methodical administrator he made his mark. He gave seventeen years' voluntary service as Hon Secretary and Treasurer (1910–27); and a further 23 (1927–50) as President: 40 years in all! Yet he still found time to umpire and steward at the All-England for many years.

Colonel Hill served in the Boer War, played Rugby for Blackheath, and cricket for the Gentlemen. A man of unusual charm, his other interests included archery and the taking of superb photographic cloud studies. He died at the age of 99!

'A man of rare parts'.

Colonel Arthur Hill: Hon Secretary and Treasurer of the BA of E 1910–27; President 1927–50. Some stint!

ERIC HINCHCLIFF

Quiet, ex-RNVR Lt Commander type, who, as 'England's most dedicated umpire' was Hon Secretary of the Badminton Umpires' Association of England for fifteen years. An almost fanatically enthusiastic administrator he clashed with his executive and was not re-appointed in 1975.

Eagle-eyed, has coolly umpired innumerable All-England, Commonwealth Games, and European Championships. His accolade: 'Fair, official but never officious'. Married to Dorothy Hinchcliff, pillar of Surrey BA, arch-enthusiast, and *Badminton Gazette* and *World Badminton* gossipcolumnist.

FRANK HENLEY, MBE

Henley emigrated to the States where he worked with the Pullman Car Company. He returned to England to volunteer for the 1914–18 War. Joined RSL in the '30s when they were advertising 'the fastest shuttle in the world'. With him as Sales Director, they certainly became the fastest selling.

As a Home Guard Captain in the Second World War he did magnificent work during the blitz. But his health was seriously undermined and by the late '40s, a 100 yard walk had become a marathon. Unsinkable, he still toured South Africa and

Malaya, in the latter country leading in a Chinese millionaire's winning racehorse.

He fostered badminton all over the world and in doing so his practical help and advice made him a respected friend of hundreds of aspiring players. His after tournament 'get-togethers' were unforgettable: witty and urbane, he also conducted his own vocal 'orchestra' with Beecham zest and discipline.

'A wonderful trouper!'

H H (BILL) HOLWILL

A former City of London 'copper' Bill Holwill never played badminton. But as RSL representative he estimates he's watched 13 000 hours of top-flight play and players of many nationalities. Not surprisingly, welcomed in every playing country in the world as a shrewd judge of the game. And, as a friend in need, nothing was ever too much trouble for 'Uncle Bill'. He liked his fellow-men—and women.

Received presentations at both European and All-England Championships.

NANCY HORNER

The Scot who put English Badminton on its feet and, as Vice-President (1967–75), the only woman in an 80-strong list of Past and Present officers of the BA of E! One of Scotland's most versatile lady players ever, she won 15 caps and every available title in both the Scottish Open and National Championships. First BA of E Coaching Secretary and then Director of Coaching, she worked wholeheartedly, effectively and charmingly for English badminton but still found time for a series of memorable coaching weeks at Inverclyde, the lovely Scottish National Sports Centre superbly situated on the Clyde at Largs.

MAUREEN HYBART

The petite blonde bombshell administrator of Welsh badminton. Never played badminton for Wales herself (though capped for netball) but her two youngsters bid fair to do so. An indefatigable worker who gets her fizz and fast reactions perhaps from a University of Wales honours degree in chemistry and Pontypool practical experience with ICI.

N P KRISTENSEN

Always affectionately known as 'Kris', a name he wore with dignity. Appointed as Hon Secretary of the Danish Badminton Forbund in 1941 and its President in 1950. But an internationalist at heart he helped to found the great exhibitions in Scot-

Air Vice-Marshal 'Larry' Lamb, top Rugby referee, and current BA of E Chief Executive.

land's Kelvin Hall, and held 'balanced views in an unbalanced world'. IBF President (1963–5); Vice-President (1950–63). Always young at heart himself, he got on particularly well with young people.

ARTHUR JONES

The fast-talking Chairman of the BA of E Council owes his badminton to the Royal Navy. It was there, whilst undergoing radio-mechanic training in 1942, that he first picked up a racket. Arctic convoys and submarines in the Pacific caused it to be a pleasure deferred. But after demob he was in the thick of it: Essex BA Chairman and Hon Secretary and Treasurer; IBF Vice-President; a leading umpire; member of six BA of E Committees. All were stepping stones to the Chairmanship of the Council in 1975 where he exercises a shrewd business-like appraisal in keeping in with the modern game.

'LARRY' LAMB

Air Vice-Marshal, CB, CBE, AFC, FBIM, RAF (Ret'd)—such are the qualifications of the 'jet-propelled' man sifted from 400 applicants by a firm of management consultants to lead English badminton through the minefields of the open game. Avowedly a man 'unafraid of change', he

J D M McCallum, CBE, DSO presented, by J L Rankin, with his portrait after 52 years as Hon Secretary of the BUI's Northern Branch!

had flown 60 different types of aircraft, researched jet-icing, organised the Nimrod Maritime patrol, rescued troops from behind Borneo insurgent lines, and—crossed the Atlantic in a sub.

Like his predecessor, Brian Bisseker, he knew nothing of badminton but had played Lancashire League cricket with Leary Constantine, climbed Lakeland hills, and was ranked by Ian Maconachie as 'the best Rugby Union referee of the lot'.

Larry Lamb has brought essential management skills to a fast expanding game and BA of E organisation.

MAJOR JOHNNIE McCALLUM, CBE, DSO
More affectionately known as the 'Wee Major'. A badminton fanatic, he started to play when he was 19 and never lost interest in the game he served so well until he died, aged 83. He was President not only of the IBF (1961–3) but also of the Badminton Union of Ireland for which he played eight times. Was presented (by J L Rankin) with his own portrait to celebrate his 52 years as Hon Secretary of the BUI Northern Branch!

His other claim to fame was as founder of 'The Strollers' (1909). Wherever badminton was teething, he took these internationals to play exhibitions on recruiting tours where time was found also for the good things of life. Denmark in particular owed much to him.

He kept wicket for Ireland, and graced its rugby trials—unsuccessfully.

D L H MERCER
'Merk', a grandson of Major-General T W Mercer (Indian Army), was born in the badminton cradle of Southsea. Educated at Warwick School, he won such practical but archaic sporting events as throwing the cricket ball and rugby drop- and place-kicking. First played badminton (1899) in a friend's flat where folding doors were pushed open and a net erected. A good club player, he was Hon Treasurer and Match Secretary of prestigious Alexandra Palace, Editor of the *Badminton Gazette*, and BA of E Secretary and Hon Treasurer (1937–45). Interested in all games, he was a member of the MCC and had been a Great Northern Railway engineer and surveyor.

Could never refuse a job!

EMIL TER METZ
Go ahead Hon Secretary of the EBU. Owed much of his interest in badminton to the enthusiasm of his two daughters both of whom became Dutch internationals. After years of administration at Haarlem's famous Duinwijck club moved on to bigger things with EBU. Wide knowledge of languages; broad sense of humour.

STELLAN MOHLIN
Being an air-line pilot curbed Stockholm-born Stellan's early successes. He did however win the Swedish Junior title with Nils Jonson. And, on becoming a ground-based business man, carried on where he had left off by winning the Senior title for 6 successive years. Though below average height he still over-topped acrobatic Nils. Represented Sweden 17 times.

A fluent linguist, he enthusiastically undertook administrative responsibilities. These culminated in his becoming President of both IBF and EBU. Greatest achievement? Reconciling WBF and IBF after lengthy negotiations. Greatest ambition? More badminton for more people in more countries!

A D PREBBLE
Captained England in their first ever international against Ireland in 1903 after just two years of play! Won the All-England Men's Doubles three times. But his proudest boast was that he won the All-England Mixed titles for *both badminton and tennis in the same year (1909)* and with the same partner, Dora Boothby. The latter also won the Singles but in 1911, again a finalist, had the unique and unenviable distinction of losing 6–0, 6–0 to fellow badminton champion Dorothea Lambert-Chambers.

Ian Goodfellow (12) became the youngest probationary member of the Badminton Umpires' Association of England.

A great player, rated by Sir George Thomas as 'a master of tactics with a complete knowledge of the finer points', he put back into the game as a Council member and officer (Vice-President 1922–46) over a period of 43 years, far more than he ever took out of it. The older generation will still have fond memories of the ADP racket.

MONA RUSSELL

Ex-WAAF meteorologist, who still mixes with the 'stars'. Round—and lively—as a ball. A loyal Kent County player in its heyday and a mixed net-player of rare delicacy. Hated coaching, but took to umpiring like a duck to water. Often in the high chair for All-England finals (including Hashman v Takagi) she rules top internationals of every nation with the same easy firmness with which she handled undisciplined East End kids during her teaching career. Imperturbably beat a TV quiz panel to reveal her WAAF job had been 'bottling fog'.

HERBERT A E SCHEELE, OBE
'Mr Badminton' himself!

Moving to the USA at 10, Herbert spent some years at Montclair Academy; more formative ones at Dulwich College, and $3\frac{1}{2}$ on the Continent where he studied languages.

In 1935, he took on three men's work: Kent Hon Secretary, Treasurer, and Match Secretary. By 1936, he was playing badminton for Kent and was a member of the BA of E Council. And in between this and playing hockey, tennis and cricket for powerful Bromley clubs he became Hon Secretary and wet-nurse of the infant IBF which was to grow steadily to lusty manhood in his devoted care.

After the War, he succeeded D L H ('Merk') Mercer both as Secretary of the BA of E and Editor of the *Badminton Gazette*. From one crowded office in his own home with only his wife, Betty, for help, he did a Herculean task. In addition, he was responsible for the organisation and refereeing of the steadily growing All-England Championships; the editing of the *Gazette* to which he himself contributed voluminously as 'Invicta', and later of his own brainchild *World Badminton*; and the refereeing of Thomas and Uber Cup matches held world-wide.

His knowledge of the game's laws, regulations, history, players and officials became encyclopaedic. In his last year of life was awarded a richly deserved OBE for his devotion and services to the game.

With advancing years he relinquished his various posts: as BA of E Secretary (1945–70); as All-

Herbert Scheele, 'Mr Badminton', BA of E Secretary for 25 years, with his wife Betty, outside Buckingham Palace and sporting his well-deserved OBE.

England Referee (1947–80); as Editor of the *Gazette* (1946–70); as IBF Secretary (1938–76). But both BA of E and IBF were loath to let him go and retained him as adviser.

Herbert Scheele employed a natural 'ball-eye' effectively in the Kent team from 1935–48. In 1946–7 and 1947–8 he was an England trialist. But his most meritorious performance was undoubtedly the defeat of no lesser pair than All-England runners-up Ralph Nichols and Jean Stewart when his nerve held in a cliff-hanging, 4-all League finish.

As a man he was forthright and did not suffer fools gladly. He had courage of body and mind. The former was underlined by his abandonment of a Thomas Cup final in the face of a raging Indonesian crowd; his self-discharge from hospital to ensure his 25th consecutive appearance at the All-England; and his flights all over the world despite pain stoically born. The latter, by the way he fought for his beliefs and principles. In later years, Canute-like he sadly had to watch the irresistible modern tide erode his rooted beliefs in amateurism and court etiquette.

Horn-rimmed spectacled, a mane of unruly grey hair about his craggy face, an inevitable cigarette dangling from his mouth, limping painfully across to congratulate or commiserate with All-England finalists: that is how many will fondly remember him. And it was on Finals day 1981, that he died.

How appositely BA of E President Stuart Wyatt summed up Herbert Scheele: 'The greatest administrator ever in any game; a man of honesty and singleness of purpose'.

A C T VAN VOSSEN

Known only as 'Uncle Van' to his friends on both sides of the North Sea. An American-born Dutchman who did much for Danish badminton in many offices including that of captain of their very first international against his native Holland. And also for world badminton as President of the IBF (1959–61) in which post he was much helped by fluency in five or six languages.

Had played only virtual battledore and shuttlecock until introduced to slightly greater reality on the outdoor court of his Malayan bungalow by RSL's long-serving H S Debnam—with an indoor shuttle.

Died within three months of his Golden Wedding and two days after making a lively speech at the All-England dinner in 1961.

STUART WYATT, OBE, BEM

Enrolled as a Special Constable in the heat of the 1926 General Strike, solid merit found him as Divisional Commander with 300 constables on his patch at the end of the War—and a BEM. Articled and practised at the same Fareham office throughout his career as a Chartered Surveyor and Chairman of Hants River Authority. No Izaak Walton but a keen club cricketer who hit a century on the County ground and adroitly contorted his 6 ft 2 in 'behind the stumps' for a quarter of a century.

Strangely, removal of a badly damaged cartilage introduced him to badminton. Forced to wear an iron-strap he had to give up Rugby. Fortunately he followed his nearly distracted mother's advice to 'stop moping and try badminton'.

He rose from club player to Championships winner and earned 72 caps for Hampshire—a number however exceeded by his wife, Mims (now a JP) who notched up over 100. In later days became a keen and efficient umpire and President of the Badminton Umpires' Association of England. A diplomatic Chairman of the BA of E Council (1961–70) he was an obvious choice as

In reaching—and winning—the 1956 All-England Men's Singles final, Eddy Choong did not meet a single seed. Unknowns had beaten all three of them.

President in 1965. Travelling the country he has filled the post for over seventeen years with distinction and a warm friendliness that never forgets even the humblest cog in the badminton wheel.

OBE (1972); IBF Council Member (1955), Vice-President (1969), President (1974–6).

Great Players

ZHANG AILING *China*

An 80 per cent victory record over Lene Köppen speaks for itself. So, in a single year (1981–2) do victories in the Friends' Provident Masters, the All-England, and the World Games. (Especially when the latter includes the doubles defeat of the world champions Nora Perry and Jane Webster). A singularly inappropriate surname for a superbly fit 24-year-old Shanghai PE teacher whose game is based on power, speed—and delicacy. And whose quiet boast is 'I fear no player'. Winner of the 1983 All-England singles title but crashed to Li Lingwei in the World Championships.

MARGARET BECK *England*

With insatiable badminton precocity, Margaret was beating internationals at 15 and was herself capped (1969) whilst still a junior. Emigrated from depressed West Cumberland to seek badminton fame in London where she and Gillian Gilks repeatedly clashed for supremacy. 'Small Maggie's' long run of national and international successes (English National (5), All-England (2), World Invitation (1), European Championships (2), and Commonwealth Games (2) ended with ironic tragedy whilst winning Bronze Medals at the first ever World Championships (1977).

Operation after operation was performed on a knee ('that of a woman of 60') shattered by remorseless training. (She even did shuttle runs on the pavement outside her flat). Gristle was removed, cartilage shaved off, bone drilled . . . to no avail.

The fatalistic hunch of her shoulders: 'The thought of no badminton scares the life out of me'. Despite brave efforts, badminton lost the joy of her easy grace of movement and classic stroke. But she is now making her mark on the golf course.

EWE BENG (EDDY) CHOONG *Malaysia*

5 ft 2 in Eddy, the 'pocket prodigy from Penang', contained huge talent in small bulk. With Malaysian titles already to his credit, he arrived in England when 19 to study law—and to bring life, laughter and vitality to England's post-war moribund game with an undreamed of jump smash, a knack for returning smashes even when flat on his back, and the tightest of drops.

Flemming Delfs (left): *the Danish Adonis with a nuclear-powered backhand; Prakash Padukone, India's master of touch and deception.*

His game could be succinctly summed up: speed and sportsmanship; fun and fireworks. He took 'the magic out of the mystic illusionist Finn Kobbero and the sting out of hurricane hitter Erland Kops'. With Wong Peng Soon at his peak, Eddy won the All-England singles four times in five years (1953–7); and the doubles outright (1951–3) with his almost equally talented brother E L (David)—the master tactician.

On retirement, coached Tan Aik Huang to exhaustion twenty hours a week to interrupt Kops' long All-England run (1966). Then took to fast dogs (Alsatians and Dobermann Pinchers) and faster cars (Lotus and Mini Cooper).

J E CRABBIE *Scotland*
An international at both rugby and badminton (1912). Might have shone still brighter had he not, as Unionist candidate for Moray and Nairn 'had to spend invaluable badminton hours weaning electors from Home Rule, Free Trade and the Insurance Act'.

FLEMMING DELFS *Denmark*
Singles was his game; Mr Backhand, his nickname. Many a player's Achilles heel was his strength, rather it seemed by some happy accident of nature than conscious practice. Indeed, Delfs disliked training and big man that he was paid the penalty in the stifling heat and humidity of Djakarta's cockpit, the Senayan Stadium. 'There it is terrible. It is so difficult to breathe'.

Elegant and casually assured, the nordic Adonis had an immaculate technique. One highlighted in cut net-shots that crawled over the tape but that could produce only what was criticised as a 'powder puff smash' for so big a man.

His peak was in 1977. In one of the finest ever Wembley finals he beat the previous year's finalist Liem Swie King (I) 15–17, 15–11, 15–8 to a standing ovation. And in the first ever World Championships, with all the shots and all the answers, slew his compatriot Svend Pri 15–6, 15–5.

Thereafter, with little money in the game, he could never again drive himself to the same heights.

FRANK DEVLIN *Ireland*
'A richly talented and likeable man; a colossus who bestrode the courts breathing fire'. An Irishman who dominated British courts from 1922–31! During that decade he won eighteen All-England titles (six singles, five in succession; five mixed and seven men's doubles) and numerous Irish caps.

Losing half a heel from osteomyelitis as a 12-year-old was a blessing in disguise. Lying in bed, using his wrist, he interminably and powerfully hit a shuttle against the wall. The peculiar mechanics of an allegedly double-jointed elbow enabled him to play accurate and audacious drops and lobs from behind him, deep in the backhand corner. Fortunate too in living near G S B ('Curly') Mack. Alternating on their home courts, they played singles early and late, each sharpening his genius on the other's.

Devlin, bespectacled, red-faced, sweat-banded, was at his best when 'steaming like mother's copper'. From intimidating crouch, he annihilated errant serves; smashed not powerfully but error-free; added contrasting and silky touches, and employed 'the most remarkable retrieving powers ever seen'. Knowing little of losing, he was always a generous winner. Not for him the often cold and silent touch with averted glance of modern tennis.

At the peak of his powers he was lured to Winnipeg Winter Club as coach. After a spell there, and a tour of Australasia and of Malaysia (where 'Europeans never play because of excessive heat') he moved to New York and then Baltimore.

There, future champions Sue and Judy (see p 153) had been born. His wife (née G Steed) had been undefeated in Bedford College doubles matches for 4 years. Her partner was the Mrs Dewhirst who in 1926 waited in vain for a Wimbledon Centre Court match. Her opponent should have been the great Suzanne Lenglen who, not getting the VIP treatment she insisted on as her right, just didn't turn up.

Found time to edit the *Gazette* (1928–9) and write *Badminton for All*.

A king amongst players!

DOROTHEA DOUGLASS *England*

Better known to tennis fans as Mrs Lambert Chambers, she won the Wimbledon singles title seven times. And yet her most memorable moment was losing to the young French challenger Suzanne Lenglen whose knee-length hemline had caused spectators to leave the court muttering 'Disgusting'.

Giving away 17 years, Mrs Lambert Chambers had hurled back her challenger from 8–10, to 6–4, 6–5 (40–15)—only to lose game, set and match after Mlle Lenglen won a net-cord point off the frame and she herself had hit the cord with her favourite drive—only to see it fall back on her own side! But perhaps the blow was softened 6 years later when, now 46, she led England to Wightman Cup victory—alongside Kitty McKane (see p 156).

Her badminton highlights were less spectacular but noteworthy. Tennis showed through all her strokes but in her second full season, 1903, the year she first won Wimbledon, she won the All-England doubles with Miss M Hardy, and the following year (another Wimbledon win), took the All-England mixed with H N Marrett. And yet she never played for England.

C P (CHICK) DOYLE *Ireland*

Broth of a boy Doyle was coached by Irish 'king' and master-craftsman Frank Peard. As crown prince, emigrated briefly to Australia in furtherance of his career as a chicken-sexer. Failed to gain antipodean honours because immediately prior to the championships he'd 'been playing every night for the past two weeks'. Anxiously wrote back to Irish title-holder Peard, 'Don't get beaten until I come back'. Returned to Ireland—and did it yeoman service.

ARCHIBALD FRANK ENGELBACH
England

Put his agility as a Schools' gymnastic champion and his all-rounder's eye to effective use on a badminton court. Won the All-England men's doubles in 1920 but never played for England

David Freeman (USA) : 'He's fabulous'.

because of the demands of his profession as a judge. A most approachable man who avoided any hint of judicial pomposity.

D F (DAVE) FREEMAN *USA*

'A perfectly balanced, precision instrument that glided on ball bearings'. Such the summing up of a lean whippet of a man, a US Army surgeon, who went unbeaten in America from 1939–49, won the All-England singles in 1949 with almost arrogant ease, dropping only 24 points in his last eight games. After retirement, made a winning comeback in Toronto in 1953 when he lost but one game —only his third since 1939! Much of this accomplished when he was stationed in the Panama Canal Zone where badminton was 'non-existent'.

Classic shots played with supple ease, and the hair-line precision of a surgeon. He lacked power but his smash (especially round the head) was steep and with poison-tipped accuracy; his retrieving, unyielding, knee-skinning!

Unhurried, calmly patient, fired by absolute concentration and driving ambition, he limited his opponents' returns and relentlessly pressured them into mistakes.

Surgeons don't make *errors*; nor did he. On those very rare occasions when he erred, they were accompanied by his own suitably pungent comments or his roar of anguished disbelief.

His greatest moments? At the age of 28, he defeated both Malayan Masters, Wong Peng Soon and Ooi Teik Hock, first in the Thomas Cup, then, allowing neither more than six points, in the All-England. In the Thomas Cup, against Wong, he was held to 4–4—then raced to an incredible 15–4, 15–1 victory! After 6 weeks' intensive neurological study he entered the Danish Open—and scored victory again over Wong Peng Soon (to win the All-England title for the next three years), and, in the final, Ooi Teik Hock.

'An amalgam of stamina, talent and unbreakable concentration'. A shooting star of unequalled brilliance that shot across the European skies just once—but never to be forgotten.

'As near faultless as any player I've ever seen'.

MORTEN FROST *Denmark*

6 ft 2 in Morten jumped his own height in Danish amateur athletics—until it was discovered he was a 'licensed' badminton player able to play for the higher Open cash prizes. But until 1981 not even his quicksilver feet and lightning defensive reflexes stopped him 'flopping' in quarter- and semi-finals. To these he added a penetrating smash, coolness and determination.

Then the Indian champion came to live in Denmark—and two hour singles practices against Prakash Padukone (see p 157) put power into his game. Defeats of his former tormentors Liem Swie King, Prakash himself, and China's Han Jian in a matter of weeks; winner of the Danish Open; runner-up in the World Games;—then, climactically, winner of the 1982 All-England.

Morten, 24 years of age, curly haired and unassuming, is a Copenhagen University 'eternal' student, seeking a history degree to qualify him for teaching—and a Derby County supporter.

GILLIAN GILKS MBE *England*

Precocious! At 11, Gillian was considered for Surrey Under 18! At 12½ (1962–3) she won the All-England Junior Under-15 Singles! At 14½ she won *both* Under-15 and Under-18 titles; later followed in Heather Ward's (Surrey) footsteps to win that title *four* times. Incredibly, her first of nearly 80 England caps came when she was only 16. Small wonder she was hailed as the 'most promising junior of all time'.

There followed a meteoric career that blazed unforgettably across the badminton sky. Stark

'I limit myself to 20-yard sprints when I'm training at home. After all Guernsey's only a small island!' Sally Podger (England).

figures (even ten All-England titles, two Silvers at the 1977 World Championships, European and Commonwealth titles, eight English National singles titles between 1969 and 1981—Margaret Beck took the others) do not tell the full story. Nor do the other honours that followed: Sportswriters' Woman of the Year; BBC Super Star; and an MBE in 1976.

All the strokes in the book were hers. Height lent pointed steepness to a smash that complemented mesmeric cross-court drops. Tight serving went hand in hand with still tighter, silken, netplay. An elegant backhand was the magic wand which wafted her out of trouble as surely did a smash-proof defence. At the net, reach and reflex made her a rampant tigress.

Tragically the comet plunged to earth in a trail of bitter recrimination with a BA of E that resented

Morten Frost (Denmark) : quicksilver feet.

any hint of dictation. A writ was issued against them; a rift created. Gillian lost her chance of a World title; England, of the Uber Cup.

A wary peace was patched up. A new look Gillian emerged: nose re-shaped; hair re-styled. Perhaps confidence returned. But things were never the same, although at the last moment the writ was withdrawn by mutual agreement.

Where lay the blame? In Gillian herself? Unlikely. In thrustful coach, Mike Goodwin; in unbending BA of E? More probable.

Once Gillian was labelled 'The Poor Man's Judy Hashman'. In truth, she lacked the latter's stubborn determination and solidity, lacked confidence, which made her brittle. But she was a greater all-rounder of flair and elegance. She was England's 'Golden Girl'.

THE HAMILTONS *Ireland*

To do justice to the Hamiltons in a single paragraph is to try to encompass the Irish badminton world in one's hand, to attempt to pour a pint of Guinness into a thimble.

Father '*Bud*' Hamilton was Ireland's first badminton champion and international. Played cricket for them too. Sport raced in the family blood. Brother W D ('Drum') kept up the cricket tradition by playing for Oxford and Ireland, and threw in amateur soccer caps for good measure.

W J ('Ghost') was another soccer international —who won Wimbledon singles in 1890, ending the run of the famous William Renshaw, who annexed seven singles and, with his twin, seven doubles titles. Strangely, as with William Baddeley, illness cut short his tennis career at its peak—but led to badminton. W J became the first Irish men's doubles champion with—why, Bud, of course.

From such strong stock sprang three of Ireland's finest players. Bud's boys *Willoughby ('Rat')* and *Arthur* collected 37 caps between them. 'Rat' might have been one of the all-time greats but he lacked the burning killer spirit—except when English players were on the other side of the net! And, not to be outdone, Mavis won 20 caps.

BRIAN 'BOMBER' HARRIS

A Sergeant PTI at RAF Innsworth. Although not a player (he probably never held a racket) he certainly taught England for the first time just what fitness really was.

Miss H Hogarth and her partner scored 35 points in one hand in a Cheltenham Handicap event in 1909.

Gunalan's lunging early-take poses problems even for eager-footed Rudy Hartono.

Of him Mike Tredgett (see p 161) said: 'He was a hard man. He pole-axed me. I was laid out on the floor unable to move. But he was a comic when you were doing it. So you did it for him'.

Graffiti summed it up: 'Never have so many been knackered by so few'.

RUDY HARTONO *Indonesia*

One of the truly greats. And the Admirable Crichton of badminton. Shrewd and cool, superbly fit (but who would not be after 8 vigorous months in an Indonesian training camp?) always on balance and gliding into instant recovery, Rudy moved like a Greek god. Court manners impeccable, sporting, modest: an unattainable example to the McEnroes and Nastases.

Though an accomplished doubles player, singles were his forte, his sole aim at the All-England. Style, classical; his smash, even from the baseline as penetrative and accurate as bazooka fire; his backhand virtually made redundant by his speed about court and leaping round-the-head interceptions; his touch at the net smooth as Eastern silk.

Formerly known as Rudy Niohapliane, he started his record breaking run of seven successive wins in 1968. Never really in danger except in 1974 when Punch Gunalan took him to the limit and in 1978 when Sture Johnsson literally had him on his knees—and (with an open court) hit out! Who better than old rival Pri to end his magic run in 1975? But he was back in 1976 to beat Kops' record seven wins.

In the 1978 All-England he played compatriot Liem Swie King with such uncharacteristic fallibility that it seemed he was 'under orders'. Thereafter he retired from the scene until, in 1980, Indonesian pride was buckled by a disastrous All-England and defeat by the Chinese. Recalled to the front, Hartono made a dramatic comeback to win the World Championship before an ecstatic crowd.

That he conceded just 44 points in 12 games in 1969 shows—the Master!

JUDY HASHMAN *USA and England*

Born of an Irish father, Frank Devlin (see p 149) and an English mother in Winnipeg, she passed much of her playing career in America; married, lived and was naturalised in England (1970).

From her Irish champion father she inherited tactical astuteness that forced opponents to play her game; from America, an indomitable determination and killer-spirit. To these she added line-to-line clearing, in-built deception, uncanny accuracy, fantastic concentration and error-free play. Her game—even her knock-up—was planned.

She swept the board in American junior badminton (13–18), won twelve American titles, and played in five Uber Cup series, helping them to victory in three and losing only one game in 14 years.

Sturdily built, beshorted and with close-cut sandy hair, 'Little Red Dev' slugged it out for world supremacy with Margaret Varner, the 'Texan Bronze'. Came out 3–2 up on her in Wembley clashes, and went on to a record-breaking ten All-England singles (the first on a first appearance at 18) and seven doubles titles (all but one with sister Sue) between 1954 and 1967: 17 in all—equal to Meriel Lucas's record and just one less than her father's tally. Virtually unbeaten, after Miss Varner's retirement, from 1959 to 1966.

In 1978 she was appointed supremo: England's team manager-coach. Sadly her career ended in dispute with the BA of E on the very day her players won the European Championships.

A great all-rounder she played also for the US Junior Wightman Cup (Tennis) and All-America Lacrosse teams.

ERNEST EDWARD HAWTHORN *England*

A massive 6 ft 6 in, Hawthorn's best strokes paradoxically were net-shots and drop-shots of exquisite delicacy. By application and joining all three of London's leading clubs, Logan, Crystal Palace and Alexandra Palace, he transmuted a modest talent into two All-England titles (in 1910 the men's with P D Fitton and in 1912 the mixed with Hazel Hogarth) and eight England caps. The last of these he won in 1925 when he was an All-England semi-finalist at 48. A fact that caused the All-England Veterans' age limit to be raised from 45 to 50 in 1927 after his three successive victories.

On retirement from active play he entered administration just as wholeheartedly. Vice-Presi-

Judy Hashman (USA): 10 times winner of the All-England singles title. 'Little red Dev, indeed!

dent of the BA of E and IBF he was also the former's official handicapper and to him are owed the BA of E differential handicap tables—baffling as racing odds to the uninitiated, invaluable to hard-pressed Tournament Referees.

As generous with possessions as with enthusiasm, he frequently gave back cups he had won and even, diffidently, his prized all-England winners' scarf and blazer to Marie Ussing and Conny Jepson, title winners themselves but deprived of that particular accolade by post-war shortages (1947). Gave cups for Junior events both in Denmark and England.

His pre-match trick-shot knock-ups with his frequent partner Frank Devlin were a tournament highlight that turned him into a minor deity for the author in his youth.

DOUGLAS HENDRY *Scotland*

Enthusiastic schoolmaster, driving force of Scottish Schools Badminton Union, selector and coach,

Hendry missed international honours through injury. As 'Scotia' and then 'Cock 'o the North' wrote for the *Gazette* with style and humour. Gave his life in a Glencoe climbing tragedy when trying to save another's.

HAZEL HOGARTH *England*
No player of the past can be ignored when hailed as 'the greatest net player ever' by Margaret Tragett and as 'murder at the net' by Frank Devlin himself. Contrary to Malayan prejudice, she was the innovator of the backhand serve. But it is recorded that 'after she had shuffled it over the net she crouched—and H S Uber, feigning a rush, would repeatedly drop it disconcertingly on her back'. Thirteen English caps in 25 years (1904–29): five All-England ladies' doubles titles and six mixed, four successfully with Sir George (1914–22). Won her first title in 1905: her last in 1927.

R J (MARIAN) HORSLEY *England*
Whilst still a schoolgirl was within a point of beating the 'unbeatable', F Chesterton and Mrs Tragett. Ahead of her time, fitness fanaticism gave her a whirlwind speed and power that won two All-England titles (1929 and 1931) and 24 caps.

Twenty years later, she won the Berks, Bucks & Oxon Restricted four times in succession. Lost her title the following year in a tight three-gamer— at the age of 61! Beaten only by an arthritic hip.

Played also for Middlesex and the Strollers—all with unequalled modesty.

HAN JIAN *China*
A footballer who shot to fame in 1980 when he defeated Liem Swie King in the second Indonesia v China clash (the 'Match of the Century') in Singapore. To do it he studied video-tapes of the Indonesian, and trained relentlessly in the 82°F humidity of a diving pool.

Such stamina is vital to enable 5 ft 7 in *2.3 m* Han Jian to maintain the pressure of a stream of 'jump' smashes and drops. But in 1981 he was in temporary decline losing easily to Prakash and Morten Frost. Has some English—and much Puckish sense of humour.

He beat Swie King in a vital match of the China–Indonesia Thomas Cup clash in 1982 but lost to him in World Championship series.

SUN AI HWANG *South Korea*
Trained from childhood at the disciplined Korean Athletic College, home of Olympic potential, and built up on 5000 calorie élite diet, Sun was kept a closely guarded secret. In 1981, with the wraps off, she swathed through world class opposition in Japan and Taiwan, before murdering Europe's favourite, and All-England holder, Lene Köppen, 11–1, 11–2 in a breath-taking display of fitness that complemented her name 'beautiful mind'. Narrowly lost in the World Games 11–9, 9–11, 9–12 to China's wonder-girl Zhang Ailing. And an injured thumb played havoc with her training for 1982 All-England. With little major success since, one wonders if Sun was just a fleeting comet.

KEVIN JOLLY *England*
England's white hope. Fast mover and faster hitter who can retract into a strongly armoured shell. Hit one of England's fastest fifties—50 caps in 6 years. (It took Sir George Thomas nearly five times as long to get half as many!) Has beaten— and lost disastrously to—some of the world's best.

All-England Junior Triple Champion in 1976–7; might well have had the European Junior Triple too had not an unnecessary 'Jolly jump' fractured his ankle.

Badminton's 'McEnroe' for some years, he was sent home for misbehaviour at the European Championships. Now reformed, and if he can throw back the menacing challenge of Steve Baddeley and Nicky Yates, may yet take over Ray Stevens' mantle as England's No 1 for which he has worked hard and long. A licensed player. Ranked No 3 in 1982, he joyously won the English National singles title only to create a stormy scene.

A D (TONY) JORDAN OBE *England*
Emerged suddenly into the limelight as All-England Junior Triple Champion (1951–2), 'the best 17 year old ever'; stayed in it when, over-ruling his mother (Cheshire) as to 'setting', they beat the redoubtable Malayan, David Choong and Miss E Windsor-Aubrey, a highly rated net-player. Has been in it ever since.

In addition to National, European, and Commonwealth Games medals, he won the All-England mixed title four times (1956–68) with three different partners: June Timperley, Sue Whetnall and Jenny Horton. His ruthless receiving, error-free accuracy, biting round-the-head smash, and subtly deceptive variations of pace and direction made him 'Master of Mixed' indeed. He had not only artistry and genius but also humility and honesty.

Won 97 consecutive English caps (a record 100 in all) in 19 years of service to his country (and his county) and took part in no fewer than seven Thomas Cup series! Richly deserved his MBE in 1970. It is recorded that he passed through Moss

Bros with all his court speed—in 3 minutes flat.

LIEM SWIE KING *Indonesia*

Swie King, Indonesia's indiarubber man, long played apprentice to sorcerer Hartono. Indeed in 1976 he seemed to be the sacrificial lamb to ensure the latter's record-making eighth All-England victory. But in the 1980 Friends' Provident Masters he ruthlessly cut down the apparently ageing maestro—only, mere months later, to be unable to match his 7-year senior in the Jakarta World Championship final. Nevertheless his whirlwind brilliance has rightly earned him three All-England singles titles but it could not enable him to overcome China's Han Jian in the key match of the 1982 Thomas Cup final or compatriot Sugiarto in the 1983 World Championships, thus becoming runner-up in that event for the second time.

FINN KOBBERO *Denmark*

'Supreme artist' and 'wayward genius'. He could play like an angel, until, concentration or interest failing, he became mortal. Born with talent, he rarely felt the need to practise.

A love of parties (with breakfast at 5 pm) and a steadfast refusal to train meant he could not effectively sustain top-flight singles. A master of the drop-shot and deception (he could hold totally wrong-footing shots longer than any one else) he still relished the smash.

But it was largely in the forecourt, with saturnine Hammergaard Hansen of the booming smash (forehand and backhand alike) at the back, that his lightning reflexes won him seven men's doubles titles (1955–64).

A master of the early-take half-court game, he played mixed with panache dividing the spoils equally with delightful Danish stars Kirsten Thorndahl and Ulla Rasmussen (later Strand) to equal Sir George's long-standing eight wins record. Tall, good-looking, he still graces Wembley—as a professional television commentator.

LENE KÖPPEN *Denmark*

The only dentist you would ever beg to visit. Lene will long be remembered for her distinguished play abroad (Danish, Nordic, European and World Champion) as well as in England (Evening of Champions; Friends' Provident Masters and All-England titles: two singles victories in the latter after an unjustly long spell of being the bridesmaid but not the bride). A player who depends more on wholehearted athleticism and determination than on finesse.

In 1982 won the 'Ekstra Bladet' (Denmark's

Giant Steen Skovgaard and graceful Lene Köppen, one of many great Danish mixed pairs.

biggest newspaper) award for most popular Danish sportsman or woman or team by polling three times as many votes as the Danish Soccer XI; and out-voted Bjorn Borg in the Volvo Cup, awarded by a panel of sports editors, for the finest Nordic achievements.

She will be remembered even longer for her charm off court and on: laughing brown eyes under a cap of dark hair and the kind of smile you'd expect, but don't always get, from a dentist. Delightful in victory; superb in defeat. When beaten by Hiroe Yuki in 1977 one could hardly tell victor from vanquished; it was Lene who raised the Japanese girl's arm aloft in salute to the thunderous applause. And in 1981, after a shattering surprise defeat by Korea's Sun Ai Hwang it was Lene who jested with reporters about the hurricane that had sunk her and paid sincere tribute to her young conqueror.

After shock defeats in the 1983 All-England and World Championships she announced her retirement.

ERLAND KOPS *Denmark*

'Erland Kops It' might have punned the *Gazette* in 1957 after he had changed his name from Olsen —and lost to Eddy Choong. But he was to win that All-England title the next year—and in another 6 to create a record beaten only in 1976 by Hartono.

Also won the men's doubles in that year—and 9 years later started a run of three with Henning Borch.

Initially owed his success—and a reputation for dullness—to tireless retrieving. After all, he trained in a weighted waistcoat. Later, having spent two years in Bangkok, he added a very powerful smash—and a complementary delicate touch.

Runs two restaurants in Copenhagen—does some of the cooking himself.

'Power, precision and ruthlessness' summed him up in his heyday.

MERIEL LUCAS *England*

Devon, long in badminton's backwoods, has had her days of glory. In an age of few international matches, Meriel Lucas more than doubled her English caps (only seven between 1902 and 1909) with no fewer than 17 All-England titles (a number exceeded only by Sir George Thomas and Frank Devlin): six singles, ten doubles, one mixed. She and her doubles partner, Ethel Thomson (later as Mrs Dudley Larcombe she won the Wimbledon tennis singles), shared the All-England singles title for 11 years and never lost a match in tournament play.

In her best year (1907–8) Meriel won the Triple Crown in England, Ireland and Scotland.

G S B ('CURLY') MACK *Ireland*

As became a double-first Scholar of Trinity College, Dublin, in Classics, Ethics and Logic, a debonair Mack glided (invariably in a heavy sweater) with a cool and unhurried elegance, born of thoughtful anticipation, that smacked of Sir George himself. Indeed he won four of his six Irish titles with the latter. And six All-England titles with fellow Irishman Frank Devlin whose restless fiery aggression his own anticipation, delicate touch and effortless smash so perfectly complemented. The finest men's pair of the Golden Twenties, their opponents found them hard competitors, 'confusing, exhausting and devastating'.

Of him (and Mrs Tragett with whom he won an All-England title (1923) and two of his Irish titles)

Within six weeks of Mrs Helen McDonald (Cheshire) winning the All-England Veterans' Mixed Doubles title, her daughter Jean won the same event at the All-England Junior Championships.

an aesthete said, 'I have seen the poetry of motion in Russian Ballet. Now I have seen it in badminton'. Tall and slender, Mack was the perfect stylist.

He was lured from ill-paid schoolmastering to more financially rewarding coaching in Montreal. And in that country tragically committed suicide.

IAN MACONACHIE *Ireland*

The man who made a billion shuttles (or thereabouts). Works Manager at RSL's Sandwich factory, Mac made the No 1 Tourney the finest shuttle in the world—and then pioneered its synthetic twin, the 'Competition-Tourney'. Only recently—after 50 years with the firm—did he decide to retire.

A 6 ft 4 in *1.9 m* giant, Geordie born but of Irish heritage, he joyously bestrode the court, with a vertical smash that did little for the welfare of his own shuttles. He forgets how many caps he gained for Ireland—but remembers winning the All-England mixed title with Thelma Kingsbury in 1937—a partnership the BA of E stretched a point to renew in 1949 when Thelma specially re-crossed the Atlantic where she had teamed up with Ken Davidson's stage show. And, more vaguely, nineteen National titles.

A born raconteur; played cricket for the MCC and was youngest ever Minor County (Northumberland) captain; drove not only a very mean +3 ball at Royal St Georges, but also express trains during the General Strike in 1926.

Personified the joy of badminton!

KITTY McKANE *England*

'An agile athlete with an eagle eye', she combined unique tennis and badminton brilliance in the early '20s. She was 'in a class of her own' when she won the first of her four All-England singles titles in 1920; was 'unbeatable' in mixed with Frank Devlin (to whom she was briefly engaged) who gave her the accolade of playing 'sides'; and she won the ladies' doubles twice with her sister, Mrs A D Stocks. Commented one opponent: 'What a reach!'

Concurrently, she was dominating Wimbledon tennis. In 1923 she was runner-up to the legendary Suzanne Lenglen who could place the ball on a handkerchief. In 1924 won the title by inflicting her only Wimbledon defeat ever on Helen Wills Moody ('Little Poker Face' who despite poor footwork hit so powerfully that she won the Wimbledon title eight times, and between 1927 and 1932 did not drop a single set). In 1926, now married to L A Godfree, they became the only married couple ever to win the Wimbledon mixed title.

In 1980, still going very strong, she was televised in action in period costume at Badminton House!

BOB McCOIG MBE *Scotland*

Non-smoker, non-drinker, fitness fanatic: he was presented with a decanter and silver cigarette box on gaining his 50th cap. Inherited his skills from international uncle R S McCoig; still competing fiercely in his mid-fifties. Bob monopolised Scottish Junior titles between 1954 and 1957; won the Kelvin Hall World Invitation Mixed title with Wilma Tyre; lost the 1968 All-England final to arch-rival Tony Jordan. Won the Scottish National singles title a mammoth fifteen times, and a host of lesser ones.

Dancing feet, laser sharp reflexes, granite defence, the early take, and Paul Daniels' deception were his weapons. His deprecating 'Aw!' and his habit of re-tieing tied shoe-laces and of demisting mist-free glasses in moments of crisis were a reporter's delight. Carried the flag for the Scots Commonwealth Team in 1974; deservedly awarded the MBE in 1975.

DR H N MARRETT *England*

A shooting star whose brilliance might have rivalled that of Sir George Thomas. Reached the All-England singles semi-final (which he might well have won had he not taken a shuttle dropping a foot out) in his second year. Made no such mistake the following year (1904) when 'by amazing activity' he took the first of his eight titles in a 'Triple'.

Then disappeared from the badminton scene absorbed in furthering his open-air cure for consumption. Emerged briefly after the War, as brilliant and agile as ever, before retiring again just as suddenly.

RALPH C F NICHOLS *England*

Spurning 'the fetish of brute force' bespectacled Nichols achieved success with a supple-wristed backhand, deceptive drops, effortless stride, stonewall defence, subtle placements using every inch of court, a scientific astuteness in reading the game, and finesse. A dour, gruff man he relished a war of attrition with slow shuttles.

Between 1930 and 1951, he won 36 caps; at one time pre-War, his record in 24 matches read: singles 22–0; men's doubles 22–2; mixed doubles 2–0.

Won the All-England singles on his second appearance and five times in all; the men's doubles

R C F Nichols (England) : dour in defence ; pin-point accurate in attack.

three times, with his brother Lesley (1936–8); and the mixed surprisingly only once (1939) with Miss B M Staples.

Played tennis at Wimbledon and reached the semi-final of the *Evening News* Trophy from a field of 2000.

PRAKASH PADUKONE *India*

The 'Bangalore Torpedo'—an Indian bank clerk whose Ranji-wrist struck sparks against the world's best. Deception, anticipation, held shots and pinpoint smashing reduced holder Liem Swie King to impotence in 1980 for him to become the first ever Indian All-England winner.

Unable to find real opposition in the whole of the vast Indian sub-continent, he migrated. In steamy Jakarta he was looked after by the Indian Community. In chilly Denmark, he was appointed coach to Hvidovre BK and sponsored by Akai and Yonex. 'I like Danish badminton better than Danish weather'.

Won Commonwealth Gold in 1978, beat Delfs in the 1979 'Evening of Champions', and Frost Hansen in the Friends' Provident Masters in the same year.

Copenhagen's Gentofte BC had 1500 members.

Awarded title Padma Shri in Republic Day Honours List.

NORA PERRY MBE *England*
Fate—or was it Ann MacFarlane—gave Nora her chance. And she seized it with both hands. When the former's car broke down, Nora, then 16, partnered USA's Tyna Barrinaga to beat Margaret Beck and Julie Rickard (internationals both). A month later Ann's leg injury gave Nora a second chance—and Judy Hashman's famous scalp.

In 1972, a Triple Crown in the All-England Junior! A year later the first of 70+ international caps. Since then there is not an honour in the game that has eluded her. All-England (7) and World (2) titles. National, European and Commonwealth—and Friends' Provident Masters too.

Her father had urged her: 'Play tennis; there's money in it'. Like all teenagers she did the opposite . . . and found success if not a crock of gold. Yet in 1974 her interest waned—and it was left to future husband Joe to shunt her back on the badminton rails. And 'as long as it's fun' that's where she'll stay.

The secret of her success? Behind the ready laughter and attractive appearance lies a shatter-proof determination.

Her low serve is not so much 'grooved' as 'tunnelled'. Her flick serve, a veritable man-trap. She is not merely an aggressive receiver but a geometrician dealing in acutely angled returns. Knife-edged reflexes and a sanguine spirit that disdains passive defence make her dangerous under pressure—and lethal in net-anticipation.

Nora has charisma. Her consolatory bottom tap with her racket, her shrill squeaks of admonition and encouragement, her ever-ready smile and blonde hair, her charming bob-curtsey and her eager stance have made her recognisable to millions.

England's 'Golden Girl' indeed—and an MBE to boot.

SVEND PRI *Denmark*
'Nastase without the nastiness'—a showman full of trick-shots, gamesmanship, and humour. 'Badminton's Houdini'—a retriever of the impossible. His fighting spirit in the sweat-bath of Djakarta's Senayan Stadium made him the idol of even its patriotic fanatics.

Born 50 metres from a badminton hall, Svend was a Danish Junior Champion from 13 to 18! An international at 19. Trained with Denmark's toughest cyclists. Won three All-England mixed titles with delightful Ulla Strand—but it took him 11 years to win the All-England singles by a memorable defeat of Rudy Hartono (1975). With tears in his eyes he ran to embrace his wife.

Loves pubs, parties and Portobello Road. Made a farewell appearance in a Copenhagen arcade. Appointed Danish National Coach.

European, Danish and Nordic titles galore.

One of badminton's richest characters—most colourful of players. Died tragically in 1983.

THE RASMUSSEN SISTERS *Denmark*
Two delightful Danish 'dishes'. Better known today perhaps as Karin Jorgensen and Ulla Strand. Together they won the All-England doubles twice; Ulla also won it once with Imre Rietveld. And she only just failed to beat Betty Uber's magnificent eight mixed titles, winning four with Kobbero and three with Pri over eleven years.

Hair now close-cut, they turned up at Wembley in 1965, solemnly to announce: 'We are de Beadles'.

GUY A SAUTTER *Switzerland*
In Debrett, Comte Sautter de Beauregard; in All-England programmes, 'Un Lapin'—a wildly inappropriate pseudonym adopted, not infrequently, when he should have been studying the art of hotel management rather than that of badminton. Sautter was before his time with rigorous fitness training and a withering round-the-head smash: 'Heavy, thoughtfully placed, and deceptive'—G A T. A keen rival of Sir George Thomas, he won the All-England singles in 1911, 1913, and 1914. Returning from Switzerland in 1922, hoping to win the trophy outright, he fell to Sir George whose third consecutive victory gave *him* the cup. Earlier in the season he had defeated Frank Devlin (with whom he won the All-England men's doubles) 15–1 in the third—though giving away 12 years.

Lived in Monte Carlo during the Second World War: suspected of helping the French Resistance, he received harsh treatment that impaired his health.

FERRY SONNEVILLE *Indonesia*
Acknowledged as one of the game's 'gentlemen', industrious Ferry was one of the best players, despite a fine Thomas Cup record, never to win an All-England title. His ability as a fluent linguist helped him as President of the IBF (1971–4) for whom he did sterling work. This included setting up the Ferry Sonneville Coaching Fund to help emergent badminton countries raise playing standards.

Danish Dishes! The Rasmussen sisters, now Karin Jörgensen and Ulla Strand—'We are de Beadles'.

WONG PENG SOON MBE *Malaya*

A small man with a great heart. The first of the Far Eastern giants. A magician. Courts shrank beneath his unhurried, gliding feet; his effortless, steel-wristed backhand clears made them appear much shorter than 44 ft *13.4 m.*

A rocklike defence, a wide repertoire of strokes and an ability to place the shuttle with uncanny accuracy in the far corners enabled him to win most games without undue use of a penetrating cross-court smash—and happily to play to the gallery with teasing cat and mouse tactics.

At his peak before the Japanese invasion, he was 31 on his first appearance in England, when he pole-axed England's best, Noel Radford, 15–0, 15–4. And yet he himself scored only a handful more points in his famous All-England final when American Dave Freeman mastered the master in one of the all-time great matches. Sportingly Wong made little play of a pulled arm muscle.

But for the next 3 years the All-England title was his. In 1950 he mesmerised Denmark's genius Poul Holm; in 1951, despite a tacky, freshly painted floor and television lights shining into eyes operated on only a month earlier, he narrowly beat his compatriot Ong Poh Lim; in 1952 he resisted the young, bouncing challenger Eddy Choong. The next two years were Choong's. Then Wong returned to the lists and at the age of 37 beat him in a 67-minute three-game marathon.

In the age of shorts, he was always betrousered. His 'nervous' racket-twiddling before serving was purely a mannerism; in play he was unruffled.

He won the Malaysian Open Championships eight times in all! Over a period of 14 years, 1940–53! And although he never won the men's doubles he did win the mixed doubles three times.

Retiring, he perpetuated the game he had so long graced, as a coach in Singapore—and received a well-merited MBE. In 1982, suffered a stroke after playing Korea's woman champion Sun Ai Hwang. 'I said I'd take on best men when young, best women when old'.

RAY STEVENS *England*

England's hard man. His all-out Basil Brush 'boom-boom' attack ranked him high in world doubles and singles.

Five times winner of the English National singles title, seven times of the level doubles, two European and two Commonwealth gold medals, and a World Championship bronze. 110 + English caps—but never an All-England title.

Fit and full of fight he invariably gave his all—especially for England. One of the first full-timers—yet finds time to help youngsters, who include in nephew Darren Hall a possible successor to Ray's England No 1 status. Modest and approachable.

DEREK TALBOT *England*

A gritty Geordie all-rounder whose record reads like advanced maths: 83 caps, 100 + open titles; 20 international titles; 10 National (including two triples); 3 Commonwealth gold; 3 European gold; 3 All-England titles and an Olympic demonstration medal! All adding up to speed, power and determination.

On the IBF Players' executive; promoter of Vicort rackets; currently promotions manager of grandiose Coventry Rackets Club; author of *Badminton to the Top*.

Derek always had what it took!

SIR GEORGE THOMAS, BART *England*

The 'Bart Cup' was how an enthusiastic American youngster described Sir George's visionary gift to world badminton. But for all that he was never a man to stand on ceremony or title.

'Records makyth not the man'. Sir George's were legion—but only a part of the whole. In his first season of play he reached the All-England men's doubles semi-final; two years later he won the mixed title (1903), the first of eight occasions. In 1906 he won the men's doubles, the first of nine victories which culminated only in 1928 at the age of 47!

And yet the Grail of the singles title eluded him until 1920 when he more than made up with four successive victories. (To make 21 titles in all). That

> *Up to 1967 Margaret Varner had never been in a losing American badminton, tennis or squash team.*

A Golden Age : Sir George Thomas, elegance and deception; J F Devlin, immovable defence and fiery determination.

of 1923 included the semi-final defeat of the redoubtable Frank Devlin whom he 'ran into the ground'—despite an age difference of 20 years.

Won his first English cap in 1902–3, aged 21; his 29th (out of a possible 29) in 1928–9, aged 47, when he also achieved his 50th victory.

With a 'virtuosity of talent' and a full range of flawless strokes Sir George was a classic stylist. Deception was the savour of the game he relished most : he would admit 'I never could resist the lure of the beautiful stroke'. An effortless but deadly smash complemented a velvet glove touch at the net. Perhaps his most memorable shot was his drive in mixed : 'hit horizontal and immediately parallel to the side-line with the speed of a bullet and, having been tested for width and length, with no possibility of going out'. The whole based on stamina and implemented by a chess master's shrewd, tactical genius.

'Willing to play on any court, in any light; to accept every umpire's decision without the flicker

Ma Khan Su Win—and she did, as Burmese Mixed Champion.

of an eyelid'. His Achilles heel? Graceful, immaculately turned out and living in a leisured world, 'he disliked being hustled'.

Nor did he shine merely at badminton. A tennis international who reached the men's doubles semi-final at Wimbledon; a chess player who was the English Master in 1922 and 1924; a Hampshire county hockey colour . . . and 'an invincible ping-pong player'.

And the man behind the player? Dignified but surprisingly shy. A man with a social conscience who encouraged boxing in boys' clubs and visited prisons. A stickler for punctuality: the only occasion he was ever late on court was at the Scottish Championships. Having speedily encompassed the downfall of 29 chess boards at Duke Street Prison he had been delayed by the cunning resistance of the 30th—a confidence trickster.

During the First World War he refused a mount when faced with a 240 mile *385 km* trek on compass-bearings across largely unmapped Mesopotamian desert. He preferred to share its rigours with his platoon—on foot.

A man too who gave service to the game as freely as he had plundered it. Editor of the *Gazette*, author of his so aptly titled *Art of Badminton*, a selector (until he resigned when his own place was at last in doubt); BA of E Vice-President for 20 years: President for 2; reviser of the laws in his own meticulous hand; President of the IBF for 21 years; founder and originator of the International Badminton Championship which popularly bears his name: the Thomas Cup. Attending every IBF meeting he was very far from a figure-head. In the early days carefully chosen dates always concluded, at Sir George's expense, with lunch—and seats at Wimbledon.

In his old age, his sight failed, and he was cruelly robbed of his trophies and mementos. He died at the age of 91.

In the words of Major McCallum: 'Un chevalier sans peur and sans reproche'.

TJUN TJUN *Indonesia*

May have a name like a panting, up-gradient railway engine but moves like black lightning. Probably the fastest, severest player ever on a doubles court. To him, serves, low or flick, are sacrificial offerings. Airborne in smashing, he disdains the ground. Defence is attack: shuttles are whipped back at speed; and uncanny intuition directs him unerringly after them for the net-kill.

With such skills it is not surprising that he and consistent foil Wahjudi won the All-England title six years out of seven (1974–80) and the world title in 1977. After back trouble—and marriage—fell to compatriots Kartono and Heryanto in 1981 at Wembley.

MARGARET TRAGETT *England*

Was categorised, rather censoriously, as 'of the dashing and brilliant school—but erratic'. The latter not surprisingly perhaps as she had a wider range of strokes—and trick shots—than any other woman—and loved to use them. Especially (much disapproved) 'a backhand drop-shot played with her back to the net and eyes on anything but the shuttle'. All delightfully in keeping with the woman who after a Strollers' match in Paris insisted 'I didn't come to Paris to sleep!' and set off without escort to see the sights.

Started her badminton in Heidelberg and played on the old hour-glass court. Her first All-England, 1902; her last, 1933, when she reached the fourth round of the ladies' doubles and played in the singles. Her greatest, in 1923 when with 'Curly' Mack she beat winners for the preceding 4 years: Sir George Thomas and Hazel Hogarth. 'Playing an inspired game she could do no wrong: her smashes completely beat Sir George and she covered every inch of the court.'

Won eleven All-England titles (3 singles, her last win 16 years after her first), 3 mixed and 5 ladies) and fifteen caps over 20 years.

Editor and eager contributor to the *Gazette* she wrote one badminton book—and a host of best-selling novels (see p 66).

MIKE TREDGETT *England*

Mike has come a long way since he first hit shuttles over his neighbour's privet hedge—and then graduated to a village hall—with a court 4ft short!

From Gloucestershire county stalwart he has risen to international status: with his 120+ caps he has slightly outgunned his men's doubles partner, Ray Stevens. (Both have now broken Tony Jordan's longstanding 100 record.)

The man behind 'Golden Girl' Nora Perry. It has been his aggressive receiving and crunching smash, his early take and angled drives which have helped make openings for her; his mobility, defence and backhand fire-power which have saved the day when womanly intuition went awry.

Unsmiling concentration is written across his pale features. Coolness is his keynote: 'He wouldn't care if there were a gorilla on the other side of the net'.

Three All-England; 12 National; 4 European and 3 Commonwealth titles; and silver and bronze at the World Championships make a very fair tally. Dramatically won the 1981 Friends' Provident Masters men's doubles with last-second substitute, virtually unknown Martin Dew.

MARGARET VARNER *USA*

Superbly built, with rich auburn hair and a languorous Southern drawl, Margaret, born at El Paso on the Rio Grande, was epitomised as the 'Texan Bronze'. When rumour whispered she toted a gun in her handbag, you believed it.

'Bronze' maybe, but her badminton was pure gold. The superbly fit PE Lecturer of Louisiana University had little competition except against her own students. But with an iron will to practise she developed an easy mobility and the heaviest smash in the ladies' game. As receiver, within a foot of the front service line, her motto was 'toujours l'audace' —but with it went coolness.

She and the great Judy Hashman fought it out toe to toe in close matched rivalry. Margaret set the pace with two All-England singles titles (1955–6) before Judy began her nine-win run. She took a doubles title too (1958) with England's youthful Heather Ward.

Thereafter, a natural ball-player, she had other peaks to scale. She and Mrs du Pont ranked amongst the very top American women's tennis players. To prove it, they reached the 1958 Wimbledon final—losing 3–6, 5–7 to Althea Gibson and Maria Bueno. And as if that was not enough she plundered the USA squash title in 1960. For fun, she raced—if not out-ran—race-horses: *Wembley Blue* and *Half Smash*.

Some girl, the Texan Bronze!

BETTY UBER *England*

Having won the Wimbledon Junior tennis title Betty Corbin, forerunner of the famous Betty Nuttall, was 'crazy to play still more tennis'. But with few opportunities, by the grace of the gods, she took to badminton instead.

Within two years she was in the Surrey team, had caught the coaching eye—and heart—of England's H S (Bertie) Uber, and moved on to the famous Crystal Palace BC where she spent interminable lone hours practising the low serve in the 'Shy Ladies' secluded court.

She caught the *Gazette*'s editorial eye too: 'a very attractive young player: good to look at'.

The first USA Championships in Chicago in 1937 were played on 21 courts.

Donald Hume, fast and powerful, and Betty Uber, supreme in serve and net-play, won four successive All-England titles.

And it gave her the mixed players' accolade: 'knows what to leave—but when she does intercept she *bullies* the opposing man'.

In 1927, scandalised voices whispered, 'Premature selection' when she made the first of her 37 appearances for England over a 26-year span. Up to 1948, she had won every one of her 51 matches! And for that feat received a silver cigarette case inscribed 'The greatest badminton personality in the world'.

If the above does not rank Betty Uber as England's greatest pre-War player, her All-England record certainly does. Seven consecutive mixed doubles wins: eight in all (3 with her coach-husband, 4 with Donald Hume, one with R M (Bill) White). Beaten only once between 1930 and

> *Much embroiled pair : 'Get into the net!'*
>
> *'I can't, you fool! You're standing on my foot.'*

1939—and that by an inspired Ralph Nichols. For good measure, throw in four ladies' doubles titles—including a 1949 come-back, the first blow against the all-conquering Danes to restore England's battered badminton pride.

She took the singles title too—just once (1935). 'I couldn't quite get the hang of singles'. In truth, she lacked the stamina.

Hers was a copybook style. Easy footwork, tape-skimming serve, line-hugging smashes and clears: all actuated by a keenly analytical eye.

Betty Uber was indeed 'great in every aspect of the game'. Not least in that 'win or lose, she never showed anything but charm and equanimity'. No wonder nations are proud to win the trophy that bears her name—the Uber Cup.

W R (DOROTHY) WALTON *Canada*

A BA and MA in political economics who preferred marriage to politics. Was persuaded to take up badminton after seeing England's Bill White looking 'ever so nice in his shorts'. Was the first overseas competitor to win, in 1939, the All-England ladies' singles, 'smashing her way to victory'. The previous year she had won the Canadian singles title—and the Canadian Lawn Tennis ladies' doubles title. As charming as she was sporting.

HEATHER M WARD *England*

A garden début at 5 led to three All-England Junior Triple Crowns (1955–7). In 1955, at 16.3, was chosen as the youngest international ever; won the All-England ladies' doubles with Margaret Varner in 1958; and in 1959, by beating the redoubtable Judy Devlin, became the first English holder of the All-England singles title for 21 years, and temporarily prevented the cup, in circulation for 29 years, going to America for good: that was the day 'the roof nearly took off'.

Sadly, emigrated to South Africa at the peak of her powers but returned 11 years after her first triumph to become All-England singles runner-up against Etsuko Takenaka. Still playing for England (1955–75) 5 years later.

Supple in action but 'Chunky' by name she allied power with touch, and bonded them with speed. Because of a model serve and smash, was chosen for a tennis film by Dan Maskell.

Pleasant, utterly unassuming, she was epitomised in the Far East as 'the tremendous sporting Mrs Nielsen'.

Now a selector, she still plays tournaments but devotes more time to grooming four potential Nielsen Champions.

R M (BILL) WHITE

The 'Gay Cavalier' of pre-War badminton; a man with a Dickensian relish for good cheer, and the hardest, shuttle-crumpling smash in the history of the game.

Deft footwork, despite his size, and a rugged defence also helped to gain him 24 caps in a decade. And, for good measure, seven All-England titles: 2 singles, 1 mixed (with Betty Uber) and 4 men's (with D C Hume).

Leather-coated, he drove to tournaments in an open 1926 Humber Hengist which replaced a Morris he gladly traded in for £1.50. The first man to bare his knees, by playing in shorts at the All-England; he also reported 'in' to the Welsh Open referee still in his dinner jacket from the previous evening's celebrations.

His party trick: holding four or five shuttles in one hand and testing them with machine-gun rapidity so that they were all in flight at one time.

One of badminton's great characters!

ZHENG YULI *China*

China's 19-year-old 'shape-of-things-to-come'! A 5 ft 1 in *1.5 m*, 97 lb *44 kg* shape at that! One blessed with fluent footwork, a suppleness that makes the 'splits' painless, a classical style, and more than a touch of oriental mystery.

Runs China's No 1 Zhang Ailing very close. Filched the Chinese National title in 1981 when Zhang was at the Friends' Provident Masters. And won the Indian Masters. China's 'secret weapon' indeed!

Now a PE student: brilliant at table tennis; devoted to embroidery.

Stars to Be?

Crowns sit as uneasily as at any time since the French Revolution. Youthful precocity is reaching for the stars.

In England, red-headed, left-hander *Steve Baddeley* and lithe *Nicky Yates* are the best singles prospects for years; *Martin Dew* won all his doubles on the China Tour; schoolboy *Darren Hall* has enormous potential—and uncle-coach *Ray Stevens*. On the distaff side, teenager *Helen Troke* and *Sally Podger* have already made distinguished heads roll.

Across the North Sea, Denmark have another Köppen in vivacious *Nettie Nielsen* who also makes a formidable doubles pairing with *Dorte Kjaer*. Good men are even more numerous: *Jens Peter Nierhoff* wields the biggest smash in the business; left-hander *Michael Kjeldsen* revels in speed;

Nettie Nielsen (Denmark) : pretty as a picture and blessed with Köppen charisma and athleticism.

burly *Mark Christiansen* springs surprises with daring unorthodoxy, and *Morten Svarrer* has a christian name he might well live up to.

The Far East holds an even greater wealth of potential. In Indonesia *Lius Pongoh*, who could be a Swie King duplicate, has been outstripped by world-ranked No 6 *Icuk Sugiarto* who won the 1983 World Championships against the odds—and Liem Swie King; petite *Ivana Lie Ing* has not yet reached her peak.

Malaysia's brothers *Sidek, Misbun, Jalani* and *Razif*, may well haul their country back to its former greatness. Japan, as ever, lacks men but more will be heard of tomboy *Saori Kondo* whilst *Sumiko Kitada, Shigemi Kawamura*, and *Fumiko Tohkairin* are likely to rank amongst her greats. With players as talented and dedicated as *Sun Ai Hwang, Yoon Suk Kim* and *Jun Ja Kim*, Korea may become a power in the badminton world.

China has an almost embarrassing wealth of talent of both sexes. To a young and victorious Thomas Cup team they can add *He Shangquan* and *Jiang Guoliang* currently ranked above them! From their gold mine of ladies they can pick two or three teams each capable of winning the Uber Cup. Wrap your tongue round, and look out for, *Wu Dixi* and *Liu Ying, Xu Rong* and *Wu Yiangiu, Chen Ruizhen, Lin Ye Skong, Wu Chen Liu, Li Lingwei* and *Han Aiping*.

INDEX

Where a number of references occur, main references are in bold type. Italicised references indicate illustrations.

Abdul Rahman Mohamed, 61, 125
Adams, Bernard, 12, 68
Ahm, Tonny, 42, 131
Ailing, Zhang, 99, *100*, 111, 113, **148**
Aizawa, Machiko, 93, 134, 135
Allen, Queenie, 42
Alston, J C, 131
Amano, H, 133, 134
Anderson, A, 53
Andrews, Keith, 93
Ang Tjin Siang (Muljadi), 123, 124
Assinder, Pat, 62

Bacher, Tom, 92, 125, 126, 129
Backhouse, Claire, 114
Baddeley, Herbert, 19
Baddeley, Steve, 114, 163
Baddeley, Wilfred, 19, **142**
Baird, Alan, 54–5
Bairstow (Palmer), Angela, 59, 74, 83, 113, 132
Baker, D, 21
Baldwin, John Loraine, 7, 9, 10
Bannister, Roger, 93
Barinaga, T, 133
Barlow, Rhona, 64
Barr, James, 63
Barrand, G W, 132, 133
Barron, Arthur, 93
Bayley, Margaret, 90
Beacom, Colin, 90, 93, 113
Beal, J R, 59
Beaufort, *Duke of*, 7, 8, 96
Beck, Margaret, 93, 113, **148**
Beckett, Barbara, *39*
Beckman, Karen, 69, 74, 93, 96
Berglund, Anni, 92
Best, John, 38, 48, 50
Betley, Derek, 14
Bhornchima, Narong, 122
Bie, Jasper, 89
Birtwistle, W Peter, 18, **142–3**
Bisgood, B L, 16, 42
Bisseker, Brian, 143
Bloomer, David, 37, 48, 49, 51, 62, 92, *142*, **143**
Boonyasukhanonda, Somsook, 122
Bopardikan, M, 90
Borch, H, 123, 126
Borg, Bjorn, 72
Bottomley, *Mrs*, 38
Bowker, T, 73
Boxall, Margaret, *67*, 92, 93, 113
Boyle, Tommy, 26, 89
Braden, Lynn, 109
Brennan, Janet, 91
Bridge, Duncan, 114
Bridge (Beckman), Karen, 69, 74, *80*, 93, 96, *115*
Brock, Ken, 68
Brown, Eric, 68
Brundle, Fred, 68
Bude, Judy, 17
Budibent, Nick, 14, 42
Bullivant, Peter, 95
Butler, R W, 45

Capon, Netta, 80
Capon, P B, 80
Carpenter, Barbara, 38, 83
Chan Kon Leong, 120, 121
Chandra, Ade, 93, 94, 109, 110, 111, 112, 116, 125, 126
Chapman, Karen, 110, 114
Charp, F C, 24
Chea Hong Chong, 126
Chen Changjie, 111, 128, 129
Chen Ruizhen, 163
Chesterton, Frank, 88
Chilton, Humphrey Farwell, 23, 73, *142*, **143**
Chitty, Pauline, 93
Choong, David, 36, 38, 46, 137
Choong, Eddy B, 36, 38, 46, 68, 121, 122, 137, *138*, 142, **148–9**
Christensen, T Holst, 132
Christian, H, 93, 94, 95, 109, 110, 111, 112, 116, 125, 129
Christiansen, Mark, 163
Chumkum, Chavalert, 122
Ciniglio, Ciro, 14, 66, 110
Clark, Gillian, *58*, 114
Clarke, David, 92
Clarke, W H, 21
Coates, Suzanne, 94
Coffin, J Pine, 73
Collier, F S, 87
Cook, B P, 63, 73
Cooley, Iris, 64, 83
Cox, Sonice, 91
Crabbie, J E, 149
Crossley, Ken, 14, 39, 64, 68
Cussen, Ollie, 14, 65

Dabelsteen, P, 120
Dalsgard, Ruth, 89
Damayanti, R, *100*, *101*, 136
Darmadi, 92, 125
Davidson, Ken, 10, 42, *51*, 63, 67, 68
Davies, Barry, *43*
Davis, Pat, 51, 56, 57, 61, 62, *67*, 68, 72, 90
Debnam, Stuart, 37
Delfs, Flemming, 61, 62, 94, 95, 96, 109, 117, 125, 128, 139–40, **149**
Denton, Cyril, 90
Denton, Robin, 43
Devlin, Frank, 19, 22, 43, 45, 46, 63, 66, *88*, 90, **149–50**
Devlin, J F, *160*
Devlin, J M, 131, 132
Devlin (Peard), Sue, 90, 91, *105*, 131, 132
Dew, Martin, 62, 96, *99*, 110, 112, 113, 114, 163
Dewi, Utama, 116, 133, 134, 135
Djamaludin, Tutang, 123
Dolby, S S C, 12, *13*, 20, 21, 46, **143–4**
Douglass, Dorothea, 150
Downey, Jake, 43, 66, 68
Doyle, C P (Chick), 49, **150**
Duff, C de V, 63

Eaton, Richard, 42
Eddy, David, 46, 56, 62, 68, 92, 96
Eilertsen, O, 121
Elizabeth II, *Queen*, *103*, *129*
Emms, Percy, 22
Engelbach, Archibald Frank, 150
Evans, H C, 63

Fairbanks, Douglas, 72
Falardeau, Johanne, 114
Felsby, M, 120
Ferrers-Nicholson, N, 63, 66
Field, 89
Fish, Geoff, 82
Fitzgibbon, Jim, 26, 45, 46
Fladberg, Steen, 96, *110*, 111, 128
Flockhart, J, 109, 114

Forgie, Hugh, *54*, *103*
Forgie, Reg, *54*, *103*
Freeman, Dave, 137, **150–1**
Freud, Clement, 50
Froman, Bengt, 96, 111
Frost, Morten, 98, *101*, 110, 111, **151**
Gardner (Perry), Nora, *see* Perry
Gathier, Rene, 144
Gem, *Major*, 7
Gilks, Gillian, *43*, 61, 64, 69, 92, 93, 94, *95*, 96, *99*, *102*, *105*, 109, 111, 112, 113, 116, 131, **151–2**
Gilliland, Billy, 96, *99*, 109, 111, 114
Gloucester, *Duchess of*, 92
Goddard, Noel, 22
Godfrey, Kitty, 43
Gonzales, Diaz, 94
Goode, Nicky, *29*, *57*
Goodfellow, Ian, 146
Goodman, C, 93
Goto, K, 133
Gowers, Gillian, 96
Grace, W G, 87
Graham, Ian, 80
Granlund, K, 131, 132
Grant, Doug, 67
Gregory, D R, 68
Gregory, Ken, 64
Grozier, Brian, 73
Gunalan, Punch, 93, 113, 116, 125
Gunawan, Indra, 125
Guntrip, Heather, 9
Gustav, *King of Sweden*, 17

Habbin, Graham, 45
Hadinata, Christian, 126
Hadivanto, 109
Hall, Darran, 163
Hallen, Bronby, 110
Hamilton family, 152
Han Aiping, 110, 163
Han Jian, 128, 129, 141, **154**
Hannington, C H, 21
Hansen, A Hammergaard, 131, 132
Hansen, Elo, 92, 94, 125, 138
Hansen, J Hammergaard, *45*, 91, 121, 123, *138*
Hansen, Morten Frost, 72, 111, 113, 128, 139
Hansen, Pernille Molgaard, 91
Hardy, M, 87
Harris, Brian, 152
Hart, J H E, *19*, 33
Hartono, Rudy, 92, 93, *94*, 95, 96, *105*, 109, 110, 111, 112, 116, 124, 125, 126, *127*, 128, 129, 138, 139, 140, **152–3**
Harvey, Mike, 66
Hashman, Judy, *10*, 38, 43, 59, 65, 66, 68, 69, 90, 91, 92, 93, *105*, *115*, 132, 133, **153**
Hasselsteen, *Miss*, 132
Havers, John, 72
Hawthorn, Ernest Edward, 153
Hay, R Bruce, 20
He Shangquan, 163
Heah, Amy, 39
Heah, H A, 122
Heah, Johnnie, 60–1, 137–8
Hedges, Sid G, 66
Helledie, Jesper, 96, *110*
Hendry, Douglas, 51, 53, **153–4**
Henley, Frank, 18, 45, **144–5**
Henry, *Sir* Edward, 11
Heryanto, Rudi, 96, 110, 128–9, 142
Heywood, Rita, *58*
Hickson, F W, 15, **144**
Hill, Arthur, *144*

Hinchcliff, Eric, 144
Hoa, I L I, 136
Hoad, Lew, 68
Hodge, Frank, 37
Hogarth, Hazel, 20, 88, 152, **154**
Holm, Paul, 120, 137
Holwill, Bill, 145
Horner, Nancy, 14, 19, 64, 82, **145**
Horrocks, Allon, 80
Horsley, Marian, 82, **154**
Horton, J, 113
Hume, Donald, 19, 24, 42, 82, 83, *162*
Hunt, David, 69
Hwang, Sun Ai, 96, 111, 112, **154**, 163
Hybart, Maureen, 145

Iino, 140, *141*
Ikeda, M, 135
Indratno, 125
Ivana, Lie (Ing), 109, 110, 163
Jacobs, Helen, 38
Jacobsen, A Schiott, 131, 132
Jennings, Harry, 66
Jensen, C, 133
Jensen, H, 132
Jensen, O, 121
Jepsen, 89
Jian, Han, 128, 129, 141, **154**
Jiang Guoliang, 163
Johnson, Olive, 64, 65
Johnsson, Sture, 95, 140
Jolly, Kevin, *80*, 83, *101*, 112, **154**
Jones, Arthur, 145
Jones, R, 133
Jones, W Basil, 63
Jordan, Tony, 73, 83, 90, 92, *105*, 113, **154–5**
Jorgensen (Rasmussen), Karin, 40, 90, 91, **158**, *159*
Jun Ja Kim, 163

Kanchanaraphi, Raphi, 122
Karlsson, S, 96, 111, 112, 113
Kartono, 62, 96, 110, 128, 129, 142
Kawamura, Shigemi, 163
Keddie, Verna, 15
Keegan, Kevin, 105
Keeling, Brian, 59
Kemp, Willie, 17
Kihlstrom, Thomas, 72, 95, 96, 109, *110*, 111, 112, 113, 117
Kilvington, Paula, 39, 80
King, Liem Swie, *see* Liem Swie King
Kitada, Sumiko, 163
Kjaer, Dorte, 163
Kjeldsen, Michael, 163
Kobbero, Finn, 36, *45*, 46, 68, 90, 91, 92, *105*, 121, 123, *138*, 139, **155**
Koestijah, Retno, 134
Koh Keng Siong, 92
Kojima, 92
Kondo, Saori, 95, 111, *135*, 136, 163
Köppen, Lene, 62, 72, 92, 95, 96, *102*, 109, 110, 111, 112, 113, 117, 140, **155**
Kops, Erland, 72, 90, 91, 93, 123, **155–6**
Kristensen, N P, 145
Kristiansen, B, 131, 132
Kurniawan, Utami Dewi, 116, 133, 134, 135

Lamb, Larry, 13, 14, *145*, **145–6**
Landrey, Larry, 14
Lane, Jim, 74
Larminie, Margaret, see Tragett, Margaret
Larsen, Kirsten, 96
Last, F W, 67
Law Teik Hock, 120
Leadbeater, Sally, 64, 74
Lee Kin Tat, 91
Li Lingwei, *110*, 163
Lianawati, Hesty, 134
Lie Po Djian, 122
Liem Swie King, 61, *71*, 93, 95, 96, 109,

110, 112, 126, 128, 129, 139–40, 141, **155**
Lim Kee Fong, 121
Lim Say Hup, 46, 122
Lin Jiangli, 128, 129
Lin Ye Skong, 163
Liu Xia, *100*, 111, 113
Liu Ying, *101*, *110*, 163
Lius Pongo, 96, 128, 129, 163
Livingstone, K G, *82*
Livingstone, Ken, 47, 66
Lockwood, Margaret, 49–50, 109
Lodge, Dorothy, 47
Loveday, C, 121
Luan Jin, *98*, 112, 113, 128, 129, 141–2
Lucas, Meriel, 21, 87, 90, **156**

McCallum, Johnnie, 18, **146**
McCallum, Mary, 25
McCoig, Robert, 138–9, **157**
McColl, Jack, 50, 60, 61, 90
MacCrimmon, Roddy, *43*, 61, 87
MacCrimmon, V, 87
McDonald, Helen, 156
McDonald, Jean, 156
MacFarlane, Nev, 65, *80*
Mack, Curly, 22, 63, **156**
McKane, Kitty, 156–7
Maconachie, Ian, 24, 33, 72, *105*, **156**
Madsen, Tage, 89, 92
Mahan, 22
Margaret, *Princess*, 95
Marie, Shirley, *54*, 61, *103*
Marjan, Ismail bin, 137
Marrett, H N, 88, 89, **157**
Marshall, E, 131
Masli, Regina, 94, 134, 135, 136
Marrs, Tommy, 14, 46, 54
Massey, S M, 10, 11, 21, 28, 40, 41, 43, 45, 47, 63, 66, 89
Massman, B, 131
Maywald, Roland, 93
Mee, Rupert, 17
Mellersh, H F, 87
Mendez, A M, 121
Mercer, D L H, 45, **146**
Mertz, O, 121
Metz, Emil ter, *129*, **146**
Mills, Roger, 14, 64, *65*, 66, 68, 74, *80*, 113, 138–9
Minarni, *Miss*, 133, 134
Minjarti, 125
Mitchell, R, 121
Mitchell, Sybil, 8
Modi, S, 114
Moeljoeno, M P, 130
Mohamed, Abdul Rahman, 61, 125
Mohlin, Stellan, *16*, *142*, **146**
Moo Foot Lian, 114, 126
Morland, Harold, 42
Moseley, E, 87
Muljadi, V, 124, 125, 129

Nakayama, N, 116, 134, 135
Natekar, Nandu, 90
Newland, John, 45
Ng Boon Bee, 61, 91, 93, 113, 116, 124, 125, 129, 138
Ng, Sylvia, 114
Ng Tat Wai, 61, 113, 125
Nichols, Leslie, *82*, 89
Nichols, Ralph C F, 63, *82*, 83, 89, **157**
Nielsen, Anders and Gorm, *74*
Nielsen, Heather, *see* Ward
Nielsen (Rietveld), Imre, 91, 92
Nielsen, Knud Aage, 62, 123
Nielsen, Nettie, 163
Nielsen, Poul-Erik, *16*, 46, 90, 111
Nierhoff, Jens Peter, 163
Njoo Kiem Bie, 122
Nurhaena, *Miss*, 134
Nurman, A, 125
Nurtjahja, Intan, 134

Oakie, Jack, 72
Olesen, I, 120
Oliff, John, 41
Olsen, Tonny, 89
O'Neill, D, 132
Ong, T B, 114
Ong Poh Lim, 120, 121, 137
Ooi Teik Hock, 120, 121, 122, 123
Oon Chong Hau, 74, 92

Padukone, Prakash, 95, 96, 109, 111, 113, 114, *149*, **157–8**
Palmer (Bairstow), Angela, 59, 74, 83, 113, 132
Palmer, Ian, 64, 66, 73
Pan Joe Hok, *45*
Parratt, Mike, 92
Paulson, J, 113
Peard, Frank, 26, 46
Peard (Devlin), Sue, 90, 91, *105*, 131, 132
Pennekett, Peter, 59
Perrin, Gillian, 74, 83, 92, 113
Perry (Gardner), Nora, 72, 83, *90*, 93, 95, 96, 109, *110*, 111, 112, 113, 114, *115*, 140, **158**
Petersen, Poul, 92, 125, 126
Petersen, Tonny, 39, 131
Philip, *Duke of Edinburgh*, 88, *103*
Phua Ah Hua, 126
Pignon, Laurie, 42
Piruz, Abdullah, 121, 122
Plomer-Walker, Ida, 63, 66
Plunkett-Dillon, John, 15, **143**
Pocock, H E D, 45
Podger, Sally, *71*, 110, 114, 151, 163
Pongo, Lius, 96, 128, 129, 163
Poulter, A, 58
Pound, Sue, 92
Powell, Robert, 46, 92
Prebble, A D, 15, 43, 89, 119, **146–7**
Pri, Svend, *24*, 28, *69*, 72, 93, *94*, 95, 96, *105*, 109, 111, 116, 125, 126, 128, 139, **158**
Prior, J H C, 66
Pritchard, Jenny, 92, 133
Purcell, Jack, 89
Puttick, Karen, *80*, *99*, 111, 112

Radeglia, Lavinia C, 45, 63, 66
Radford, Noel, 42, 67
Rahman, Abdul, 61, 125
Rangecroft, C G, 68
Rankin, Jim, 89, *146*
Rasmussen (Jörgensen), Karin, 40, 90, 91, **158**, *159*
Rasmussen (Strand), Ulla, 40, 90, 91, 92, 94, 116, **158**, *159*
Ratanasaengsuang, Channarong, 90, 122
Redhead, Kath, 73
Reedie, Craig, *16*, 17, *129*, *142*
Rickard, Bill, 59
Rickard, Julie, 92, 93, 113
Ridder-Luesken, M, 109
Rietveld (Nielsen), Imre, 91, 92
Ripley, Sylvia, 90
Robertson-Glasgow, R C, 38
Robinson, Maurice, 65, 66, *115*
Rogers, Iris, 90, 113
Rogers, Wynn, 120, 121, 132, 133
Ropke, Lene, *see* Köppen
Ross, Louis, 45, 68
Rowan, Ronnie, *16*
Ruffle, H W, 84
Rugani, Frank, 33
Russell, Marjorie, 139
Russell, Mona, 147
Rutnagur, Dickie, 42

Sadek, Jalaini, 96
Sadek, Razif, 96
St John, R F StA, 21
Samaranch, Juan, 110
Sansom, Herbert, 73

Sartika, Dhany, 141–2
Sautter, Guy A, 88, **158**
Saw Swee Leong, 126
Scheele, Herbert A E, 13, 15, 16, 17, 18, 37, 39, 40, 45, 46, 89, 92, 114, 129, 130, *147*, **147–8**
Scheele, Velma, 45
Schiott Jacobsen, *see* Jacobsen
Scott, Gary, *75*
Selby, S S C, 11
Selveraj, J, 126
Seto, T, 49–50
Sharp, Ray, *67*, 92
Shaw, John, 73
Shedd, Marjorie, 40
Shute, Warwick, 18, 90
Sidek, R, 114
Skaarup, Jorn, 120, 121, 137
Skovgaard, Steen, 62, 109, 128, 140, *155*
Smith, Frank, 50
Smith, Sidney H, 87
Smith, Ursula, 90, 91, 113, 131, 132, 133
Smythe, Donald, 60, 137–8
Soedaryanto, M, 135
Soemasto, Padmo, 129, 130
Somerset, Geraldine, 8
Somerset, *Lady* Henrietta, 8
Sonneville, Ferry, *45*, 46, 72, 122, 123, 124, *142*, **158**
Soon, Wong Peng, *see* Wong Peng Soon
Soong, D, 126
Sperre, H, 90
Starkey, C, 132
Statt, Ann, *105*, 114, *115*
Steden, Barbara, 93
Stevens, Ray, 28, *42*, 72, 83, 93, 95, 109, 111, 113, 114, *115*, **159**
Stewart, H McG, 131, 132
Stewart, Jean, 19, 82
Stouse, Ivan, 59
Strand (Rasmussen), Ulla, 40, 90, 91, 92, 94, 116, **158**, *159*
Streeton, Richard, 42
Stuart, Elliott, 93, 113
Sudirman, *Dr*, 16
Sugiarto, Icuk, *110*, 163
Sumirah, T, 134, 135, 136
Sumirat, I, 93, 128
Sun Ai Hwang, 96, 111, 112, **154**, 163
Sun Zhian, 111, 129
Supatera, Darmawan, *see* Tan King Gwan
Susanto, A, 124, 129
Sutton, Barbara, 96, *115*
Sutton, Ed, 93
Sutton, Phil, 96
Svarrer, Morten, 163
Swie King, *see* Liem Swie King

Takada, Mikiko, *59*, *135*, 136
Takagi, Noriko, 92, 134
Takahashi, T, 133, 134
Takasaka, K, 134
Takenake, Etsuko, 92, 93, 134, 135
Talbot, Derek, 68, 72, 93, 109, 113, 114, *115*, 116, **159**
Tan Aik Huang, 91, 113, 124, 125
Tan Jin Eong, 121
Tan Joe Hok, *45*, 46, 62, 122, 123
Tan King Gwan (Supatera), 122, 123, 124
Tan Soon Hooi, 61, 113
Tan Yee Khan, 91, 113, 124, 129, 138
Tanagi, N, 133
Tautz, Gerald, 22
Taylor, Bernard R, 42
Teh, Katherine, 114
Teh Kew San, 46, 122, 124
Teh Soo Gwan, 62
Teoh Seng Khoon, 120, 123
ter Metz, Emil, *129*, **146**
Thomas, *Sir* George, 8, 15, 16, 19, 20, 42, 43, 45, 46, 66, 72, 81, 87, *88*, 112, *118*, 121, **159–60**

Thomas, G A, 66, 89
Thomson, Ethel, 87
Thorndahl, K, 132
Tier, Niel, 96
Timperley, June, 90, 92
Titherley, Alan, 83
Tjan So Gwan, 136
Tjun Tjun, 93, 95, 96, 109, *124*, 126, 128, 140–1, 142, **160–1**
Toganoo, E, 109
Tohkairim, Fumiko, 163
Tragett (Larminie), Margaret, 11, 19, 20, 23, 40, 45, 66, 88, **161**
Trapnell, A G, 119
Travers, 96
Tredgett, Kathy, *10*
Tredgett, Mike, 62, 69, *90*, 93, 95, 96, 109, 110, 111, 113, 114, *115*, 140, **161**
Trevor-Williams, E, 42
Troke, Helen, *102*, 110, 114, 163
Tsuchida, 140, *141*
Tumengkol, P, 133, 134
Turner, Pat M, 45
Twedberg, Eva, 92, *105*

Uber, Betty, 11, 18, 19, 24, 42, 43, 60–1, 63, 67, 89, *131*, **161–2**
Uber, H S, 67
Ueno, Emiko, 95, 109, *135*, 136
Unang, A P, 123, 124

Vallet, M, 59
van Beusekom, Joké, 94, 109, 110
van Vossen, A C J, 18, **148**
Van Winkle, Ted, 22
Varner, Margaret, *131*, 132, 159, **161**
Vatanatham, Chucart, 122
Verawaty, Wiharjo, 95, *100*, *101*, *104*, 109, 110, 112, 136
Vidal, G W, *19*
Vincent, John, 72
von Maltzhan, *Baron*, 13

Waddell, Peter, 90
Wadsworth, Barbara, 14, 66
Waldheim, Kurt, 49
Wahjudi, J, 93, 95, 96, *124*, 126, 128, 140–1, 142
Wallace, Roy, 32
Wallwork, Brian, 69
Walton, Dorothy, 89, **162**
Ward (Nielsen), Heather M, 61, 74, 83, 90, 93, **162**
Warrington, 89
Webb, G A, 68
Webster, Jane, *31*, 69, 96, 109, 110, 111, 112, *115*
West, Vic, 36
Whetnall, Paul, 14, 66, *67*, 68, 72, 74, 90, 113
Whetnall, Sue, *67*, 68, 90, 92, 93, 113, 131
White, Bill, 38, 89, 92, **163**
White, Brian, 82
White, June, 73, 83, *105*
White, R M, *88*, 131
Whittaker, Cecil, 69, 73, 89
Whittaker, S, 113
Widiastuti, Teresa, 94, 135, 136
Wigoeno, Imelda, 95, 110, 111, 112, 135, 136
Wiharjo, V, 136
Wilks, Mike, 95
Willard, Jess, 41
Williams, R, 121
Willis, C Dudfield, 43, 46
Willis, Ron, 46
Wilson, Adam, 37
Wiltshire, Bill, 74
Wingfield, John, 7
Wingfield, Tom, 42, 81
Wingfield, Walton Clopton, 7
Winther, A, 132

Wong Peng Soon, 26, 42, 91, 121, 137, *138*, 142, **159**
Wood, Christina, 42
Woolcott, Ken, *64*, 65
Woolhouse, John, 62
Wright, Len, 68, 79, 80
Wright, Les, 65, 68
Wu Chen Liu, 163
Wu Dixi, 96, *101*, *110*, 163
Wu Yiangiu, 163
Wyatt, Stuart, *142*, **148**

Xu Rong, 96, 163

Yao Ximing, 111, 129
Yates, N, 114
Yates, Nicky, 163
Yeoh Teck Chye, 120
Yew Cheng Hoe, 91, 113, 124
Yokoi, F, 133
Yokoyama, M, 133
Yonekura, Yoshiko, *59*, 96, 111, 112, 113, *135*, 136
Yoon Suk Kim, 163
Young, Daphne, 41
Youngberg, J, 114
Yuki, Hiroe, *70*, 92, 133, 134, *135*, 136, 140
Yun Ya Kim, 110
Yusuf, E, 122

Zhang Ailing, *99*, *100*, 111, 113, **148**
Zheng Yuli, 163
Zizman, M-L, 93

Index by
David Wilson.